MW00809981

CHINESE
ASTROLOGY
FOR
2020

THE YEAR OF THE METAL RAT

鼠
年
運
程
上
卷

庚子年

The Year of the Metal Rat

Chinese Astrology for 2020

All intellectual property rights including copyright in relation to this book belong to Joey Yap Research Group Sdn. Bhd.

No part of this book may be copied, used, subsumed, or exploited in fact, field of thought or general idea, by any other authors or persons, or be stored in a retrieval system, transmitted or reproduced in any way, including but not limited to digital copying and printing in any form whatsoever worldwide without the prior agreement and written permission of the copyright owner. Permission to use the content of this book or any part thereof must be obtained from the copyright owner. For more details, please contact:

JOEY YAP RESEARCH GROUP SDN BHD (944330-D)
19-3, The Boulevard, Mid Valley City,
59200 Kuala Lumpur, Malaysia.
Tel   : +603-2284 8080
Fax   : +603-2284 1218
Email   : info@masteryacademy.com
Website : www.masteryacademy.com

DISCLAIMER:

The author, copyright owner, and the publishers respectively have made their best efforts to produce this high quality, informative and helpful book. They have verified the technical accuracy of the information and contents of this book. However, the information contained in this book cannot replace or substitute for the services of trained professionals in any field, including, but not limited to, mental, financial, medical, psychological, or legal fields. They do not offer any professional, personal, medical, financial or legal advice and none of the information contained in the book should be confused as such advice. Any information pertaining to the events, occurrences, dates and other details relating to the person or persons, dead or alive, and to the companies have been verified to the best of their abilities based on information obtained or extracted from various websites, newspaper clippings and other public media. However, they make no representation or warranties of any kind with regard to the contents of this book and accept no liability of any kind for any losses or damages caused or alleged to be caused directly or indirectly from using the information contained herein.

INDEX

PREFACE

Towards the end of the year, we invariably start to think about the future. I am often approached by people who want to know whether the new year will be good or bad for them. People who have experienced heartbreak, loss or injury frequently wonder if the coming year will be easier. Others have more specific questions about what the new year will bring in terms of their career, business, marriage and social life.

Traditional Chinese Astrology gives us the power to answer these questions. I published the first incarnation of this book on Chinese Astrology way back in 2006. In the years since, interest in the subject has continued to grow and grow, and the positive reviews have kept coming.

Most people know that Chinese Astrology focuses on the twelve animal signs. With a traditional forecast, results are ultimately based on the year that a person was born. What is less well known is that animal sign forecasting is actually a form of BaZi Destiny analysis.

The word BaZi means "Eight Characters" and in a full BaZi reading, one must analyse all Eight Characters in a person's chart. Together, they paint a complete picture of that person's destiny. In BaZi, everyone has a Destiny chart which is derived from the Year, Month, Day and Hour of their birth.

Forecasting using a person's animal sign alone (which is assigned by the Year of birth) only makes use of 12.5% of a BaZi chart. By using more of a BaZi chart, we can draw more accurate and tailored conclusions. A large section of this book focuses on how to analyse the Day Pillar or Jia Zi (甲子) in a person's BaZi chart. You won't find this feature in any other book and it can make a big difference to your forecasts.

I've studied Chinese Metaphysics and provided BaZi consultancy services for over two decades now. I can say with complete confidence that there is no such thing as a truly good or bad year. We are not helpless with regards to the future. To make the point, imagine if a person's outlook for the year ahead was favourable but they chose to spend the entire year on the sofa. What would come of their good fortune? Very little! The importance of mindset and effort should not be underestimated. Conversely, if a person's outlook is poor, they must not be deterred. With adequate preparation, we can always minimize hardship and loss and come out on top. Equally, knowing that an opportunity is coming let us prepare for it and make the most out of it.

It is important to stress that even with the techniques herein, an astrology reading can really only offer a glimpse into the future. The gold standard for Destiny analysis will always be a professional BaZi consultation, because Destiny analysis is inherently complex and nuanced. From there, Feng Shui and Qi Men Dun Jia can help one act on what they learn. If BaZi can provide the diagnosis, then Feng Shui and Qi Men Dun Jia are like the prescription!

With all that being said, you can still significant insight into the year ahead with the help in this book. Nonetheless, it should still provide a useful analysis on the yearly general prospects for you. Knowledge really is power, and with the right attitude and information you can make 2020 the very best year it can possibly be.

Whatever the future may hold for you, I wish you good luck!

Warmest regards,

Dato' Joey Yap
July 2019

Connect with us:

www.joeyyap.com   JOEYYAP **TV** www.youtube/joeyyap

@DatoJoeyYap   @RealJoeyYap   @JoeyYap

Academy website:
www.masteryacademy.com | jya.masteryacademy.com | www.baziprofiling.com

The Earthly Branches

In BaZi, the Earthly Branches on the BaZi Chart consist of the Four Pillars namely, the Hour, Day, Month and Year Pillars, as illustrated below. You need to refer to the forecast of each of the Animal Sign that appears on the respective Pillars of your BaZi Chart in order to derive a more comprehensive outlook for the year.

Each Pillar signifies a different aspect in life:

Internal Your inner personality and behaviour that are hidden from and not openly revealed to others.		External The personality and behaviour you exhibit outwardly and can be seen by others.	
Hour Pillar denotes a person's dreams, hopes and inspirations.	**Day Pillar** represents an individual's relationship with his or her spouse.	**Month Pillar** reveals one's career and business outlook.	**Year Pillar** shows a person's state of health and social circle (i.e. friends).

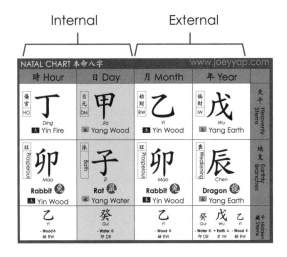

庚子年 The Year of the Metal Rat

Do This First

Print your Free BaZi Chart at the URL below:

www.masteryacademy.com/regbook

Here is your unique code to access the BaZi Calculator:

CA12BZ68

Sample: This is how your BaZi Chart will look like

Exclusive content available for download with your purchase of the Chinese Astrology for 2020 book.

Claim your FREE ONLINE ACCESS now at: www.masteryacademy.com/bookbonus2020

BONUS CONTENT

FREE
DOWNLOAD

CAR93AC8

Expires
31st December 2020

The Year of the Metal Rat Outlook

The Metal Rat, Geng Zi 庚子 year can be likened to a rollercoaster ride – characterised by a few sudden drops, turns and shake ups that is sure to keep your mind sharp and senses switched on. Nevertheless, the year is bound to be exciting and fun for those who crave challenge and adrenaline rush. Some of the upheavals from 2019 may also follow through in 2020.

With that said, remember that behind chaos there is always subtle opportunities for those who are vigilant and are prepared with clear strategy before they hit the proverbial iceberg. The year of the Metal Rat will not be conducive to speculative endeavours. The global economic outlook isn't exactly vibrant despite the best efforts of various governments. Instead, the year is best spent focusing on the fundamentals, stocking up on financial immunity and awaiting opportunities while waylaying disruption.

The Day Pillar of the year 2020 is Ding Chou 丁丑. The year may seem to lack a sense of stability and the reason for this lies in the fact that the Ding stem is not rooted which denotes a wavering year, much like a weak candle flame – bright on the outside but hallowed on the inside. The presence of the Seven Killings Star 七殺 is hidden inside in the Day Pillar which further serves as a time bomb, waiting to put out the impending fire.

Seven Killings Star also symbolizes potential turbulence or internal pressure. Although the Day Pillar combines with the Year Pillar, it unfortunately may not produce the harmony and balance it should rightfully create, but is rather a sign of conflicts to come. This is pictured as an outward smile on a person's face while internally, they are consumed by fear and insecurity. This is evidenced by many powerful world powers in their display of external calm and control, yet behind the curtains they are dousing fires and closing brewing lids.

The year ahead sees Chou 丑 (Ox) and Yin 寅 (Tiger) together forming a 'Hidden Combination' in the BaZi Chart. This combination denotes power plays, perhaps manipulation of the judiciary system and creating a fair amount of public angst. A hidden combo such as this as seen with a Seven Killings Star which denotes sudden and abrupt changes which doesn't bode well for economic stability and peace.

The challenges of 2020 is further indicated by the presence of Yin 寅 (Tiger), a Solitary star that repels cooperation with others. This will perhaps see many prominent figures being questioned on their values, ideals and the manner in which they choose to help the people. In 2020, the Year Branch Zi 子 (Rat) and the Hour Branch You 酉 (Rooster) forms a 'Destruction' combo. This may signify an increase in mass protests, particularly in places where the people have been oppressed and do not have access to their fundamental rights. In essence, there is a fair bit of political turbulence in store. Fortunately with the help of the Nobleman star, if this turbulence comes to be, it would be shortlived.

The strongest element in the chart for the Year of the Metal Rat is Earth, Ding Fire's Output element. As the output element is associated with appearance, this suggests that the economy merely looks good on the surface exterior due to the weaker Metal element which represents Wealth. The Metal element's lack of strength is likely an indication of a potential global economic downturn which could manifest possibly as a recession. A 'trigger' of course is needed to activate this timebomb and hopefully the strength of the Nobleman star residing in the Rooster would be able to soften its explosion for yet another year. But the best strategy is still to be fully prepared and to strike hard while others retreat.

The Water element would be at its weakest in 2020 due to the abundance of Earth element suppressing and "blocking" its flow, as it were. As such, faster moving industries influenced by the Water element like tourism, journalism and e-hailing services are likely to suffer some setbacks.

It is important to note that many millionaires and multimillionaires founded their empires during tough times. You cannot drive a car while looking in the rear-view mirror. Therefore, while the global economy may be unstable with many uncertainties, this may be the best time for those who are prepared to take advantage of the fluctuation in the market to amass great resources for the future. While there may be a possibility of a decline towards the end of the Metal Rat or Early Metal Ox next year, the best long-term strategy would be to prepare for a "long-winter" financially which may last a couple of years.

One suggestion would be to begin the year on a clean financial slate: work to clear any existing big long term debts and aim to put at least 3 - 6 months' worth of cash reserves in the bank to serve as emergency funds.

Adaptability and innovation are the driving forces behind every success in 2020 and 2021. One of the most favourable things to do is to work on expanding your immediate skillset. The best time to get ahead of challenging times – is BEFORE it comes challenging – become better, faster and add more value to what you are doing. Increase your level of expertise. Instead of trying to hope that the year's outlook and the circumstances become better, the best thing to do is to make yourself become better. Remember that those with weaker skillsets always gets eliminated first in a downturn.

Since the year contains "Combination", this is the best time to do some worthwhile networking. In the coming new economy, it's WHO you know that will set you apart from the rest. In fact, one should start to network with key business leaders or important "noblemen" right away. The best time to FIND a job (or business deal) is to look for one is when you STILL have a job (or a current project). Meaning – start networking with potential bosses or business leaders, get yourself known to them, exchange contacts and establish a relationship. Don't wait for the absence of work before looking for one. By then it will be too late. In the event of an abrupt change in economic or financial situations, these connections will help you get out of the rut easily.

Like a well-trained boy scout, be prepared with all the metaphorical muscle you need to master 2020. Best of luck to you all, I hope that I've been able to point you in the right direction where success awaits you.

Forecast for the 12 Animal Signs in 2020

Rat 子

鼠

Year of the Rat							
1936	1948	1960	1972	1984	1996	2008	2020

A person's Chinese age is obtained by adding one year to their Western birthday. For example, if you were born in 1976, your Western age in 2020 is 44, but your Chinese age would be 45.

Overall Forecast For The Year

Abundance is just a matter of perception. Instead of remaining idle, try to put in some effort and begin to notice it in every aspect of your life. It has always been there. In fact, it is your birth right, but perhaps you were too busy to notice its existence due to lack of awareness.

Information regarding auspicious stars and inauspicious stars serve only as a guideline to help you navigate this year's ups and downs with ease. What's more important is to detach yourself from any commotion that may arise in life and find the silver lining in every situation. Life is too short for you to be in a constant mode of negativity or selfishness.

The presence of the Golden Lock Star (金匱) gets you into the flow of receiving gifts. When the good fortune kicks in, and more wealth starts to come your way, it is better if you start positioning yourself in a way that not only benefits you but also benefit others. One way to do this is by donating a percentage of the extra income that you are entitled to receive to an organisation that is known for improving people's lives. When you put your plans into action, you make a positive difference in other people's lives which does not only have a positive impact on them, but also on yourself.

This year, there is also high potential for you to be the recipient of money in the form of a reward for something that you have done. With this in mind, taking on a new job or role with added responsibilities would benefit you immensely.

Throughout your life, you may have experienced coming across someone that you probably have negative karmic affinity with and although he or she may have seemed helpful in many ways, his or her assistance unfortunately came with ulterior motives. Fortunately, this year, the General Star (將星) ensures that you are lucky enough to receive assistance from individuals with good intentions. Their kindness and sincerity will be very obvious to you and due to this star's auspicious energy of leadership, authority and power, you will also have potential to take on the leading role of managing a team. Everything will be easy for you as you will be surrounded by good people.

Speaking of people, when you come to a point in your life when you start to realise that all eyes are on you, and people are drawn to you like a moth to a flame, it means that the Duke's Arrival Star (歲駕) is playing its significant role in your life. Its presence this year is especially beneficial for you if you have something to offer to others. The energy it emits is similar to the rank of an emperor who is arriving to an event – someone everyone wants to look at.

With all of the positivity in your life that is coming one after another, you may think that everything has fallen into place, but the Grand Duke Star (太歲) will not allow it to happen as it displays its duty by swiftly bringing to you a number of problems to overcome. The star challenges you to think out of the box and pushes you to understand that being rigid and overly focused is not the way to go. Disruptions to your life and plans will only upset you if you are not prepared for it.

You may also end up getting into squabbles and clashes with family members as well as butting heads with loved ones over trivial issues, but these issues are connected more to the Hidden Corpse Star (伏屍) which has its own way of highlighting life's difficulties throughout this year.

The presence of the Sword Edge Star (劍鋒) may bother you with health implications which revolve more around stress and depression, but if you know how to take care of your overall health by signing up for wellness, stretching or meditative type of classes and being more mindful of your diet, you will be able to get positive results.

Instead of rushing to do all of life's duties or tasks, take things one step at a time. A slower pace will ensure that the star's negativity won't adversely affect you this year.

The Forecast for Individual Aspects of the Year

 **Wealth**

Although this year brings in new energy, unfortunately, il will not bring in the type of energy that will manifest as streams of financial wealth into your bank account. That's why it's best to watch how you spend your money and be cautious not to overspend. It helps to list down items you need to buy prior to shopping to help you focus on important things first. It's also better if you maintain a laid-back attitude in terms of making investments and completely avoid gambling to prevent further monetary loss.

 **Career**

It's common to have ambitions when it comes to work, but try not to be over-ambitious as it will not lead to anything worthwhile or pleasant. It's best to display an earnest gesture of goodwill and maintain a down-to-earth attitude. Forming harmonious relationships should be your goal especially at your workplace. And this is not something out of your reach if you are courteous. If you come across negative situations that might nudge you in the wrong direction, pause for a while, take a deep breath and make an effort to take a peaceful approach as quarrelling in the workplace is going to work against you, this year.

 **Relationships**

Although this year's forecast shows a rather dull and ordinary overall relationship cycle for you, it is up to you to take action and focus on the positive aspects in your relationships to create better experiences for yourself where relationships are concerned. If you are in a romantic relationship with someone, you should pay attention to it. Allow it to grow and strengthen by making plans to foster a closer bond with your significant other through relaxing getaways or romantic dates. If you have not met the person of your dreams yet, make an effort to expand your social circle. A potential partner will cross your path sooner or later, and when that happens, take your time to get to know him or her.

 **Health**

Health is very precious because once you lose it, it will affect your whole life. It will be difficult to enjoy life with a lot of health issues. It's important to never take health advice with a pinch of salt especially this year because 2020 is a time when health matters should be taken into serious consideration as there may be potential issues related to your urinary system. If you are a lady, it would be better if you pay special attention to potential gynaecological issues that may arise. And if you have to use sharp metals this year, be extra cautious to avoid any injuries.

Monthly Luck

農曆正月 (February 4th - March 4th) 戊寅

Sometimes people rely solely on good fortune and expect instantaneous results in all areas of their life. This is not wise. Although lucky items and the good energy they may emit is good, it is better if you focus on hard work because the rewards you get will be based on your efforts. You reap what you sow. If you deliberately make your goals happen, you can expect the best outcomes. They will unfold before your eyes in unexpected ways. And if there are people asking you to be part of a funeral or burial arrangement this month, it is better if you avoid being involved in it.

農曆二月 (March 5th - April 3rd) 己卯

This is the best month for you to carry out important tasks because due to the good energy that is supporting you, you will yield twice the result with half the effort. Although gossips and rumours should be of concern, and there is high potential for people with ill intentions to stab you at your back, you will have a great month as long as you stay humble and modest. Don't worry, nobody has the ability to hurt you if you maintain a positive mind set.

農曆三月 (April 4th - May 4th) 庚辰

You will be connected to outstanding improvements where career and relationships are concerned during this lucky month. If you are in a committed relationship, you will be enjoying a blissful and stable month, but don't close your eyes and take things for granted. Pay attention to your partner's needs and desires. Address any misunderstanding before it takes root. If you are single and looking, there is a strong chance for you to bump into your Mr or Miss Right.

農曆四月 (May 5th - June 4th) 辛巳

More career and financial luck are in store for you this month. Although good energy is on your side that can help you reach a higher level, don't rely on the good energy alone to succeed. Write down your goals on a piece of paper and figure out how to move towards them in the best possible way. Be more action oriented by forging good relationships with your clients, and further enhance good ties to make way for more opportunities.

鼠

農曆五月 (June 5th - July 5th) 壬午

According to this month's forecast, you should refrain from doing anything major or important. Be extra cautious if you need to make small decisions. Try not to express your feelings or thoughts to anyone you admire as there is high potential for you to face ordeals in your relationships this month. To change your overall luck, it is advisable for you to plan a trip to a different state or country and absorb the experiences as well as the good energy that abounds.

農曆六月 (July 6th - August 6th) 癸未

This month consists of mixed fortune that will come to you at varying degrees. Joyous events will shift bad fortune tides, but that should not upset you in any way. The key to better life experiences is to continue to be grateful for what you have and learn from past mistakes. Embrace the good and the bad with a positive attitude and mind set. This month, you should also stay away from extreme and dangerous activities as there are high chances for you to be injured.

農曆七月 (August 7th - September 6th) 甲申

This is another good month for you to carry out important activities or tasks as you will be able to yield twice the result with half the effort. A lot of doors will open up for you. But remaining idle or waiting around for someone to help you out won't yield the best outcome. As long as you take a chance, know your place and work hard towards your goal, you will reap the rewards and be happy. Keep your eyes open to any good opportunities and seize them at the right moment after weighing the pros and cons.

農曆八月 (September 7th - October 7th) 乙酉

This month is related to the infinity symbol as it symbolises a smooth and steady month for one's career as well as love life. Expect a positive shift at your workplace and be creative when it comes to expressing your love and affection towards your loved ones. With a strong Peach Blossom luck backing you up, you will never go wrong. So, what are you waiting for? Write that poem, seal that love letter with a kiss or buy the most gorgeous bouquet of flowers to impress your special someone.

農曆九月 **(October 8th - November 6th)** 丙戌

Although you will be facing a lot of unexpected obstacles during this month, many people will come to your rescue. You should be thankful, but don't let this information get to your head, thinking that you should just sit around and wait. You should take the necessary actions to prevent or rectify any problem. It's also important to be wary of legal matters and refrain from being anyone's guarantor to prevent further hurdles in your life.

農曆十月 **(November 7th - December 6th)** 丁亥

This month, you will be able to bask in the fruits of your labour. Anything that needs to be solved at your office will take place with ease. And this ease or support will be clearly seen in other areas of your life. Being earnest and down-to-earth will lead to more positive effects that will be more prevalent in your life this month. It's better if you share the abundance that you have with others and be grateful for this month's pleasures.

農曆十一月 **(December 7th 2020 - January 4th 2021)** 戊子

Work this month seems to bog you down. It's not supposed to cause you stress, so try working in a smart way instead of a hard way that will enable you to get your tasks done more easily. Be extra cautious when dealing with work related matters. When dealing with the opposite sex, it is best to approach them with tolerance. The same goes when communicating with your superiors. Always exercise tolerance when trying to connect with them to get the best results. You should be able to extract some good memories from this month if you are careful enough to notice the signs that can nudge you in the right direction.

農曆十二月 **(January 5th - February 2nd 2021)** 己丑

All will be well for you this month. Since you have a lot of good energy backing you up, it is best for you to outline and reorganise your goals especially if they pertain to your career. It is also a good month to collect debts. Although these are more focused on and highlighted to a certain extent, every area of your life will show improvements and will yield positive outcomes much better than you expect. But for sure, you will see greater success with emphasised intensity in your finances and career life above everything else.

Ox 丑

Year of the Ox							
1925	1937	1949	1961	1973	1985	1997	2009

A person's Chinese age is obtained by adding one year to their Western birthday. For example, if you were born in 1976, your Western age in 2020 is 44, but your Chinese age would be 45.

Overall Forecast For The Year

This year, with the rise of three auspicious stars, worry will be replaced with optimism and fear will be replaced with hope. Although inauspicious stars are lined up to potentially derail you from your dreams, a positive and focused mind will ensure that the stars' negative effects won't cause tears to roll down your cheeks. You won't be able to run away from problems, but instead of being turned down like you have experienced in the past, you will get all of the love and support that you need.

When this happens this year, it is a sign that you are enjoying the benefits from the Grand Duke Combination Star (歲合). Expect your sphere of influence to grow. It will be easy for you to mingle with people of high quality, and also people of power and authority this year. If you happen to need approval for a licence or a permit, this is definitely a good year for you to make that happen.

The Sun Star (太陽) is also taking the spotlight this year and as a Nobleman Star, it is connected to being of service to others. Instead of you seeking for other people's help, this year, other people would actually be seeking out for your help. Perhaps it is time to be the sun in the life of your colleagues, friends and superiors. When you help others, it not only ensures that you make a positive difference in other people's lives, but also ensures that you receive the abundance that you need along with an abundance of good karma and merits. Assisting others simply puts you in a position of activating this star. It shows progression, social networking and financial gains. One door after another will open up for you in terms of career and business.

Apart from this auspicious star, the Heavenly Yi Star (天乙) is another lucky star for you this year that gives you the edge to hire, befriend or partner with the right people. If you have been thinking about starting up a business, go ahead and do it. You will get the support that you need. Unfortunately, your path will not be as smooth as you have expected and although it is difficult to steer clear of the three inauspicious stars this year, you can make an effort to adjust the way you perceive and approach them to experience positive results.

The Bad Qi Star (晦氣) ensures that you pay extra attention to your health. Frequenting the gym would also show a lot of positive results and if time does not permit for you to partake in any of these healthy activities, it is recommended that you squeeze in at least other forms of exercises. In fact, simple activities such as brisk walking can also give you a major health boost. If you are taking medications, make sure you take them as prescribed by a doctor and do not skip any meals.

Another inauspicious star showing up this year for you is the Yin Sha Star (陰煞). With this star in its position, you will be offending women in ways that you won't even be able to comprehend. Apart from women, it would also be easy for you to offend those who are easily angered or those who have a personal vendetta against you. To avoid unwanted situations, all you have to do is stay away from these types of people. If that is not possible, try to maintain a polite attitude when you are around them and apologise if you cross any lines. If you watch what you say with the intention to keep your interactions harmonious, they will reciprocate.

You, like everyone else, just want to be happy regardless of what is going on in your life, but the Sky Emptiness star (天空) won't make that easy for you this year. If you have even an inkling of emptiness or loneliness, this star will fortify those emotions. This star also indicates meeting someone with big dreams, but no action. In other words, he or she lacks the drive to move forward in life. While his or her excitement or passion exists, it is not strong enough for them to maintain it. With that in mind, try not to depend on anyone at work or at home. If you totally rely on friends, there is high potential for them to betray you.

Basically, this year should have an overall positive effect on your life that is capable of bringing you a wealth of knowledge and pleasant experiences if you keep your eyes open for any warning signs, weigh the pros and cons prior to making any important decisions, focus on the positive aspects in life and simply be aligned with love.

The Forecast for Individual Aspects of the Year

 **Wealth**

Your income is expected to grow exponentially in 2020. This means you are headed towards experiences that may help you increase your financial wealth. In relation to this, you won't have difficulty in obtaining more money on top of your usual monthly income, but it's best to maintain a sense of balance in life by taking care of your overall health at the same time. Of course, it is good to accumulate financial wealth but not at the expense of your own health. This also means that you should try to manage your stress and try not to let work overwhelm you too much. It's also better for you to stay away from any form of speculative investments or gambling.

 **Career**

This year bodes well with your career goals as a harmonious bond with your superiors and colleagues will easily be achieved. When a good working relationship is established, it is easy for you to climb the corporate ladder. If the work that you are assigned to do involves communicating with clients, gaining performance recognition would be easier for you to grasp this year. Do not postpone any new plans or goals as this year is a good year for you to make an effort in this direction.

 **Relationships**

The possibility for you to bump into your potential partner this year is very high. This would certainly be good news for you if you happen to be under the category of single and looking for quite some time. Your searching days might come to an end this year and soon, may even be able to take your relationship to the next level. As long as you are bold and sincere when it comes to matters of the heart, you will see your love life unfolding in the right direction. If you happen to know someone in a committed relationship, they may be inviting you to their wedding reception some time this year to share the journey of their love.

 **Health**

This year, your overall health is expected to be in tip-top condition. Although that deserves a thumbs-up, you should not take things for granted. It's better if you keep paying attention to your health regardless of the condition that you are in because there is still potential for you to contract minor diseases. A good way for you to keep your body active and in shape is through working out on a daily basis. Being aware of the food you eat, taking sabbatical from work or your studies and being mindful of the weather can do wonders for you in terms of overall health.

Monthly Luck

農曆正月 (February 4th - March 4th) 戊寅

This month, fortune in your career will show off its prominence in a very strong way if compared to other types of fortune that are also present in other areas of your life. You won't need much assurance where good luck is concerned because everything will be fine for you throughout this month. As your work performance ascends, your position at work has high potential of being elevated to a higher level. This is the right time for you to reap what you sow.

農曆二月 (March 5th - April 3rd) 己卯

A change of fortune towards the negative side is expected this month. But it's not something you should worry about because it all depends on what you choose to do about it. The main issues for you to focus on this month are related to health and relationships. You should not neglect your health due to work commitments or anything else. It's also important to exercise tolerance in the workplace to avoid arguments and unnecessary hard feelings between colleagues.

農曆三月 (April 4th - May 4th) 庚辰

Positive outcomes in the areas of financial wealth and relationships are more prevalent throughout this month if compared to the previous month. But you should not take this for granted or keep your focus only in these areas. It's better to make necessary efforts in other areas of your life to reap overall benefits and see positive outcomes in all areas of your life. Since this month is a month for you to be easily injured, you should be extra cautious when making the decision to take part in any dangerous or life-threatening assignments.

農曆四月 (May 5th - June 4th) 辛巳

As a month with reasonably good fortune to tap into, you can bet that your daily undertakings and work plans will come to fruition much easily. However, it is best not to leave it to fate or good energy alone. Fortify these possibilities through positive actions, efforts, thoughts and feelings to enable more of its goodness to intensify in your life. If you have been putting effort towards something but have not seen it materialise yet, this month is most probably the right month for you to see it actually unfolding in a positive way.

農曆五月 (June 5th - July 5th) 壬午

If you are expecting good fortune this month, you are lucky because it is definitely yours for the taking if you are willing to shoulder the responsibilities that come along with it. Although there are months where you have been forecasted to have good luck that came with ease and less effort, this month, your version of good luck comes only when you put in some effort. Basically, the more hard work you put in, the luckier you will get. Helpful people will also be on your side this month, setting the perfect tone for more success to come your way.

農曆六月 (July 6th - August 6th) 癸未

Let's face it, nobody likes to encounter obstacles in life, but sometimes it is inevitable. When you are in these types of situations, especially this month where hurdles seem to take over and are part and parcel of life, it is better if you refrain from making big decisions and be wary of potential monetary losses. Keep your expectations low to ease the stress and restore your peace of mind. Although everything may seem to be on the rocky side, everything will eventually fall into place in time.

農曆七月 (August 7th - September 6th) 甲申

Everyone dislikes monetary issues. But unfortunately, that is not something you or anyone can avoid sometimes especially throughout this month where minor monetary losses are expected. Prior to this, you are advised to purchase items that you love at the beginning of the month as a gesture of good tidings to prevent further financial losses. When it comes to career, it is good for you to have a positive outlook as it increases your chances to climb the corporate ladder in a reputable way.

農曆八月 (September 7th - October 7th) 乙酉

Within this period from September to October, Peach Blossom Luck's presence fortifies the love that married couples have for each other. This means that throughout this month, married couples will enjoy a stable love life. If you are single, this may be a good chance for you to confess your affection to your loved ones. And in terms of work, you can get the best results due to the harmonious relationship that you are capable of achieving whenever you are working with the opposite sex.

農曆九月 (October 8th - November 6th) 丙戌

Be aware of the type of words that come out of your mouth. Careless talk can lead to a lot of trouble this month. If you feel the urge to express yourself or give a negative opinion, think of the impact it may have on other's thoughts or feelings. Put yourself in other people's shoes first before vocalising your thoughts and feelings to anyone. Only a fool would rush into things. You would not want to be categorised as one, especially this month.

農曆十月 (November 7th - December 6th) 丁亥

Although this month is considered a tiring month for you, it is important to remember that work is not everything. Do not let it occupy your whole life to the extreme. All work and no play will sooner or later take a toll on your health. It is advisable for you to take some time off to travel and relax. During your sabbatical, reconnect with yourself and loved ones. Allow yourself to experience the pleasures that life has to offer. Do things that make your heart sing.

農曆十一月 (December 7th 2020 - January 4th 2021) 戊子

A merry heart makes a cheerful countenance. This seems the best theme for this month's situation as pleasant surprises become part of your daily life. To elaborate further on this, your career and relationships will be in fruitful conditions and is expected to unfold more beautifully if you maintain a positive and cheerful attitude. Couples who are in a relationship should consider tying the knot this month as they have a strong backup support in terms of positive energy.

農曆十二月 (January 5th - February 2nd 2021) 己丑

Due to this month's overall good fortune, positive outcomes are expected in all areas of your life, especially in terms of career and relationship. If you are in a stable romantic relationship, this month is a good month for you to consider tying the knot with your partner. Be creative in expressing your romantic proposal to your partner and you might get a positive response. As for those in a stable marriage, they have the opportunity to see their relationship flourish and live a blissful married life. But it's important for them to make an effort in this direction to enhance their bond with each other.

Tiger 寅

虎

The Tiger in 2020

Year of the Tiger							
1926	1938	1950	1962	1974	1986	1998	2010

A person's Chinese age is obtained by adding one year to their Western birthday. For example, if you were born in 1976, your Western age in 2020 is 44, but your Chinese age would be 45.

Overall Forecast For The Year

寅 Good luck awaits you this year in the form of travel and money-making opportunities. While it is always good to adopt an attitude of gratitude when you come across favourable situations, it is also important to remember that these lucky chances may not come your way twice. Pay attention to people or situations that may present them to you in unexpected ways and simply be prepared to be the recipient of such tremendous luck.

This year's inauspicious stars revolve around feeling lonely and coping with health problems that involve family members. You can either view these issues as obstacles to push against or as blessings in disguise to approach with love and kindness. The Sky Horse Star (驛馬) moves you towards a prosperous direction where there is great expansion for growth and even a chance to start a business. If you love the thought of travelling abroad, you will be pleased to know that there is potential for you to travel extensively this year for your career or education.

This star shows the need for you to cross borders and even gives you the opportunity to go to a different state. When the right set of circumstances arise and you seize them, make sure you complete each task given to you and also take your time to get to know new people. Striking up a good conversation with one of the team members in your group may lead to a long-lasting friendship. If time permits, it is better if you go the extra mile to brighten someone's day through a local charitable organisation because it would be a waste of time to travel but not even try to make a positive difference in other people's lives.

When it comes to money, your financial struggles are over as this year, you will have the chance to start online businesses that have the potential to succeed on an international level. Basically, with this star on your side, earning extra income is more than possible.

You have high potential to accumulate wealth from abroad or at least, a different industry. When this comes to fruition, save some cash for a rainy day and do not forget to share a portion of it with the less fortunate.

And when your financial success does not seem enough to make you happy, learn to appreciate the more meaningful aspects in life. If feelings of loneliness and isolation starts to creep in, you know the Solitary Star (孤辰) is the real culprit. Instead of entertaining these low emotions, perhaps it is better if you shift your focus elsewhere and show more of your sweet self towards an elderly relative as the appearance of the Funeral Door Star (喪門) and the Earth Funeral Star (地喪) indicate that an elderly relative may need more health support from you this year.

Savour the good moments you spend with them and help them avoid injuries as well as health problems. If you have been neglecting your health, it is time for you to pay attention to it as this year, you may have to deal with a lowered immune system which means you might fall sick far easier than before with the appearance of the Funeral Door Star.

This, however, can be avoided if you are picky when it comes to food choices and make an effort to get involved in healthy physical activities. A better approach would be to focus on a healthier lifestyle for the sake of your overall wellbeing. When you are healthy in mind, body, soul and spirit, it would be easier for you to help other people.

Logically, if you cannot get rid of stress and constantly struggle with negative emotions, it would be difficult for you to give advice to loved ones or brighten someone's day. The same goes with feeling sluggish, looking unhealthy and displaying an overall negative attitude. You won't be approachable and instead of drawing people near you, you would push them far away. The more you nurture yourself, the more you become capable of caring for others.

The Forecast for Individual Aspects of the Year

 **Wealth**

If you have been wanting to splurge in 2020, it is best to put that thought on hold as monetary loss would be an inevitable part of your life throughout this year. To avoid its negative effects from escalating, it is advisable for you to purchase items that you love as a symbol of good tidings. And although financial difficulties may come, heaven luck is expected to be drawn to you in the most surprising ways if you are open and receptive to it.

 Career

The possibility for you to go through a rough patch is very high, but if you make an effort to communicate well with others, you should be able to eliminate misunderstandings that could lead to potential problems. And although effective communication is imperative in the workplace especially this year, unfortunately, no matter how much effort you put into your work, your talents and skills would go unrecognised. In fact, you can only achieve half the result with double effort. But there's more to life than work. At least, you have a job and you are doing the best you can. When you adopt a positive attitude, you will be surprised at how easy it is to meet your targets.

 **Relationships**

Emotions are barometers that we use throughout the day to determine our well-being and degree of happiness. If you are upbeat most of the time, your weak Peach Blossom Luck may have little to no effect on your relationships. All you have to do is put in some effort. When it comes to matters of the heart, it's best to show people your true colours and allow them to love you for who you really are. Wedded pairs and romantic duos should pay more attention to their partner's health this year.

 **Health**

This year's overall health fortune falls on a low scale, but problems in any area of life actually exist to teach you to face them and appropriately address them. When you start perceiving everything as a blessing, your whole life starts going in that direction. A good way to fortify this new positive mentality is by acting out on it. The best way to be healthy is by following a health regime on a daily basis. It may be difficult for you to cope with sad news that may involve the death of a relative or family member this year, but the strength to go on usually comes from embracing the situation. It's also best to avoid any assignments or tasks that pose a threat to your safety or health.

Monthly Luck

虎

農曆正月 (February 4th - March 4th) 戊寅

This month's overall fortune falls on a moderate scale, but fair fortune is still good fortune and that means you are headed towards quite a good month even if you have to go through a few obstacles. Stumbling blocks actually exist to teach you to face your fears with boldness and give you the opportunity to shift your negative thoughts. When you start perceiving everything as a blessing, your whole life starts going in that direction. A good way to fortify these positive traits is by being around positive people.

農曆二月 (March 5th - April 3rd) 己卯

This month's forecast shows that you have potential to experience smoothness in the area of work due to the help of colleagues. Although difficulty may arise, helpful people are willing to lend a helping hand and when that happens, acknowledge and appreciate their kind gesture. Let them know how touched you are by their assistance and if help does not happen automatically for you when you need it the most, ask for it. This month is also a good month for you to attend social networking events to expand your social circle.

農曆三月 (April 4th - May 4th) 庚辰

Although there is less fortune in store for you this month, it should not stop you from making plans and enjoying life to the fullest. The thought of having less fortune should not scare you or worry you. In fact, it should propel you to take more action. Instead of moping around, go out there and be the best version of yourself. But be careful how you spend your time and money as there is potential for unexpected events to delay your plans this month.

農曆四月 (May 5th - June 4th) 辛巳

You should be more focused on tolerance throughout this month, not that it was not important during other months. It's just that during this month, there is higher potential for you to be involved in arguments. Therefore, the quieter you are, the better the outcome. Try to always take a positive approach. If someone seems to sway you in a negative direction, quickly turn the other way or completely avoid them whenever they show the slightest negativity. Being around these types of people won't do you any good anyway.

農曆五月 (June 5th - July 5th) 壬午

Emotions are barometers that we use throughout the day to determine our well-being and degree of happiness. For some people, however, their emotional life tends to resemble more of a roller coaster than a barometer, with ups and downs that leave them feeling wiped out and drained. If that is how you feel, the best way for you to cope with it is through total relaxation. This month is the best month for you to take leave from work and simply unwind. It is advisable for you to start making plans to travel to a familiar or new destination.

農曆六月 (July 6th - August 6th) 癸未

Solid wealth fortune is yours throughout this month. Your sphere of influence also resembles that. If you are contemplating on what you should do next, perhaps it's best to choose the selfless route and help others out of their problems. Whether your assistance is more focused on finances, food or even a kind word, sometimes that's exactly what others need to nudge them in the right direction and help them shift their life's purpose.

農曆七月 (August 7th - September 6th) 甲申

This month is about working hard to get rewards. If your superior instructs you to go outstation or travel for work, do not think twice as it could benefit you in the long run. If you are in a relationship, this month shows high potential for you to experience a lot of drama. Therefore, the best approach would be to focus more on the positive aspects of your partner. Although you may feel the urge to express your feelings to someone you admire, this month is not a lucky month for you to take that step. It's best to put that thought on hold for a while.

農曆八月 (September 7th - October 7th) 乙酉

Health may start to deteriorate this month. Fortunately, only minor illnesses with a fast recovery rate is expected due to your potential to meet with the best doctors or healers. A decline in health, however, does not mean that everything else would start going downhill as well, as career and work have strong potential to benefit you.

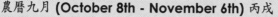

農曆九月 (October 8th - November 6th) 丙戌

Career and wealth fortune are meant to soar this month through the help of nobles. You have high potential to be at the right place at the right time to meet the right people. When you are fortunate enough to come across people with good intentions, you know you are on the way to success. The only problem that may steal your joy this month is related to your relationships. But through positive communication, even this can be rectified very quickly.

農曆十月 (November 7th - December 6th) 丁亥

There is strong fortune for you throughout this month to increase your wealth and the best part of It all, is the high potential for helpful people to move obstacles out of your way for you. Everything is meant to flow effortlessly in the right direction. But you have to sacrifice your negative patterns and push your ego out of the way. While there is nothing wrong with the information that you currently know, being open to other people's advice and ideas exposes you to a whole new world.

農曆十一月 (December 7th 2020 - January 4th 2021) 戊子

Although this month is labelled as a disastrous month with unexpected financial losses and stressful moments in relationships, you have the ability to navigate through the rough waters with ease if you dwell on positive thoughts and feelings. Be more compassionate when dealing with others. When the situation calls for you to make a decision, think twice before you act. It's important to remember that the best decisions are usually made when one is calm. You can move mountains when you have the right attitude.

農曆十二月 (January 5th - February 2nd 2021) 己丑

This month's experiences revolve around stability in terms of career and wealth. But effort and determination both go hand in hand when it comes to fortune in these areas. Although there is potential for you to see slight improvements with less setbacks, it should not disempower you from going after what you want in life. You have the right to live a better life and more than enough abilities to make this month better than it was meant to be.

Rabbit 卯

Year of the Rabbit

1927	1939	1951	1963	1975	1987	1999	2011

A person's Chinese age is obtained by adding one year to their Western birthday. For example, if you were born in 1976, your Western age in 2020 is 44, but your Chinese age would be 45.

Overall Forecast For The Year

For better or worse, the theme of Rabbit's forecast in the year of the Metal Rat is all about relationships. Almost all of the annual stars, both auspicious and inauspicious, touches upon your relationship aspect in one way or another. Though the current is looking to be less auspicious than the previous year, how it would actually play out depends on your decisions. If you are able to make wise choices, it can definitely be a good year for you.

The Moon Star (太陰) allows you to find opportunities that can expand your wealth. If you have considered making investments such as acquiring properties, now would be a good time to do so. It's all about who you know; if you wish to get ahead, listen to what others have to say. They may have input that would be valuable to you or can connect you to mentors. Additionally, you'll be able to gain the help of Noble People in the form of women if you have the Moon on your side.

What enhances the relationship aspect would be the Red Matchmaker (紅鸞). For Rabbits who are single and ready to mingle, you might find just the right partner with the help of this particular star. Overall, it's a star that can boost your likability factor, making you more easy-going when it comes to socialising with others. If you're not looking for love, it's also a good star to have in terms of networking, attracting new customers and building your fanbase.

When your social life is enhanced, it does bring its fair share of problems. The Piercing Rope Star (貫索) may hint at how exactly it may happen. This inauspicious star indicates that there are petty elements in your environment and it is likely you'll hear all sort of gossip and people being vindictive to one another. This doesn't bode well for those who can't handle stress. If you let it get to you, you might even develop stress-related illnesss. Fortunately, the negative effects of this star won't be able to affect you if you keep a strong mind and learn to ignore the negativity around you.

The Triple Punishment Star (三刑) indicates that trouble brews on the domestic front as well. It's a star that foretells clashes and arguments between family member. Rabbits simply have to be mindful with their speech and interaction. Think before you speak, choose your words carefully and try to have an idea on how others might perceive you. Handle your family with care, focus on your bonds and don't let petty squabble put strains on your relationship.

A good reason for you to remain focused would be because of the presence of the Hook Spirit Star (勾神). It is an inauspicious star that indicates a confusing and uncertain year; or at least you might feel like it. The problems associated with this star is generally minor. If you have made promises in the past, be prepared for people asking you to make good on your words. If not, be prepared for angry people. If it is clear that it is something you have promised, just get it done and over with.

What you should really be looking out for however is the Great Assembly (卒暴). This inauspicious star on its own denotes you being accident prone; which is not a surprise considering everything else that's happening at the same time. Try to look after your well-being, both mental and physical. These two aspects correlate to one another so it's advisable for you to strike a healthy balance in your life. This way, come what may and you will still be able to overcome it in one piece.

Like it or not, you'll be able to meet more people this year. Even if you find the problems that comes with it to be a hassle, it's all a matter of perspective and mindset. Rather than dreading the fact that you'll be dealing with people problems, there are silver linings in sight. You'll be more well-connected this year and these new people are also opportunities for new endeavours in the future. In order to access this valuable asset, you have to overcome a couple of small challenges. When describe the year as such, it's not so bad after all.

The Forecast for Individual Aspects of the Year

Wealth

There is superb wealth fortune in store for you throughout 2020. First of all, there is an opportunity for you to get a raise, but this can only be part of your delightful experience after you do all of the necessary tasks at your workplace and refrain from participating in any high-risk investments. If you really want to get involved with it, it's best to select low risk investments. Aside from that, it is also advisable for you to purchase real estate or assets with growing value to allow more financial wealth to flow into your bank account.

Career

Although your career fortune is ordinary this year due to obstacles that may come in the form of rumours, helpful people are keen on helping you out. Learn to focus on the bigger picture and feel genuinely thankful that you have a job. Think about other individuals out there who are suffering due to the fact that they are jobless. Put yourself in their shoes and realise how lucky you really are. This may give you a motivational boost to do better at your workplace.

兔

The Rabbit in 2020

Relationships

Instead of being someone's maybe, you'll actually turn out to be someone's baby. In other words, there is strong peach blossom luck for those who are single, this year. However, you should not remain idle and wait for someone to sweep you off your feet. Of course, there is nothing wrong with letting the love of your life come find you, but it is better if you also take action by frequenting potential places that may allow you to meet him or her. Committed couples on the other hand may consider tying the knot this year due to the presence of auspicious stars.

Health

This year is not a good year for you in terms of health. But that can shift if you are willing to change your lifestyle and daily habits. After all, prevention is way much better than cure. It's best for you to commit to a scheduled health regime and indulge in holistic practices which involves a lot of self-care than actually trying to fix a dire condition when or if it ever arises. A balanced daily food intake and adequate workout are among the best ways to keep your body active and prevent illnesses.

Monthly Luck

農曆正月 (February 4th - March 4th) 戊寅

Although rumours are trivial when it comes to work related matters, it can bother you if you focus on it too much. This month can be considered a smooth month for you to accumulate wealth and an even better month for you to experience success in your career. But it has the potential to surpass your expectations if you put in extra effort. The presence of helpful people around you are meant to assist you in ways that you have never even thought possible. With their assistance, problems that may seem difficult to rectify would not only be easy to solve, but would only take a short amount of time to see the positive results coming to fruition.

農曆二月 (March 5th - April 3rd) 己卯

Instead of responding negatively to people who are so keen on spewing hatred, realise that this type of people are actually unhappy and miserable. That is why they have no capacity to be kind or respond in loving ways towards others. That is why they come up with silly or nasty rumours to hurt others. Try to understand their situation and start feeling compassion for them. It's best to take care of your overall health and wellbeing this month and refrain from focusing on rumours. Let the negative karma that they have accumulated through their actions come back to them and it's best to refuse to partake in any dangerous activities to avoid any injuries.

農曆三月 (April 4th - May 4th) 庚辰

It looks like you will be able to mingle with ease this month as everything concerning relationships will be working out just fine for you. This also includes your relationships with the people you work with and on top of that, women will find it easier to relate to men. If you are romantically interested in someone, this is a good month to confess your feelings to him or her. Both of you might end up taking your relationship with each other to the next level.

農曆四月 (May 5th - June 4th) 辛巳

This month's theme is centered around rewards and trips. Although the workload at your workplace may overwhelm you, you will be rewarded for your hard work. There is even an opportunity for you to go on a pleasant trip. How about a trip to a desired location or country with all expenses paid for? Well, that is something that you can definitely look forward to this month. But why wait for other people to give you what you want? You can do your own research, book your own flight, accommodation and tours, and still go on a pleasant trip.

農曆五月 (June 5th - July 5th) 壬午

Good fortune this month won't be as strong as you have experienced it during other months. It may seem strange at first, as if you are on a roller coaster ride, so it's best to refrain from making major decisions. If you are in a committed relationship, you should be careful because there is high potential for someone to interfere or pose as a third-wheel, causing you heart ache and suffering. If you suspect any early signs, it's best to have a heart to heart discussion with your partner or totally avoid it by paying attention to your partner's needs and desires. There is high chance for your partner to stay loyal if he or she has a strong, special bond with you.

農曆六月 (July 6th - August 6th) 癸未

This month is considered to be a lucky month for you due to the consistency you will receive in terms of getting assistance from others. When it comes to work, you will have to toil this month and get rewards only after working very hard for it. Although that is the situation, it is important to remember that when people lend a helping hand to you, it is better if you acknowledge their help and show your appreciation towards them through both action and speech.

農曆七月 (August 7th - September 6th) 甲申

Pay attention to your health to prevent illnesses this month. You can jog or do brisk walks on a daily basis to keep your health in tip-top condition. And although health is not a strong point for you this month, favourable conditions will start making its way to you through your career as you have very strong good fortune in this area. You need to be healthy in order to perform well at your workplace, so take note on the importance of having good health.

農曆八月 (September 7th - October 7th) 乙酉

Refrain from making any investments this month to avoid monetary losses and think twice before making any decisions. If you are scheduled to attend any tests or sit for any exams this month, try to prepare everything beforehand which among them includes conducting your own research, arriving to the exam hall a few minutes before the examination starts and avoiding careless mistakes. When it comes to tests and exams, enough rest is needed to perform well and achieve high marks.

農曆九月 (October 8th - November 6th) 丙戌

This is considered a pleasant month for you because you will receive assistance from helpful people. There were times when you were required to put in a lot of effort to see visible results, but this month, that is not necessary as favourable situations will be unfolding very easily for you. Noticeable good fortune in relationships in particular will be present throughout this month. If you want to make new friends or have good connections with VIPs, there are plenty of social networking opportunities for you to tap into. The best part of this is your strong ability to attract their attention and support to accommodate you in every way.

農曆十月 (November 7th - December 6th) 丁亥

You should be aware of the fact that not everyone in this world can be trusted. Let's face it, appearance can be deceiving sometimes. There are many layers to a person and this, unfortunately is even more noticeable throughout this month – a month full of fraud traps. Keep your eyes open and be alert at all times. If anyone approaches you with a proposal to become his or her guarantor, it would be better if you turn the person down to avoid unnecessary monetary losses. If you need more information about this, it's best to conduct your own research, ask around or seek for professional advice.

農曆十一月 (December 7th 2020 - January 4th 2021) 戊子

Love will come knocking on your door this month. Superb Peach Blossom luck awaits you which will make it easier for you to find the right partner. But it's best not to leave it to luck and actually go out there and find ways to expose yourself to the possibility of love. If you know what to do, it's best to go in that direction and allow your love story to unfold naturally. This month is also a lucky month for rabbits to show their affection and confess their admiration to someone they think highly of.

農曆十二月 (January 5th - February 2nd 2021) 己丑

Prepare to welcome wealth fortune with arms wide open throughout this month as you are more than capable of receiving heaps of it together with ample stability from known and unknown sources. Although a minor monetary loss is expected, this can be avoided if you purchase items that make your heart sing at the beginning of the month - a sign of good luck and a symbol of good fortune to prevent further losses. And since rabbits are expected to be easily injured this month, it is advisable for you to say no to any proposals that require you to be involved in extreme and dangerous activities.

Dragon 辰

Year of the Dragon							
1928	1940	1952	1964	1976	1988	2000	2012

A person's Chinese age is obtained by adding one year to their Western birthday. For example, if you were born in 1976, your Western age in 2020 is 44, but your Chinese age would be 45.

Overall Forecast For The Year

辰 A journey like no other is this year's theme for the Dragon's forecast. The way you respond to a situation and the meaning you give to each moment is what really matters as it determines how your year will unfold. There will be challenging times, but remember no matter how tough a situation may get in life, you still have the power to turn the tides in your favour. It is just a matter of shifting your way of thinking.

The Three Stages (三台) calls you to career success and work advancement this year. But if you are slow to act when an opportunity arises, that moment may just pass you by. Those on the entrepreneurship path may be drawn to a business expansion and if you are looking forward to a promotion, this star will help you get the recognition you need for that to come to fruition. If there were doors that kept shut for you in the past, get ready to choose which door to go through this year because all of them will open wide for you without you even having to knock on each one of them.

If you have your heart set on a career advancement, the Elegant Seal (華蓋) will most likely make that happen for you. It's also a good star to have if you are involved in sales and marketing. Having it on your side this year gives you more opportunities in terms of professional interests while highlighting the positive aspects of confidence and independence.

As an artistic star, it imbues you with the inspiration to show more of your creative side and finds its way of illuminating an important part of you that makes you eccentric and at the same time strange to the public eye.

The National Treasure Star (國印) has its own style of bringing you a whimsical feeling of being fortunate all of the time and whenever it is around, it increases your opportunity to gain power and authority at work, especially among male superiors. This is a good star to have when you are working for someone. It is associated with a rise in rank and a possible increase in income.

This year, your sensitivity to supernatural energies will be heightened due to the Five Ghost (五鬼), a star that has the ability to open you up to the possibility of witnessing mysterious and supernatural events. Another downside to it is having to deal with suspicious people which may involve one's spouse in particular. This is due to its ability to stir emotional volatility and instability.

When there are legal entanglements and documentation problems, it is not fair to blame it all on the Officer Charm Star (官符) even if these affairs are strongly linked to it. Of course, it is always easy to point fingers at something or someone when a problem occurs in your life, but if you get your act together and deliberately make an effort to pay attention to anything that would get you in muddy waters where these issues are concerned, you may be able to turn the tides in your favour. Should any unfulfilled promises come to mind, it is best to sort them out quickly.

The Flying Charm Star (飛符) and The Year Charm Star (年符) are both coming into view to make matters even worst as they eagerly present themselves as fearsome heartbreakers with potential legal entanglements attached to them. A combination of these three stars make negative effects even more severe. Bankruptcy and unwanted chaos are connected to the Year Charm Star – a sign to be extra careful where finance is concerned.

The Yellow Flag Star (黄幡) on the other hand shows you how important your overall health is although it has the potential to give you concerns in this area. And unfortunately, that's not the only thing it is famous for. It also indicates troublemakers. Although this is bad news, at least, you will know who they are as they will not be lurking around, but instead, will be in your face as you pursue goals or make plans to get married.

Visible troublemakers may not be able to bother you as much as the gossip that is brought in by the Pealing Head Star (披頭). However, if you continue to focus on the important and meaningful aspects of life, you will come out as a winner. While this star is also associated with ill health and the death of a family member, your main focus should be on maintaining a healthy lifestyle and appreciating life on a daily basis.

The Forecast for Individual Aspects of the Year

 **Wealth**

Although financial strife after incurring a significant loss is expected this year, visible signs to gain from this loss is also expected. It is advisable for you to spend money on assets or make investments into fixed deposits or saving plans to prevent further losses from occurring. The trick is to transform this financial drought into something more positive, tangible and profitable. Deal with it wisely by asking people for in depth insight on possible financial developments. Do not remain idle and leave everything to fate. Be the captain of your own ship.

 **Career**

Miscommunication and backstabbing take the spotlight in your life this year. While these situations are certainly not good for your career progress, it has the ability to strengthen you in many ways if you are willing to see the blessings that come along with it. For instance, through the possibility of miscommunication, you are able to learn that respecting others is vital and that genuine communication involves more than just words and non-verbal gestures. Backstabbing is a difficult experience to embrace, but it just makes you think about the deeper meaning of life and appreciate your real friends or the genuinely kind people around you even more.

 **Relationships**

You can garner your partner's attention this year to the point of drawing in a romantic marriage proposal. As long as one of you bring up the subject, there is high chance for you to tie the knot especially if you are in a committed relationship. This year's relationship forecast does not show much progress if you are a single individual keen on meeting the right person. However, if you have a crush on someone, expressing your admiration towards him or her may lead to favourable and surprising results.

 **Health**

Although you would probably feel uncomfortable to change your habits this year to be more in alignment with good health, it is vital for you to do it as your overall wellbeing depends on it. This year, it would be easy for you to fall sick and sustain injuries. Although only minor issues are tied to these scenarios and the negativity surrounding them are miniscule in nature, you should not ignore this aspect of your life. It's best if you pay special attention to potential issues that are related to your waist and stomach area because there are high chances for these issues to become severe if left unattended. In relation to this, it is advisable for you to refrain from extreme activities or exercises and avoid eating fried food.

Monthly Luck

農曆正月 (February 4th - March 4th) 戊寅

Since this month is considered as a laborious month, be prepared to work extra hours to complete any tasks or assignments. Although you have potential to fall ill due to the presence of the illness star this month, it won't be much of an issue because it is so miniscule in nature. There is nothing to worry about where health is concerned especially if you maintain a healthy lifestyle on a daily basis. The best way to minimise its negative effects is by keeping yourself busy throughout this month.

農曆二月 (March 5th - April 3rd) 己卯

Let the rumours and backstabbing that are expected to happen reveal who your true friends are and unveil the actual, accurate information that is needed. Approaching these types of circumstances with tolerance is usually the best approach for anyone to take. Although you have a chance to provoke arguments this month, refrain from doing it even if you are on the winning end. This month, any slip of the tongue can cause you unwanted trouble. Only a fool would indulge in such foolish activity.

農曆三月 (April 4th - May 4th) 庚辰

It's better to set the tone of this month by having more low expectations than what you are normally used to. Of course it is good to have goals in life and be more ambitious, but this is not a good month for you to be in that stance as it would only bring you heart ache and disappointments. If compared to other months that are usually productive, this month tends to be non-aggressive. Perhaps it is better if you remain nonchalant about it to reap its full benefits.

農曆四月 (May 5th - June 4th) 辛巳

Unpleasant events may take place this month, but nothing major or life threatening are meant to happen. If you are a single dragon, you may have had difficulties meeting the right person, but this month is a good time for you to be on the lookout for the opposite sex. You do not even need to look so far as the person you are looking for is most probably within your social circle. Contemplate on the type of person you want and make efforts to meet him or her. Everything else will fall into place once you make a decision.

農曆五月 (June 5th - July 5th) 壬午

Your luck to receive extra amounts of money is already written in the stars. But if you do not make an effort to make it happen, you won't be able to see it come to fruition. When it comes to financial matters this month, you should refrain from making any high-risk investments and remember that being generous is a positive way to live a better life. It may seem that you are losing money, but that is further from the truth as greedy people are actually the real losers.

農曆六月 (July 6th - August 6th) 癸未

You may encounter some speed bumps in your career this month. But if you work hard enough, it is not impossible for you to go through it and even solve any problems that may come along the way. Pay extra attention to your health this month as there is an increased risk of experiencing various types of illnesses. Whether you want to rectify these issues immediately or completely prevent them from happening is totally up to you. If you have enough commitment, you will see visible results.

農曆七月 (August 7th - September 6th) 甲申

This month is all about having good fortune especially in terms of career, health and relationships. If you have been thinking about purchasing a house, there is high chance that you may find the house of your dreams this month. Strong Peach Blossom luck is on your side if your relationship status is either single or married. But you would be more entitled to receive the blessings if you are in a receiving mode or have a mindset that makes you more receptive to its flow.

農曆八月 (September 7th - October 7th) 乙酉

Minor illnesses may negatively affect you this month. But if not addressed properly, the intensity of this negativity could escalate to an unbearable level. On top of that, it's also important for you to be wary of accidents related to road and traffic to be on the safe side. If you are a parent, it is advisable for you to know your children's whereabouts and circle of friends to prevent them from mixing with the wrong crowd. Equip them with the correct perception and knowledge to help them make good decisions.

農曆九月 (October 8th - November 6th) 丙戌

It's time for you to reap the rewards from what you have sown in the past. You could even see signs of it about to materialise which will further assure you of what you are about to receive. Basically, this month is a month of delightful pleasures. But it depends on how you want to use your time and it also depends on how you want to perceive everything that comes into your life. When you are in a readiness type of mode, it would be easier for you to enjoy the fruits of your labour.

農曆十月 (November 7th - December 6th) 丁亥

Stagnation and boredom take the spotlight throughout this month. Yes, unfortunately, it is a rather dull month with no risks and no surprises. But the good part is, you can spruce it up by planning interesting activities and simply spice up your life through positive actions, thoughts and feelings. The moment you do this, positive shifts will take place and instead of experiencing the dull month that you were supposed to experience, you will end up giving testimonies about the fun experiences that took place.

農曆十一月 (December 7th 2020 - January 4th 2021) 戊子

Unlike other months throughout this year, this particular month is actually the best time for you to start working on any collaboration projects that you might have thought about doing but have not dared to do yet. And due to the strong Peach Blossom Luck this month, there is high chance for you to succeed when you confess your admiration to your crush, so go ahead and make your first move!

農曆十二月 (January 5th - February 2nd 2021) 己丑

The speed bumps in your career should not derail you from your dreams. In fact, it should be able to make you stronger and actually help you deal with any hurdles that you may come across from time to time. Although your career life may not show favourable results this month, you are guaranteed a smooth life where love is concerned, so start expressing your undying love towards your partner and show more passion when it comes to making decisions to spend more time with each other.

Year of the Snake							
1929	1941	1953	1965	1977	1989	2001	2013

A person's Chinese age is obtained by adding one year to their Western birthday. For example, if you were born in 1976, your Western age in 2020 is 44, but your Chinese age would be 45.

Overall Forecast For The Year

巳 This year presents many opportunities for you to find the silver lining in every situation. Although good luck will come to you in the form of support and new relationships, the way you approach every situation will determine its final outcome. Life can be filled with so much drama due to the presence of the inauspicious stars this year, but if you choose to look at life in a more positive way, you could turn the tides in your favour. Take time to contemplate on life's blessings that you have the pleasure of encountering on a daily basis.

Positive thoughts can help you navigate through life's ups and downs with ease, while at the same time nudging you to make good choices and eventually, realising your goals. This year's auspicious Monthly Virtue Star (月德) takes the spotlight to rectify any problems that tend to escalate with time. Since this star is related to relationships and is strongly linked to support, rectifying problems will be such a breeze for you this year.

This also means that if you are in need of solving issues that revolves around people, this star shows that you are much closer to a desired conclusion than you think you are. At least, it has a strong ability to reduce the severity of this year's negativity where relationships are concerned.

And although doom and gloom seems to get in the way of your life this year with the presence of the three inauspicious stars - the Death Charm Star (死符), the Robbery Sha Star (劫煞) and the Solid Killing Star (的煞), you won't see them as huge or miniscule problems if you keep an open mind and heart.

The Death Charm Star suggests that you pay more attention to elderly relatives especially senior males as they might need you to support them in terms of health-related matters. Since this star is also related to common illnesses, when this star comes into the picture, it is best to pay attention to your overall health with emphasis on your throat, respiratory system and big intestines.

Your reputation is unfortunately at risk this year due to the presence of the Robbery Sha Star. Watch your words and behaviour when you are out in public and you may be able to safeguard your reputation.

And when the coast is clear, start paying attention to your personal belongings. Anything cash-based has the potential to be stolen this year. If you happen to be a business owner, it is wise to monitor your bank account on a daily basis and keep your password in a secure place.

With the appearance of the Solid Killing Star, potential theft or robberies may even take place within your household. You should put in extra effort to prevent this from happening through enhancing your home's security with burglar alarms, CCTV and security systems.

In terms of finances, The Lesser Consumer Star (小耗) indicates that more cash will flow out of your pocket and bank account throughout this year. If you are not mindful of your finances, you may end up experiencing financial losses as a result of cheating, swindling or extravagant spending.

A breakdown in communication due to factors beyond your control may happen with the appearance of the Broken Star (破碎) and although you may feel a strong urge to ignore these types of situations, pretending that everything is alright when they are not could lead to more harm than good.

When this star starts to subjugate you and causes your status or reputation to suffer, imagine the life of a caterpillar that turned into a butterfly. You too have the ability to break free from the chrysalis prison of your former life to become someone new. You have the power to choose good thoughts, and fly away into a life filled with flowers, nectar, wind at your back, while being appreciated for your overall beauty as you soar from one phase of your life to the next completely changed.

The Forecast for Individual Aspects of the Year

 **Wealth**

This year, you'll have more chance to accumulate, save and spend money in a more relaxed way compared to last year. Although there is progress and good fortune in terms of financial status awaits, you should not go overboard when it comes to spending. It's also important to keep an eye on your possessions as this year, more people will give their attention on your personal belongings with ill intentions of stealing it away from you. Your cards should also be placed in a safe place to avoid any unwanted occurrences.

 **Career**

You will start this year with a solid foundation where career is concerned and with unbelievably strong good fortune headed your way. As a result of this, you will see great cooperation between you and your superior. This is a thumbs-up for you as from there, you can only go up and with the good energy supporting you, there are high chances for career advancement. The only thing you should watch out for is your health. A busy schedule will most likely cause a lot of stress which will unfortunately lead to health issues.

Relationships

Negative situations may strike a deep chord within causing you to feel helpless, and in certain cases, miserable or ill tempered. But it's important to remember to anchor your thoughts with love and appreciation. If you follow this as your guideline, it will enable you to refrain from getting involved in a lot of arguments this year especially if you are in a committed relationship or a blissful marriage partnership. Should an argument still take place, it won't leave a scar due to the help of mediators. And if you happen to be single, tolerance is the keyword for you to keep a new relationship moving in the right direction.

 **Health**

This year, you are required to pay extra attention to your health. If you are not mindful enough, you may contract illnesses related to the urinary system and perhaps even suffer from foot problems. In situations like this, it is better to light a candle than to cruse the darkness. There are many ways to address these health issues. However, preventing an illness is far better than curing one. All health issues can be addressed appropriately when you have a better attitude towards health by maintaining a healthy, balanced diet, treating minor illnesses before they become worse and getting involved in holistic activities that are more centered around improving people's overall wellbeing.

 **Monthly Luck**

農曆正月 (February 4th - March 4th) 戊寅
Resounding success in terms of career will be experienced this month in the most profound way. If you've been longing for a promotion, this month is the time for you to see that goal or intention come to fruition. It's best if you execute your plans accordingly. However, due to the possibility of having minor setbacks in your health, it is best to prevent it from happening through habits that revolve around good health. Parents are also required to focus more on their children's overall wellbeing and academic matters more than anything else.

農曆二月 (March 5th - April 3rd) 己卯
Although you have been exercising tolerance and endurance in your life, and you have experienced the positive impact that this combination brings, you may feel that you need to intensify your efforts and be even more patient especially when everyone is pointing their fingers at you. This month, the best approach for you is to focus on the bigger picture and adopt an attitude of gratitude. Learn to detach yourself from any negative situation that you may encounter and instead of adopting a victim mentality, try viewing it through the eyes of a loving and compassionate person.

農曆三月 (April 4th - May 4th) 庚辰
There is strong relationship fortune in store for you this month. This means that there is high potential for someone out there to tell you that both of you make the right combination. And instead of being someone's maybe all of the time, you have high potential to actually be their baby. People are more drawn to you this month and you have the ability to get along well with people from different cultural and racial backgrounds which means all types of relationships are easily forged and strengthened.

農曆四月 (May 5th - June 4th) 辛巳
Solid good fortune awaits you in terms of career throughout this whole month, but although progress is seen in this area, it is rather weak in the area of health. It is advisable for you to practice stretching exercises to improve your health, relax your muscles and avoid the risk of easy-spraining. Other health related activities can be done by joining classes related to Pilates or yoga. The simplest form of happiness inducing healthy habit that you can do is smile more often. That in itself can elevate your mood which leads to stress-free situations and a healthier outlook in life.

農曆五月 (June 5th - July 5th) 壬午

Life is not always predictable and this month, represents this even more as according to this month's forecast, you have a high chance of experiencing a roller-coaster-ride type of fortune. Although unwanted, these experiences should be acknowledged and embraced. And eventually, in the end, you are expected to come out of each experience, stronger than you were before. Committed couples should be aware of any signs of another person in your relationship because this month is a month which has a strong possibility for the appearance of a third-wheel.

農曆六月 (July 6th - August 6th) 癸未

While you may plan on working laboriously this month, it is advisable for you to take some time off and treat yourself to a nice, relaxing getaway to take your mind off work. If you refuse to follow this advice, there is high potential for you to fall sick. Although it is good to use your talents for a good cause and work hard, do not overdo it. You need to maintain a sense of balance in order to come to the conclusion that you actually had an overall good month. Do not let the bumpy road in your career derail you from your intended path.

農曆七月 (August 7th - September 6th) 甲申

Your bad luck has been reversed during this entire month which means Instead of dealing with ordeals and heart ache, everything will finally work out as they should especially in the areas of career, relationship and wealth. Your fortune star is back and thanks to its presence, you will be overflowing with joy especially if you appreciate all of the different types of abundance that comes to you regardless of whatever form it takes. Pay attention to every little good thing that happens in your life and you will end up having more chances to experience more of it on a continuous basis.

農曆八月 (September 7th - October 7th) 乙酉

A mixed of fortune is expected to invade your life throughout this month and although there are ups and downs, you should not use it as an excuse to feel upset. The wisest approach would be refraining from making any high-risk investments. In fact, any step you choose to take this month should be done with extra caution. Weighing the pros and cons on your own won't be the same as asking someone who has been through the situation. Although thinking about it is indeed very good, asking someone for reliable advice is even better.

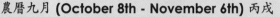

農曆九月 (October 8th - November 6th) 丙戌

This month is a blissful month for couples especially for those who are in a committed relationship. If you are single, you may be surprised with the pleasant situations that keep unfolding in your life. Although that may be a treat, love should not be the only thing on your mind as having good health is vital and without it, you won't be able to enjoy life. This month is the perfect time for you to pay more attention to it. You should be particularly cautious of mouth related diseases and choose to eat food based on its nutritional value and hygiene.

農曆十月 (November 7th - December 6th) 丁亥

If you are not strong enough, this month, you'll fall down real hard to the point of no recovery or perhaps slow recovery. This, however, should not hinder you from having a good time. After all, life unfolds in alignment with the quality of your thoughts. It is not necessary for you to be worried because you can shift your situation into a more positive state by shifting your focus. All of the issues, stumbling blocks, rumours, backstabbing, arguments and instability in relationships can be fixed when you have the right attitude and mind set.

農曆十一月 (December 7th 2020 - January 4th 2021) 戊子

Congratulations for making it through quite a rough month! This positive transition allows you to sit back and relax as it unfolds with wonderful surprises due to the presence and prevalence of a very prominent wealth fortune. It's time for you to welcome it back into your life with glee. Its absence in previous months caused difficulties here and there, but this is a month where you can think back and view those months in a much more favourable light as you will be in a far better condition this month. Since there is sufficient good energy backing you up, it will be a good month to execute your plans and goals.

農曆十二月 (January 5th - February 2nd 2021) 己丑

Since part of the best aspect of this month's highlight is good fortune in relationships, you will see a positive outcome in your relationships and it is going to be so significant that it will be hard not to notice. Although relationships should be given priority, it's best to pay attention to other aspects in your life to maintain a sense of balance. For instance, health should not be the last thing on your mind. Make sure you take sufficient rest to ensure your body gets enough rest.

Horse 午

Year of the Horse							
1930	1942	1954	1966	1978	1990	2002	2014

A person's Chinese age is obtained by adding one year to their Western birthday. For example, if you were born in 1976, your Western age in 2020 is 44, but your Chinese age would be 45.

Overall Forecast For The Year

Your aim for this year should revolve around being patient, kind and appreciative because everything else will fall into place once you get into that type of mind set and attitude. In other words, you will step into a much more comfortable scenario even when life seems to lean towards a negative direction due to the presence of inauspicious stars.

After all, there is more to life than making sure you get everything you want. Shift your focus onto helping others and making them happy, and see life unfolding with more meaningful moments that infuses you with joy.

When problems arise, the Monthly Emptiness Star (月空) has the capability of dissipating them before they even reach you. This star has your back with its own way of dissolving negative situations in ways that you have never even thought possible – a star with a strong indication that lofty goals and a long list of wishes are going to be fulfilled.

The only factor you should take into consideration is transforming your unrealistic views because if you are too fixated on your own ways and perceptions, you may not even notice the star's positive effects in your life.

Unfortunately, the inauspicious Year Breaker Star (歲破) takes the lead this year with enough power to sting and create problems for you in the form of unsettling and unexpected changes. If you do not handle your money properly, you will end up losing a lot of it this year. The wisest choice for you would be to invest your money and refrain from overspending it. You should also remember that money is not meant to be hoarded. Always give a percentage to an NGO or charity that supports a good cause. As you become a blessing to others, you will be entitled to get more blessings in return.

And while nobody likes the idea of being associated with natural calamity or experiencing calamity first hand, that is exactly what the Calamity Sha Star (災煞) brings. With this star coming into view, there is a high possibility for you to come face to face with nature's wrath. This means, when you arrive at a certain location, you may end up getting stuck in a typhoon, a hurricane or a massive flood. Help may always be available to get you out of the situation unharmed, but it is always better if you check the weather forecast prior to going out and should travelling be on your list of important plans this year, it is best to consider buying a travel insurance first.

The effort you put in towards that and other situations may not yield proper results, but do not let these difficulties stop you from giving everything your best shot. You may notice that nothing you do seems enough this year.

And the presence of the Obstacle Star (關干) will further aggravate this. Without further explanation, this star's name already shows what it represents and although it has a bad reputation of giving you challenges, you still have the ability to succeed.

Its prominent emergence this year is not meant to halt your progress or keep you away from getting what you want, but it will make sure you know it is around and make you work really hard to achieve your goals. Keep in mind that all of the hard work actually leads to satisfaction when results are accomplished.

The Sky Cry Star (天哭) is capable of making matters even worse because not only will life turn into a roller coaster ride because of it, this star influences your emotions during these situations and make you more prone to being extra sensitive when you are within your sphere of influence. If tears suddenly roll down your cheeks due to trivial matters, or you suddenly cry for no reason at all, you know that the heightened sensitivity that you feel in response to your surroundings is due to this star's existence this year.

The impulse to spend money aimlessly may come due to the Greater Consumer Star (大耗) and the huge expenses that comes along with it will have a long-term impact. Your ability to spend money wisely, however, will come only when your emotions are balanced and when your mind is alert.

The Forecast for Individual Aspects of the Year

 **Wealth**

Your income is expected to grow exponentially in 2020. This means you are headed towards experiences that may help you increase your financial wealth. In relation to this, you won't have difficulty in obtaining more money on top of your usual monthly income, but it's best to maintain a sense of balance in life by taking care of your overall health at the same time. Of course, it is good to accumulate financial wealth but not at the expense of your own health. This also means that you should try to manage your stress and try not to let work overwhelm you too much. It's also better for you to stay away from any form of speculative investments or gambling.

 **Career**

This year bodes well with your career goals as a harmonious bond with your superiors and colleagues will easily be achieved. When a good working relationship is established, it is easy for you to climb the corporate ladder. If the work that you are assigned to do involves communicating with clients, gaining performance recognition would be easier for you to grasp this year. Do not postpone any new plans or goals as this year is a good year for you to make an effort in this direction.

Relationships

The possibility for you to bump into your potential partner this year is very high. This would certainly be good news for you if you happen to be under the category of single and looking for quite some time. Your searching days might come to an end this year and soon, may even be able to take your relationship to the next level. As long as you are bold and sincere when it comes to matters of the heart, you will see your love life unfolding in the right direction. If you happen to know someone in a committed relationship, they may be inviting you to their wedding reception some time this year to share the journey of their love.

Health

This year, your overall health is expected to be in tip-top condition. Although that deserves a thumbs-up, you should not take things for granted. It's better if you keep paying attention to your health regardless of the condition that you are in because there is still potential for you to contract minor diseases. A good way for you to keep your body active and in shape is through working out on a daily basis. Being aware of the food you eat, taking sabbatical from work or your studies and being mindful of the weather can do wonders for you in terms of overall health.

Monthly Luck

農曆正月 (February 4th - March 4th) 戊寅

This month, fortune in your career will show off its prominence in a very strong way if compared to other types of fortune that are also present in other areas of your life. You won't need much assurance where good luck is concerned because everything will be fine for you throughout this month. As your work performance ascends, your position at work has high potential of being elevated to a higher level. This is the right time for you to reap what you sow.

農曆二月 (March 5th - April 3rd) 己卯

A change of fortune towards the negative side is expected this month. But it's not something you should worry about because it all depends on what you choose to do about it. The main issues for you to focus on this month are related to health and relationships. You should not neglect your health due to work commitments or anything else. It's also important to exercise tolerance in the workplace to avoid arguments and unnecessary hard feelings between colleagues.

農曆三月 (April 4th - May 4th) 庚辰

Positive outcomes in the areas of financial wealth and relationships are more prevalent throughout this month if compared to the previous month. But you should not take this for granted or keep your focus only in these areas. It's better to make necessary efforts in other areas of your life to reap overall benefits and see positive outcomes in all areas of your life. Since this month is a month for you to be easily injured, you should be extra cautious when making the decision to take part in any dangerous or life-threatening assignments.

農曆四月 (May 5th - June 4th) 辛巳

As a month with reasonably good fortune to tap into, you can bet that your daily undertakings and work plans will come to fruition much easily. However, it is best not to leave it to fate or good energy alone. Fortify these possibilities through positive actions, efforts, thoughts and feelings to enable more of its goodness to intensify in your life. If you have been putting effort towards something but have not seen it materialise yet, this month is most probably the right month for you to see it actually unfolding in a positive way.

農曆五月 (June 5th - July 5th) 壬午

If you are expecting good fortune this month, you are lucky because it is definitely yours for the taking if you are willing to shoulder the responsibilities that come along with it. Although there are months where you have been forecasted to have good luck that came with ease and less effort, this month, your version of good luck comes only when you put in some effort. Basically, the more hard work you put in, the luckier you will get. Helpful people will also be on your side this month, setting the perfect tone for more success to come your way.

農曆六月 (July 6th - August 6th) 癸未

Let's face it, nobody likes to encounter obstacles in life, but sometimes it is inevitable. When you are in these types of situations, especially this month where hurdles seem to take over and are part and parcel of life, it is better if you refrain from making big decisions and be wary of potential monetary losses. Keep your expectations low to ease the stress and restore your peace of mind. Although everything may seem to be on the rocky side, everything will eventually fall into place in time.

農曆七月 (August 7th - September 6th) 甲申

Everyone dislikes monetary issues. But unfortunately, that is not something you or anyone can avoid sometimes especially throughout this month where minor monetary losses are expected. Prior to this, you are advised to purchase items that you love at the beginning of the month as a gesture of good tidings to prevent further financial losses. When it comes to career, it is good for you to have a positive outlook as it increases your chances to climb the corporate ladder in a reputable way.

農曆八月 (September 7th - October 7th) 乙酉

Within this period from September to October, Peach Blossom Luck's presence fortifies the love that married couples have for each other. This means that throughout this month, married couples will enjoy a stable love life. If you are single, this may be a good chance for you to confess your affection to your loved ones. And in terms of work, you can get the best results due to the harmonious relationship that you are capable of achieving whenever you are working with the opposite sex.

農曆九月 (October 8th - November 6th) 丙戌

Be aware of the type of words that come out of your mouth. Careless talk can lead to a lot of trouble this month. If you feel the urge to express yourself or give a negative opinion, think of the impact it may have on other's thoughts or feelings. Put yourself in other people's shoes first before vocalising your thoughts and feelings to anyone. Only a fool would rush into things. You would not want to be categorised as one, especially this month.

農曆十月 (November 7th - December 6th) 丁亥

Although this month is considered a tiring month for you, it is important to remember that work is not everything. Do not let it occupy your whole life to the extreme. All work and no play will sooner or later take a toll on your health. It is advisable for you to take some time off to travel and relax. During your sabbatical, reconnect with yourself and loved ones. Allow yourself to experience the pleasures that life has to offer. Do things that make your heart sing.

農曆十一月 (December 7th 2020 - January 4th 2021) 戊子

A merry heart makes a cheerful countenance. This seems the best theme for this month's situation as pleasant surprises become part of your daily life. To elaborate further on this, your career and relationships will be in fruitful conditions and is expected to unfold more beautifully if you maintain a positive and cheerful attitude. Couples who are in a relationship should consider tying the knot this month as they have a strong backup support in terms of positive energy.

農曆十二月 (January 5th - February 2nd 2021) 己丑

Due to this month's overall good fortune, positive outcomes are expected in all areas of your life, especially in terms of career and relationship. If you are in a stable romantic relationship, this month is a good month for you to consider tying the knot with your partner. Be creative in expressing your romantic proposal to your partner and you might get a positive response. As for those in a stable marriage, they have the opportunity to see their relationship flourish and live a blissful married life. But it's important for them to make an effort in this direction to enhance their bond with each other.

Goat 未

Year of the Goat							
1931	1943	1955	1967	1979	1991	2003	2015

A person's Chinese age is obtained by adding one year to their Western birthday. For example, if you were born in 1976, your Western age in 2020 is 44, but your Chinese age would be 45.

Overall Forecast For The Year

The essence of the infinity symbol seems to have a strong connection with you this year, where issues tend to subside and absolute truths are revealed, thanks to the five lucky stars' ability to tune you into this year's miracles and wonders. A smooth path ahead is definitely anticipated, but if life takes a detour, it would be best to lean more towards the positive side. After all, lighting a candle is always much better than cursing the darkness. You may want to try shifting your perspective to see each situation as a blessing in disguise that was deliberately put on your path to help you become a better version of yourself.

If you anchor new positive beliefs into your subconscious mind, life may to take on a new meaning. Perhaps it's time for you to live a heart-based life where you make it a priority to discover your passions, go after your dreams and be of service to others. Let love be the mantra that accompanies you on your journey this year and onwards regardless of the inauspicious stars' ability to show themselves as harbingers from hell from time to time.

If you suddenly feel as though life is falling apart, and the whole world is against you, the right people will appear to lend you a helping hand. And you may even come to a point where you feel as if helpful people are coming out of the blue, or somehow, dropping from the sky to assist you – a clear sign that shows you the Nobleman Star (貴人) is around. Expect promotions, extra income, strong relationships and basically, overall success this year due to this star's strong, gleaming presence.

The appearance of the Jade Hall Star (玉堂) on the other hand highlights this year's excellence in terms of asset acquisition and increase in overall value. Since it is also one of the four wealth stars in Chinese astrology, it brings along with it a superior type of wealth luck.

If you are into good omens and favourable encounters, you will be pleased to know that everything positive is labelled under the Dragon Virtue Star(龍德). At least you won't have to think too hard to come up with a plan to rectify any problems that may occur as its potent and prominent debut is strongly linked to swift assistance and positive transformations.

Fortunately, it shares a lot of similarities with the Emperor Star (紫微) that conjures up the feelings of love, happiness and utmost appreciation as it assists you to receive desired outcomes. A lot of opportunities and benefits in all areas of your life may show up due to its appearance this year.

The Earth Relief Star (地解) indicates more good luck for you on the highest level. Apart from being associated with property, investment and land, it also gives you an extra edge on problem solving and the type of skills to turn a negative into a positive.

With all the good luck flowing into your life this year, it may be difficult for you to accept negative occurrences or obstacles that come from the three inauspicious stars – The Dark Sky Star, the Brutal Defeat Star and the Six Harm Star.

If you are convinced that the project you're working on is going to flop, this mechanism leaves you with a soured view of reality that wreaks havoc in your life. The trick is to not let negativity stick on your mind too much by imagining the worst case scenarios.

The Dark Sky Star (天厄) can aggravate negative situations to the point of causing minor accidents for you, but since the Emperor Star is around, there is a high possibility for you to stay safe.

When you have set your heart on something and have planned it to the point of microscopic detail, The Brutal Defeat Star (暴敗) may derail them and cause you a lot of heart ache. This star is a huge sign of severe obstacles. You may end up going through unexpected twists and turns because of it.

And if you suddenly get the feeling of being lonely or isolated, it is due to the presence of The Six Harm Star (六害). While it is okay to feel negative once in a while, dwelling on negativity for too long may cause a lot of trouble. Instead of wallowing in self-pity, it's best to get involved in charity. There are lonelier people out there than you. These people are abandoned for various reasons and if you look at their conditions, and help them out, you will see how fortunate you really are and at the same time, make a positive difference in other people's lives.

The inauspicious Year Sha Star (歲煞) may make you doubt love's powerful force due to jealous individuals. But it's important to remember that people who are filled with so much negativity are capable of showing it through their words and actions. Vibrate love and those who don't vibrate on that level will vibrate out of your experience. Although you may come across stumbling blocks once in a while, this year ensures that no stone would be left unturned.

The Forecast for Individual Aspects of the Year

 **Wealth**

This year, you are blessed with another year full of wealth in all areas of your life. The only downside to this good news is your potential to experience a minor loss where finance is concerned. But don't let it steal your peace because with careful financial planning and an attitude of gratitude, you will be able to sail through all of the difficulties with ease. Instead of noticing lack here and there, try shifting your focus into paying attention to how lucky you are. The truth is, you are always surrounded by infinite amounts of abundance. The quicker you notice and perceive that, the better your life will be.

 **Career**

When it comes to career, it is not wise for you to expect instantaneous results. You need to build a strong foundation during the first half of the year through hard work and determination. If the opportunity for you to start any new plans or projects arise while you are focused on completing your work assignments, it's important to approach each one with careful evaluation and consideration. Although your overall career fortune is fair, this year, a stronger career fortune will make its way to you in autumn. You will, however, reap more rewards if you put in more effort. If you give more than what is expected of you, you will be surprised with the positive results.

Relationships

Love is in the air and Peach Blossom luck is in the house– It's time for confessions and courtships. Couples in a stable relationship have a high chance to walk down the aisle to exchange wedding vows this year. Although wedded pairs are advised to be on guard to prevent the intrusion of a third-wheel, they should be more focused on reigniting their passion for each other by planning a blissful, sweet date or escape. And due to the strong Peach Blossom Luck this year for singles, there is high potential for them to meet someone special. Their potential partner might just be around the corner.

Health

While health issues related to the stomach won't be a problem for the younger generation throughout this year, it can negatively affect the older generation. When it comes to stomach issues, it won't be enough for you to just maintain a healthy balanced diet. You should also be mindful about where and what you decide to consume. If you prepare your own food, this won't be much of an issue because you are able to make sure everything is clean prior to cooking. The problem only arises when you decide to eat at a café, restaurant or stall. Wherever you choose to enjoy a meal, it is best to confirm the cleanliness of the place and food preparation first.

 **Monthly Luck**

農曆正月 (February 4th - March 4th) 戊寅

The new year is usually connected to ushering in new beginnings, new luck and new hope. This month in particular is all about attracting fair fortune in terms of career and wealth. But it depends on how you contemplate on this. Do not let this information cause you to be worried. Although the forecast refers to moderate fortune, it does not mean that you are unable to get more than that. If you are willing to put in more effort, there are wonderful surprises that are waiting to unfold for you.

農曆二月 (March 5th - April 3rd) 己卯

This month, you'll bask in the good fortune of your career that has been brought forward from the previous month. You can look forward to the fact that every little effort that you put into will be paid back with rewards, but do not just contemplate on its benefits without being thankful. Adopt an attitude of gratitude as life's difficulties that may arise in the early phase be solved in no time. Have patience and strive to do a good job regardless of how difficult it may seem at first.

農曆三月 (April 4th - May 4th) 庚辰

Career fortune this month is not too intense, but you can still enjoy a moderate splash of its goodness. Luckily, any obstacle that tries to get in your way will soon be met with a helping hand. Although you won't have any idea on how to solve your problems, other people are most accommodating during the whole month to ensure you achieve positive outcomes. The luck that is entitled for you is enough to lead you to the right place at the right time and enable you to meet the right people.

農曆四月 (May 5th - June 4th) 辛巳

This is a month full of activities. Investing in your personal health has the ability to take you from one successful accomplishment to another. When you are healthy, you are able to complete your tasks easily and properly. If anyone approaches you with a proposal to be their guarantor, it's best to refrain from accepting. Think twice prior to any decisions even if you think that by doing it you are helping someone out of trouble. Aside from this, it will be good if you can take some time off from work to go on a short trip as it will help you get some rest.

農曆五月 (June 5th - July 5th) 壬午

This is considered to be a month of great tidings. Since the forecast shows that all be well for you, this is a good month to work on new projects and assignments that involve a group of people. It is also a good time to confess your admiration towards someone you are fond of. If you are a man who happens to be in a romantic and stable relationship, this is the best time for you to pick a ring and propose to your girlfriend! Let the good energy of this month support you in your romantic endeavours.

農曆六月 (July 6th - August 6th) 癸未

Since health is wealth, you should focus on improving it because it might be a big problem for you this month. Therefore, it is best to be mindful of your overall health so that you will be able to do your daily tasks properly. And although the workload at your office may overwhelm you, it is another good way to keep your body active and healthy. Apart from that, it is advisable for you to refrain from any extreme and dangerous activities due to potential bleeding.

農曆七月 (August 7th - September 6th) 甲申

Love is in the air and Peach Blossom luck is in the house– It's time to pay attention to the people around you especially if you are single. If you have been admiring someone, confess to him or her because this month, you have energetic support to assist you. Lovers have a high chance to walk down the aisle to exchange wedding vows this month while married couples have potential to spend more romantic times with each other. When it comes to career, there will be no setbacks or surprises.

農曆八月 (September 7th - October 7th) 乙酉

It's best if you figure out the best way to manage your finances and refrain from partaking in any investments throughout this month. Dangerous activities should be the last thing on your mind to avoid any injuries. Those keen to pass their exams should not study too hard because instead of getting the high marks that they want, they will end up getting less rest and more stress. Besides, if they do not get enough rest, they have high potential to make careless mistakes during their examination which could jeopardise their academic success.

農曆九月 **(October 8th - November 6th)** 丙戌
You will be swirling in unpleasant gossip this month, as you learn of the rumours that others have been spreading about you. It would be wise to ignore these trivialities and focus on important things. It is also a particularly good month to exercise tolerance to avoid from getting involved in arguments with people around you. If you happen to come across negativity in any form, it is best to calm down and approach it with a positive and rational mind.

農曆十月 **(November 7th - December 6th)** 丁亥
This month, you will be experiencing fair fortune in terms of career advancements. However, do not work too hard to get ahead to the point of ignoring your health. In fact, health should be your main concern during this month. If you are not in tip-top condition, it will negatively affect your work performance. Another area that you might want to focus on is making sure that the food you consume is hygienic to avoid food poisoning. If you're preparing the food with your own two hands, it's easy to make sure everything is clean, but once you decide to eat at a restaurant, you should observe the quality of the food and place.

農曆十一月 **(December 7th 2020 - January 4th 2021)** 戊子
Your attempt to do better in your career may meet with failure, but you have a choice whether to let this forecast take root and allow it to manifest, or take steps to improve the current situation to influence the potential condition in order to prevent it from unfolding. One way to do that is by maintaining a calm and peaceful attitude. This can easily be achieved through positivity and gratitude. You can't be negative and positive at the same time and you certainly can't be thankful and hot-headed at the same time either, so this is a perfect way for you to set the right tone for this whole month.

農曆十二月 **(January 5th - February 2nd 2021)** 己丑
This month is set to bring you various types of experiences, but unfortunately, it does not include the wealth fortune that many people are longing for. However, this does not mean that you will have a hard time accumulating wealth. It just means that you have to work a little harder than before and refrain from making high risk investments to make sure you are on the safe side where money is concerned. Instead of mindless spending or splurging, try to get into the habit of purchasing things based on your needs first.

Monkey 申

猴

The Monkey in 2020 —

Year of the Monkey							
1932	1944	1956	1968	1980	1992	2004	2016

A person's Chinese age is obtained by adding one year to their Western birthday. For example, if you were born in 1976, your Western age in 2020 is 44, but your Chinese age would be 45.

Overall Forecast For The Year

申 2020 is shaping up to being the year that would truly test your resilience in life. This is a great year to learn and grow through the many challenges that may come your way. Most people take their joys and blessings for granted and start grumbling about what they do not have when they are faced with problems and troubles. In times like this, think of those who are less fortunate than you. There are many ways a situation could have been worse than it is now. This is the year that will help you see the glass half of the glass for satisfaction and the empty half with a resolve to fill it.

There are several negative stars lining up in 2020. None of them are too hot for you to handle and all of them easily countered by a Monkey's sheer brilliance and perseverance. The first two stars that may bring with it some misunderstanding, malicious gossip and rumor is the aptly named Back Poking (指背) and Sky Warrior Star (天雄) star. Be careful with whom who share personal information with and be selective with whom you trust particularly at your workplace and on social media. When faced with gossip, there is only so much you can do about the situations you face, but there is a lot you can do about how you respond to them. There are many ways to handle the rumour mill. The idea is to get on the path that proves the least resistant and the most helpful to you.

With the prevalence of the White Tiger (白虎) and the Flying Chaste (飛廉) this year, you will need to be a little extra watchful with things that may bring you harm. The star is indicative of accidents and bodily harm. Be watchful of your surroundings and make sure to avoid dangerous places. Certainly drinking and driving is a big no-no this year with these stars sitting in your corner. If you have been thinking of adding some adventure to your life this year, it is best to reconsider that idea. With both these stars sitting at your heels, high risk activities such as bungee jumping, surfing, sky diving, and other extreme adventures should be put on hold.

The Monkey in 2020

As the year progresses, you may turn to retail therapy as a form of soothing your troubles away and consoling yourself on the challenges you may have to wade through. Be very selective on how you spend your money this year as the Greater Consumer (大耗) star will leave you with the tendency to spend money aimlessly. Retail therapy has its benefits – however keeping a check and balance on things is highly crucial to your economic well-being. Huge credit expenses will leave a black hole size impact on your wallet which is something you do not need to add to your troubles.

The arrival of the Great Sha (大煞) this year asks that you take careful care of your reputation. Building a good reputation requires effort, patience, and time. Destroying a good reputation only requires a single moment's misstep. With this star, you need to keep yourself in check and refrain from being reckless and impatient. Our reputation represents the way others look at us and as such if we were to behave or carry our ourselves and the things we represent in a careless and reckless manner – this is calling on trouble to your potential and current endeavours.

Life has its ups and downs. It's perfectly normal. Trying to find the source of your unhappiness will only bring you even more unhappiness. There isn't a single event in person's life, good or bad, that isn't placed there for a reason. Challenges and difficulties are there for us to confront and for us to grow. The year might see a little more upheaval, but remember Monkeys are patient and optimistically resilient. You might not be able to change the direction of the wind, but you can certainly adjust your sails to get to where you need to go.

80 Chinese Astrology for 2020

The Forecast for Individual Aspects of the Year

 **Wealth**

The flow of wealth fortune this year that you have the potential of receiving is quite on a medium scale, but that does not mean you can't accumulate more than that if you put in more effort. It is still possible for you to get into the flow of more wealth luck and gain unexpected remuneration with the help of other people. This year, you will meet helpful individuals who are willing to assist you with financial matters. But don't forget to acknowledge and appreciate their help and be more generous towards the less fortunate. A waterfall of wealth is just waiting for you to tap into it.

 **Career**

This year, there are many opportunities for you to showcase your talents. This is good for you as it will open up a lot of doors that will lead to resounding success. Unfortunately, the improvement in performance might make you a victim to jealousy and backstabbing. If this is what you are up against, you should be careful with the type of information you share with people. During these conditions, it is also best to avoid any miscommunication with your superior and colleagues especially if both parties hold a difference in opinion. Try to create stronger bonds with the people you work with by engaging in non-work-related matters outside of your workplace.

 **Relationships**

If you and your partner's actions for each other are birthed from love that is not just on a romantic or sexual level, but also on a friendship, soul to soul basis that is deep and meaningful, then marriage is a good way to take your relationship to the next level. Although this year is a romantic year if you are in a stable relationship to exchange wedding vows, it is not such a promising year if you are single and looking. However, the good news is, if you have been admiring someone from afar, this is the best year for you to make the first move. Go ahead and ask him or her out for a cup of coffee.

 **Health**

This year, expect visits to the doctor, but don't worry, no major illnesses or anything out of the ordinary are expected to happen to you. It is best to refrain from consuming too much fried food to totally prevent health problems. Although fried food may seem appetising to you at first, it can cause various unwanted illnesses such as diabetes, high blood pressure and gastritis. Unfortunately, there is a long list of other health problems that can come from this. It is an even better idea to be mindful of your overall health. Make sure you get rid of stress in a smart way. The best way is to sign up for a yoga class or practice meditation. It's also very important to choose a healthy diet and exercise on a regular basis. All of these efforts will eventually lead to a healthier, better version of yourself.

Monthly Luck

The Monkey in 2020

農曆正月 (February 4th - March 4th) 戊寅

This month is apparently not a month for you to rest and relax. In fact, it is an important month for you to step up a notch where work is concerned. As long as you pay attention to details, focus on given tasks and meet deadlines, you'll be fine. Unfortunately, in regards to finances, losses are expected, but as a lucky symbol to minimise this potential negative outcome, it is advisable for you to purchase items that you love at the initial stage of the month. In terms of relationships, it is best to maintain a positive mind set and attitude while observing the types of interactions that takes place.

農曆二月 (March 5th - April 3rd) 己卯

You will have more than enough money to fulfill all of your needs and desires and the needs and desires of others during this month – a month that promises you a good wealth fortune. Doors will also open up for you to earn unexpected extra income. Although it won't necessarily fall onto your lap, it is better if you are open to the unlimited possibilities in which it can come to you. Aside from this aspect, the period from the fifth day of March until the third day of April is forecasted to be a time where Peach Blossom Luck comes into full bloom which denotes a rather blissful month for couples.

農曆三月 (April 4th - May 4th) 庚辰

The good wealth fortune that you experienced last month will continue to help you prosper during this month which makes it also a great time to kick start a new project. Apart from luck in the area of wealth, this month also brings luck in the area of marriage for married couples. If you are single, it's a great time to ask your crush out. There's no use holding back thinking that he or she would say no. Be positive! If he or she decides to turn you down, at least you won't be wondering what would have happened if you dared to make the first move. There is high potential for you to be successful in your endeavour, but in case it doesn't turn out the way you had hoped for, don't be disappointed. At least, the person you approached will appreciate you for having the guts to come forward.

Chinese Astrology for 2020 83

農曆四月 (May 5th - June 4th) 辛巳

Career fortune is on your side as everything work related will be smooth sailing for you throughout this month. You will receive help from colleagues and superiors that will contribute to your success. But don't just sit around waiting for others to help you out. If you have been pondering on the thought of making certain decisions, you will suddenly see everything unfolding with ease for you this month. When it comes to relationships, you will see positive improvement to a certain extent among family members.

農曆五月 (June 5th - July 5th) 壬午

The theme for this month has a lot to do with experiencing a mixture of different types of fortune and various types of rewards. If you put your best foot forward, you will not have to wait for so long to see positive results springing out from that. This can be experienced in all areas of your life. The best part is, the favourable outcomes will keep on coming to you throughout this month. Although you should enjoy the endless streams of positivity, you should also remain humble and feel enormous gratitude for the good fortune and rewards that have come your way.

農曆六月 (July 6th - August 6th) 癸未

This month is a great month for love to blossom. This means you will have great luck with the opposite sex. If you were nervous to ask your crush out on a date, this month is the time for you to put that emotion aside and take action because there is high potential for your request to be accepted. If you are in a stable relationship and have thought about proposing to your sweetheart, you are most likely to succeed in your romantic endeavours.

農曆七月 (August 7th - September 6th) 甲申

You can label this month as a month for you to practice more patience and if you have not been serious with listing positive aspects as part of your daily routine, this month might be a good time for you to start. Although you won't be experiencing severe problems, and they will most likely be resolved quickly with the presence of helpful people, it is better for you to be in a positive state of mind to ease your way through all of your problems. Apart from this, there is high potential for you to sustain injuries which is a warning for you to refrain from getting involved in any dangerous activities or assignments.

農曆八月 (September 7th - October 7th) 乙酉

This month does not guarantee the type of good fortune that will make your cup overflow, but it is quite a good month for everything career related. You might have to deal with the ups and downs in your relationships and see a slight rise in terms of reputation and status, but that's about it. No matter how important you think you need to have good fortune on your side, it is best to not rely on luck alone. Of course, it helps due to the energy support, but if you try making your own effort, you will see that the probability of you having a fantastic month will increase.

農曆九月 (October 8th - November 6th) 丙戌

If you rest on your laurels, you will end up having a tough time at your workplace. It's best to put in extra hours, keep to yourself and deal with people harmoniously so that those that harbour ill intentions towards you will automatically lose. Although there is potential for nasty rumours and backstabbing that has a lot to do with you take place, it is best to redirect your focus on fully completing your work on a daily basis. After all, your main intention to work is to acquire more valuable experience and earn money. Always focus on the bigger picture. What people think or say about you is not important. You have true friends outside of work.

農曆十月 (November 7th - December 6th) 丁亥

Your patience will continue to be tested this month with more rumours and a lot of back stabbing that will eventually bother you in one way or another. Although positive thinking is the best way to deal with this, it won't be easy to maintain a positive outlook during severe negative conditions. As long as you watch every step you take and watch every word you say, you will not suffer in any way. And in order for you to come out as a winner in this situation, you should continue to focus on your daily tasks, meet deadlines and always remember to keep your eyes on the bigger picture.

農曆十一月 (December 7th 2020 - January 4th 2021) 戊子

This month is a month that allows you to shift to a positive state of mind due to the series of good experiences. With this in mind, it is important to remember to be thankful. These types of opportunities should be savoured and thoroughly enjoyed. And although the forecast is not detailed to the point of revealing everything that will happen, anything that is destined to take place will be to your liking. Contrary to the previous month, your good luck is back, so it's time to milk it!

農曆十二月 (January 5th - February 2nd 2021) 己丑

Waves of good luck from the previous month will flow into your life this month. It's time for you to celebrate because you are entitled to experience great fortune not only in one or two areas of your life, but in all areas of your life. Everything will fall into place due to help from the right people at the right place and time. You can surrender and allow the beauty of this month to unfold right before your eyes leaving you with the best memories.

Rooster 酉

雞

The Rooster in 2020

Year of the Rooster							
1933	1945	1957	1969	1981	1993	2005	2017

A person's Chinese age is obtained by adding one year to their Western birthday. For example, if you were born in 1976, your Western age in 2020 is 44, but your Chinese age would be 45.

Overall Forecast For The Year

While many people out there are looking for ways to find the light which represents solutions, happiness and fulfilment, they often overlook the most important part of all which is to actually become a light unto others. With enough support from four auspicious stars - The Heavenly Virtue Star (天德), The Fortune Virtue Star (福德), The Sky Happiness Star (天喜) and The Prosperity Star (福星), serving others will be much easier for you as you will be experiencing quite a smooth year in 2020.

In other words, despite the odds that are against you, this year foresees that you will be activating good memories, building long term relationships, progressing professionally and basically, achieving overall happiness.

If it was probably difficult for you to see commitment from your partner in the past, the Heavenly Virtue Star (天德) is coming out this year to help you patch things up. The more you reveal the selfless side of you to your partner, the more he or she will reciprocate. This star steps into your experience with its ability to remove obstacles in the form of assistance from friends, family members and colleagues. if you wish to be in full alignment with it, it is best to show your desire for improvement.

The good tidings that are continuously on its way to you this year is further magnified through the Fortune Virtue Star (福德). Since it is also a star known for prosperity, when it appears, good food, fun gatherings and a chance to explore the world appears along with it. Get ready to be spoiled rotten this year without forgetting to be selfless and showing compassion towards others. Perhaps it would be a good idea to consider getting involved in meaningful activities with your family because when the benevolent and happy evoking events start to take place, it will seem like there is no end to it.

The Rooster in 2020

Let another auspicious star known as the Sky Happiness Star (天喜) takes its course by magnifying these seemingly endless joyous occasions. As a star that is strongly linked to happy escapades which also happens to be a positive Peach Blossom Star, there is high potential for you to be in the presence of good company at gatherings such as weddings and graduation ceremonies.

If you are single, you should consider reaching out and connecting to others as you may end up finding someone special. This is a year where long-term relationships are forged. If you need important connections to get your projects done, this year may also be a good year for you to do that. Should romantic twosomes in a committed relationship bring up marriage as a topic in their conversation, they might end up exchanging wedding vows with each other this year.

In terms of career, the Prosperity Star (福星) magnifies your ability for professional progress which is connected to promotion and salary increment. But that does not mean you can just sit around and wait for the star's lucky energy to help you out. You yourself must get up and make things happen.

Inauspicious stars will be present, but they won't be able to influence you if you do not allow them to. The Salty Pool Star (咸池) will definitely create opportunities for you to be in unexpected intimate relationships. Although this is an excellent star to have when you are single, it does not create such a benevolent outcome for couples in a committed relationship. You should try to spend more quality time with your partner to avoid infidelity issues. You also need to beware of various types of disputes and slander brought in through the Annual Sha Star (年煞) and the Curled Tongue Star (卷舌).

Remember, you have the power to change situations in your life. If the story of your life still does not make you feel happy, go ahead and rewrite it. After all, you are the master of your destiny. Stars won't be able to get in your way if you have a strong desire to overcome obstacles.

The Forecast for Individual Aspects of the Year

 **Wealth**

A year of average wealth fortune may best describe your year, but that does not mean that you only have the ability to acquire wealth on an average scale. It just means you need to put in more effort. What you want is definitely not far-fetched. In fact, if you study the various methods that are available in the market on how to increase your wealth while getting advice on the best one for you, your wealth will eventually grow. As long as you plan and manage your money well, you will be able to acknowledge with conviction that by the end of this year, your wealth luck was actually not that bad.

 **Career**

Despite being an arduous year, you are likely to gain some wealth through your line of work. Prepare to receive some wonderful news in the form of a special career development opportunity or bonus that revolves around company trips and company dinner invitations. Although these are all very enticing, it's important to remember that you did not achieve all of these based on your own merits. If you want to continue the cycle of good relationships with people, put your attention on tolerance and endurance. It's best to refrain from nit-picking to create a conducive atmosphere for good communication to flourish.

Relationships

There's good news for Roosters who are focused on love, this year. You will meet the right person if you are single. But don't wait around thinking he or she will somehow drop out of the sky and into your lap. Go out there and find him or her, or at least expose yourself through dating sites and places of interest. You might even meet your potential partner through friends or family members. If you happen to be interested in someone, this is the year for you to ask him or her out because there are high chances for you to take the relationship to the next level. Twosomes in a stable relationship may end up tying the knot this year if one of them brings up the subject.

 **Health**

Health should be on your list of top priorities, this year. It is advised that you maintain a balanced diet and be mindful of your eating habits. You will be amazed to see how far it will go towards improving your health. If you have the chance to expose yourself to nature on a daily basis, that is even better as it is capable of helping you rejuvenate. Another way to maintain good health is by keeping yourself active through working out. This helps boost your immunity against diseases. If you think wealth in the form of finances is important, that is true, but so is wealth in the form of health because it helps you enjoy everything else.

Monthly Luck

農曆正月 (February 4th - March 4th) 戊寅

Those focused on love will find it pervasive due to the escalation of the Peach Blossom Luck throughout this month. If you have been intending to ask someone out, there is high potential for you to get positive feedback if you take appropriate action. While your love life may outweigh other areas of your life, your health should be your main concern. There is high potential for it to decline to a critical level if you don't pay attention to it. After all, you are the master of your destiny. Make sure you grab the steering wheel and make an effort to go towards a desired outcome.

農曆二月 (March 5th - April 3rd) 己卯

Your wealth fortune this month is growing strong. There are tons of opportunities for you to gain unexpected wealth or earn extra income. What you need to do is just open yourself up to the many possibilities. One way is by sending your resume out to companies that need part-time staff members or freelance workers and wait for their response. To avoid getting hurt, you should probably refrain from getting involved in any dangerous activities as the chance of you sustaining a serious injury is higher than normal. Being vigilant especially when you have to deal with any kind of sharp implement should ideally reduce the odds of an accident occurring.

農曆三月 (April 4th - May 4th) 庚辰

It is possible that you will suffer a small financial loss this month, but this is still a relatively great month for you as it won't cause you to cross out any items on your shopping list. You can still purchase anything you need and want. Should you come across any obstacles, you will also cross paths with helpful people. These people will not only offer you a particular boost that can help you out of your misery, but also steer you in the right direction to the point of rectifying all of your problems at the maximum level.

農曆四月 (May 5th - June 4th) 辛巳

Despite being an arduous month, you are likely to go through it with pleasant emotions and experiences due to your ability to look at everything through a different angle. When you start perceiving everything in a positive way, everything around you will transform. After all, isn't it better for you to be busy doing work to earn a living instead of being jobless? Always remember to be thankful for what you have. Many people out there are not as fortunate as you are.

農曆五月 (June 5th - July 5th) 壬午

You can look forward to this month's good energy. Everything pertaining to work will progress in a remarkable way. However, you must play your role to work hard and adhere to the rules at your workplace. In terms of relationships, you will be able to maintain a desirable camaraderie with friends and the people around you which will give you more positive energy. This makes it a suitable time for you to indulge in group activities with your friends. Planning a short trip or gathering somewhere nice would be able to further strengthen your bond with them.

農曆六月 (July 6th - August 6th) 癸未

This month, the bad luck revolves around health and travelling. The health fortune of either your parents, children or spouse may start to decline, but don't worry, this just means you need to put in extra effort towards your loved one's health. You can either purchase multi vitamins, nutritious food and drinks for them to consume or even bring everyone out for a healthy get together that involves healthy munchies or fun aerobics. Apart from that, you should try your best to avoid travelling. If you must do it due to work related matters, you can shift the negative energy by participating in regular prayers, meditations or mantra chants.

農曆七月 (August 7th - September 6th) 甲申

Although the road may not be as smooth for you this month, doors will still open up for you. It's best for you to watch every step you take. This means you need to ask for reliable advice or think carefully while weighing the pros and cons. And when an opportunity comes knocking on your door, don't wait for too long to take action. Of course, it is wise to give yourself a certain amount of time before you make the decision to proceed, but not to the point of missing out on a great chance to experience something life changing.

農曆八月 (September 7th - October 7th) 乙酉

According to this month's forecast, Roosters will be experiencing a rollercoaster ride type of fortune, but don't let the ups and downs upset you. If you are willing to grab the steering wheel, you can arrive to a better future. After all, you are the master of your destiny. Although rumours and arguments are expected to happen this month, it is not a good idea to retaliate. When you approach negativity with more negativity, you will end up dealing with the same type of energy over and over again. To be on the safe side, it is best to watch every word you say this month. This is more than just an advice for students.

農曆九月 (October 8th - November 6th) 丙戌

When the going gets tough, the tough gets going. But it should not be that way. In situations like this, it is important to remember to pause and think back about the good moments that have happened. Although this month shows signs of another rough month of career for Roosters, don't allow it to steal your joy. People with ill intentions may try to halt your progress, but if you strive to do better in your career, and show improvement via hard work, you will be rewarded for it.

農曆十月 (November 7th - December 6th) 丁亥

If you've been wanting to earn some extra income, but have no idea on how to generate the finances, the ideas might come pouring in and opportunities may come from every direction due to the good energy that is present for you throughout the whole month. It's up to you to assess each opportunity that comes to you and take action in order to see positive results. As for finances, money will come to you in abundance, but also flow out from you in abundance. It won't be easy for you to save money. But through this knowledge, you can try to move towards the idea of trying your best not to let your money flow out of your pocket or bank account too easily.

農曆十一月 (December 7th 2020 - January 4th 2021) 戊子

Despite the moderate career fortune that's in store for you during this month, you may gain appraisal from your superior. In fact, a lot of other doors will open up for you if you make an effort to be a better employee. When it comes to love, women are not as lucky as men are due to the Peach Blossom luck's potent energy which is entirely on the men's side this month. This usually means that there is a high chance for guys to win the heart of someone they admire. It is definitely a great time to take things to the next level.

農曆十二月 (January 5th - February 2nd 2021) 己丑

There is awesome ascending fortune in terms of career and wealth for you this month. However, you should not only pay attention to material gain and ignore your health. It's important to remember that health is also a form of wealth. It's best to shift to healthier habits that eventually leads you to a better and healthier version of yourself. If you are the person behind the steering wheel in a vehicle, make sure you obey the traffic rules and be fully present while driving. It's best for you to be focused to prevent any accidents.

Dog 戌

Year of the Dog							
1934	1946	1958	1970	1982	1994	2006	2018

A person's Chinese age is obtained by adding one year to their Western birthday. For example, if you were born in 1976, your Western age in 2020 is 44, but your Chinese age would be 45.

Overall Forecast For The Year

Nothing is ever achieved without some trials and tribulations. The first step in moving beyond those circumstances is to remain positive. When you reverberate positivity – the quality of your thoughts and feelings improve. Remember that you can't control everything in life, relationships or business, so embrace the adversity and dig in even further to drive a positive outcome. The harder you work for something, the more rewarding it is in the end.

This year, the many auspicious stars' strength will propel you forward, which is a true blessing. Keep in mind that with good there is also evil and with darkness there is always light. It would be best to learn to accept changes and challenges when negative aspects of the inauspicious stars rear their heads to balance out the aces in your stack.

The signature style of the Eight Seats Star (八座) can be seen through one's enhanced learning capacity, good fortune and progress of personal development. This star opens a portal for you to receive ample, noble support and unexpected opportunities for advancement. If you have this star in your Destiny Palace, you may even experience overnight fame. One way to tap into its abundant energy is by exposing your talents and skills on social media. And although this act alone won't necessarily bring you expected results, at least, you have started a ripple for things to go in a positive direction.

No matter how benevolent this year's auspicious stars might be, none of them are capable of putting an end to all of your problems. But the good news is, whenever life presents you with challenges, someone will always be around to help you. This is due to the emergence of another auspicious star known as the Relief Star (解神). It enables any type of problem you encounter to be rectified in the best possible ways. Whatever life throws at you this year; the right person will come to help you out of life's predicaments. Basically, you will be protected from all of the evil effects that come from the inauspicious stars.

This year also, you may need to pay close attention to your finances as the Leopard Tail (豹尾) star will be paying you a short visit in 2020. The star brings with it some minor financial issues in the likes of monetary losses and misplacement of valuable objects, partly due to your own carelessness. For your own peace of mind know where things are at any given time. The Leopard Tail may also result in you offending a few more people that you might be comfortable with. Therefore watching your manners, movement and communication, particularly with sensitive, is vital in keeping your sanity.

An important subject to bring up and pay attention to this year revolves around safety as two stars - the Blood Knife Star (血刃) and the Instability Star (浮沉) have potential to cause you harm. Since the Blood Knife Star makes you prone to injuries and accidents particularly during physical activities, it is better for you to be extra careful when you choose to get involved in any type of physical activity.

And while the Instability Star can cause water-related accidents and injuries, you may also find yourself having difficulty when it comes to making decisions when a situation prompts you in that direction. It would be difficult for you to make up your mind due to this star's presence which leads you to fluctuate between decisions most of the time.

The Funeral Guest Star (吊客), on the other hand, reminds you to avoid funerals in general as they have potential of leaving a negative impact on your wellbeing. The appearance of the Sky Dog Star (天狗) also comes as a warning of the ill side effects of attending a funeral. Apart from that, it is a star that bears a message for you to avoid being involved in anything that can be categorised as dangerous.

If you are not careful, the results are non-life-threatening, but you could still sustain injuries, cuts, scars and may even go through minor surgeries. Unfortunately, the plethora of negative news does not just end here as the Lonesome Star (寡宿) brings you the feeling of being lonely and unwanted. This is the type of feeling that you may want to escape from, but the best way to approach it is through acceptance because the more you push against it, the more it tends to escalate.

The only way to soothe yourself when you are feeling this way is to embrace it. Give yourself some space and enable it to gradually subside. Another way to address these emotions is by doing charity work. When you see others who are far more unfortunate than you, and you make an effort to brighten their day, your emotions will shift.

The Forecast for Individual Aspects of the Year

 **Wealth**

This year, you might have to go through a bumpy road where finance is concerned. Expect constant monetary losses, but with a solid financial backup plan in your hands. Maybe you think investing your money would be a wise approach to face this challenge, but instead of rectifying the problem, it would further aggravate it. The best way to prevent further monetary loss is by refraining from any high-risk investments.

 **Career**

Although there is potential for you to deal with backstabbers at your workplace, influential people will come to your rescue and vouch for you. Express gratitude to these people and keep in mind that the most important thing for you to do this year in terms of career is to be in alignment with your employer's goals and strive to become a better employee to transform whatever negativity that may come your way into something more positive. Sincerity also plays a major role in shifting your luck into a more pleasant one.

 **Relationships**

Due to the weak Peach Blossom Luck this year, those without a partner should not be in a hurry to tie the knot but focus more on improving themselves. Love-struck twosomes and wedded pairs, however, are prone to illnesses which means, this year is a good time for them to show more of their love and care for each other. It is advised to be more considerate with one another as even the simplest misunderstanding could lead to a decline in relationship. While it is good to listen to your partner's words, it is wiser to pay attention to your partner's body language.

 **Health**

Health is a form of wealth. Sometimes you won't notice its benefits until it is completely gone. But don't wait for it to slowly deteriorate or end before you start appreciating it. Although it might be nothing to worry about, and you will be lucky enough to find the best doctors or healers if your health starts to decline, it is best to be mindful of your overall health and safety. Try to avoid participating in extreme activities if you have not adequately prepared any essential safety measures beforehand because you may end up getting a minor injury this year.

Monthly Luck

農曆正月 (February 4th - March 4th) 戊寅

Congratulations, you will stand out this month in terms of career, but don't be a top employee with health problems. Pay attention to your overall health. Although you might want to impress your boss, overworking yourself to the point of constant stress is not the answer. It's important to remember that balance is key. To get into this stress free, healthy, balanced routine, you can join a spiritual centre to learn how to meditate properly or sign up for a yoga class and really practice it on a daily basis. If you don't have time, going to a nearby gym or brisk walking will also do wonders for your overall health.

農曆二月 (March 5th - April 3rd) 己卯

Get ready to be invigorated this month with the arrival of more auspicious luck. If you're head over heels in love with someone, and feel tongue tied whenever you are near him or her, this is your chance to get closer. Putting in effort at the right moment will yield fantastic results. Go ahead and ask him or her out for a cup of coffee. Although the success rate is relatively higher for him or her to say yes, don't be disappointed if he or she declines your offer. At least, you tried and believe it or not, that is the most important thing.

農曆三月 (April 4th - May 4th) 庚辰

Don't let minor obstacles in the form of physical health and workplace problems cause you to be upset. There's no use losing sleep over these difficulties. Do what needs to be done and simply surrender to a higher power. Everything will eventually work out for you and the good part is, it will work out for your highest and greatest good. You don't need to fight or struggle in any way. Be positive and focus on positive aspects in life to enable you to go through these minor obstacles with great ease.

農曆四月 (May 5th - June 4th) 辛巳

More than one joyful occasion will occur this month and you could be in store for a pleasant surprise. Ignore rumours that may negatively affect your positive frame of mind. It is best to focus on the good career fortune that is open to you that may come in the form of a sought-after promotion at your workplace. As a symbol of readiness, it is best to continuously adopt an attitude of gratitude. Those intending to get married will see their plans unfolding with success. Bottom line is that it is better for you to be focused on success and fortune not only throughout this whole month, but throughout your whole life.

農曆五月 (June 5th - July 5th) 壬午

A continuous flow of good fortune is coming your way this month that may lead you to bigger and better opportunities. To ensure that you experience its benefits and give way for more fortune in your life, you should learn to juggle the work load given to you with wisdom and care as every opportunity that you will come across is accompanied by another new opportunity for development. Although the forecasted career fortune for you is fair, it is not something that you should take for granted. Apart from this, you might want to take a chance on new challenges that may yield unexpected rewards.

農曆六月 (July 6th - August 6th) 癸未

Your interaction with different types of people will be more harmonious if you master the art of communication. It's not about being on your toes, but it is more about maintaining a humble and respectful attitude towards others to avoid arguments or misunderstandings. Usually, we get something by sacrificing another thing in return. This sacrifice could involve sacrificing our time or certain things we like in order to get what we want. During an argument, what needs to be sacrificed the most is your ego and your eagerness to be a winner regardless of what happens. It's important to take note on the positive aspects of making an effort and making a sacrifice while having a positive attitude towards what's coming next.

農曆七月 (August 7th - September 6th) 甲申

This month your schedule will be packed with a lot of activities and in a way, may cause you to be exhausted and quite stressed out. But the stumbling blocks you will come across at work will be far more negative and nerve racking as it will lead you to a series of disappointments. Females are forecasted to encounter more mood swings than usual. Unfortunately, emotional turmoil that comes from these experiences could cloud your judgement and interfere with your decision making. This is not a month for you to put yourself down. Instead, try to allow yourself to feel the hurt, slowly pull yourself out of it and reach out for relief.

農曆八月 (September 7th - October 7th) 乙酉

This month's theme is centered around health and hygiene. If you've been ignoring your health, this month is the perfect time for you to start paying more attention to it. You can start by examining your daily food intake and making sure it contains the necessary vitamins and minerals. The next part is by ensuring that everything you consume is prepared in hygienic ways. There are other steps for you to take, but these two aspects should be your main focus before becoming a permanent health junkie.

農曆九月 (October 8th - November 6th) 丙戌

Although you will experience less fortune this month, instead of worrying excessively about what might happen, it is better for you to be cautious when crossing the road and be even more careful when driving to prevent any unnecessary accidents. Although there is high potential for you to be injured this month, you should not focus on that. Instead, focus on positivity and be involved in charitable projects. It is advisable for you to give donations whether in the form of items, skills, money or blood for you to come out of these possibilities with success and ease. Your generosity, however, should not only be extended to others on a temporary basis. Continue to be generous regardless of the circumstances.

農曆十月 (November 7th - December 6th) 丁亥

It looks like your luck will continue to dip this month with more than just monetary loss. But don't worry, if you lose money, there are high chances for you to gain something else in return. Basically, you won't be empty handed. Although this has been forecasted, you should not use this opportunity to whine, but instead use this chance to come up with a plan and continue helping others. If you feel that you are suffering, it is time for you to realise that there are other people out there who are in far more dire conditions than you. If you don't have enough money to donate, you can contribute in many other ways. Stop thinking only about yourself, be open to helping others and watch what happens.

農曆十一月 (December 7th 2020 - January 4th 2021) 戊子

After going through the previous months that tested your patience, expect far better situations throughout this month as it can be labelled with great certainty as a month of great wealth fortune. Be open to extra income or even better, multiple streams of income through part-time jobs or gigs. Surprisingly, someone might come across your path to clear your debts. In fact, that person may even help to cancel your debts. And if that happens, be thankful and acknowledge that person for coming to your rescue. Appreciate him or her for their help.

農曆十二月 (January 5th - February 2nd 2021) 己丑

It's good to have goals to help you navigate through life, but it certainly is not good when they are blown out of proportion. After all, too much of something is not good for you. To avoid being over-ambitious, it is best to keep your feet on the ground and refrain from making aggressive decisions. Come to think of it, it's better if you carry out your plans based on the appropriateness of time. Although you have a nagging feeling that you should go in a certain direction or the thought just crosses your mind, it is wiser for you to review your plans accordingly, think about them carefully by weighing the pros and cons prior to making any important decisions.

Year of the Pig							
1935	1947	1959	1971	1983	1995	2007	2019

A person's Chinese age is obtained by adding one year to their Western birthday. For example, if you were born in 1976, your Western age in 2020 is 44, but your Chinese age would be 45.

Overall Forecast For The Year

Great year ahead in terms of wealth and learning with a good star that would boost your monetary gain, particularly through information gained through carefully researched investments. There are many ways of looking at your life this year and the outcome is determined by your state of mind and the actions you choose to take during every moment. You can either perceive life as a way to accumulate more wealth or a platform to be a blessing to others. If life gives you lemons, you can either complain, make an effort to get something else or simply make lemonade.

This year, when inauspicious stars are taking the spotlight and throwing all sorts of negativity at you, how you respond or react to them will determine how your life will unfold this year.

If you find yourself enjoying the moment with your loved one and then five minutes later, bickering over trivial matters, you may want to pause for a while and take a deep breath. Think about what you want out of life and simply shift your focus.

Although the Death God Star (亡神) is obviously playing its role in this situation, there is no reason for you to be so engrossed with it. Try to be more understanding and forgiving. If you are not focused on resolving an issue with loving intentions, it would be difficult for the other person to reciprocate.

Apart from putting you at risk of causing offence, outbreaks of arguments, this star is also considered a forgetful star that has the ability to cause you to overlook details, dates and information. Refrain from trying to memorise every data that you come across and instead, make an effort to record them by using modern technology as an aid.

The Surpassing Path Star (陌越) has the ability to negatively influence you to the point of giving you tendencies to be anxious or agitated. Unfortunately, mental and emotional anguish are both strongly linked to this star. This, however, should not be an excuse for you to be negatively affected by it. Approaching these matters through meditation retreats and yoga classes will be able to help you find solutions in the long run.

Agitation and anxiety aside, this year you will be blessed with a star that will serve as your ally. The Intelligence Star (文昌) is one star that will give you an edge over everyone else. The star aids you in the ability to understand complex information and the opportunity to learn critical concepts and find answers that may aid you in your quest to garner wealth. This is a great star in your corner particularly if you are a solo entrepreneur. It helps you achieve better business skill while obtaining relevant knowledge. For those under a boss, the star will serve you with the ability to solve problems and up your leadership and management game.

You may also want to include health regimes as part of your health goals for this year, but make sure you take a moderate and balanced approach. Going to extremes in diet, fitness or detoxification practices strips you of the healthy life you are aiming for. If you want to detox your body, start by giving it what it needs to do the job that it was designed to do.

The Sickness Charm Star (病符) aims to create health problems for you which means there is a strong possibility for you to fall ill this year, but if you regularly go for health check-ups and follow a healthy lifestyle, your health results will surpass your expectations in a positive way.

Another star that has a high probability of stealing your joy is the Swallow Trap Star (吞陷). It is coming into view with a negative impact on your finances. This means that if someone approaches you with a proposal to borrow your money or nudge you to make a major investment, you should apologise, say no and turn down the offer.

Remember that life is sometimes enjoyed by taking baby steps. The problem with many people is that their primary aim in life is to get to places fast, be it a physical location or mental goal. Sometimes looking at a situation through a big picture focus can get overwhelming. When you try to move, think, talk, eat fast things don't go too well. Stress builds up. Negative thoughts about just about anything start to well up and your personal power decreases. Remember to slow down just for a few minutes. It becomes easier to think things through clearly again and easier to find the optimistic and constructive perspective.

The Forecast for Individual Aspects of the Year

 **Wealth**

This year, you have high potential to accumulate an abundance of wealth. While you won't experience it right away, you will see a lot of positive shifts where wealth is concerned. Although unexpected wealth fortune will open doors for you to get part-time jobs and multiple streams of income, it will only be on a moderate scale. But that would be enough to propel you forward and give you peace of mind. You should, however, keep an eye on fraud traps. And it's best to refrain from gambling or getting involved in high risk investments to prevent financial losses. This will ensure stability in your life and a stronger wealth luck for you, this year.

 **Career**

Although success in this area won't be too profound to make you jump up and down with joy, the presence of the lucky vibration this year is sufficient to elevate you to a distinguished position. The fortune available to you is on a medium scale, but it will be more than enough to attract a lot of needed assistance into your life. The good part is, you won't have to struggle. You'll achieve desirable results with half the effort and you'll get along well with your superiors and colleagues. Obstacles are miniscule compared to the career luck you are destined for.

Relationships

Get ready to fall in love if you are single because the Peach Blossom luck is in your favour this year. However, it is best for you to get to know him or her on a deeper level before you start confessing that you are head over heels in love. If you have a partner, this month is a good time to pay extra attention to your relationship and try to refrain from committing to a complicated twosome. Although it may seem like it won't bother your daily undertakings, if not approached in the right way, it will be a nuisance to you and trouble you in the most upsetting ways.

 **Health**

If you've been thinking of taking action to be aligned with better health options but have postponed due to your busy schedule, this year is the time for you to step up a notch and get really serious. Make sure your food intake contains the right amount of vitamins and minerals. And although there is high potential for you to get cardiovascular and ophthalmic diseases as well as experience problems with high blood pressure, you can reduce that possibility if you visit a doctor on a regular basis for check-ups and health advice.

 **Monthly Luck**

農曆正月 (February 4th - March 4th) 戊寅

This month is a month of good tidings for you as good fortune in terms of wealth and career are very high. Your goals will come to fruition very easily and the continuous flow of getting along well with your colleagues and superiors at work will be more magnified this month. However, you should not ignore the fact that you need to respect everyone you meet to maintain harmony in your relationships. It's time to acknowledge and appreciate people wo have helped you because although good luck is your constant companion this month, success may seem far-fetched without their help.

農曆二月 (March 5th - April 3rd) 己卯

Don't worry, the stories you hear are just rumours. When you hear information without solid evidence, try not to believe in it too much. Instead, pause, think and be aware that it lacks substance. This month, it's better if you avoid unnecessary arguments and practice tolerance to those you come across. And when it comes to knowledge, be aware of the fact that a wise man is humble and acknowledges that he knows nothing while a fool will be quick to praise himself, showing off that he is an expert that knows everything.

農曆三月 (April 4th - May 4th) 庚辰

The suitable theme for this month is associated with healing and love for your body and overall health. Minor health issues may trouble you and while that might seem uncomfortable as you'll end up visiting the doctor and taking medication, it is actually a blessing in disguise as it allows you to take some time off of work and nurture yourself back to better health. It also prompts you in the right direction where health is concerned. You have probably been neglecting your health for a long time. This situation is perfect to get you back on the right track.

農曆四月 (May 5th - June 4th) 辛巳

This month is not a month for you to relax. Instead, it actually will squeeze out the hard worker in you and earn you the title of a workaholic. When that happens, it is important to maintain a positive frame of mind at all times. Arguments and conflicts can cause more stress in your life if you are not careful. Activities that promote relaxation and peace should be on your list to anchor you into this vibe. If any legal problems and issues arise, don't let it worry you as if you respect and abide in the law, everything will turn out better than you expected.

農曆五月 (June 5th - July 5th) 壬午

While there were good times in your life where you have experienced good luck on a consistent basis, this month, you will experience it in a different way. The circumstances will still be as rewarding, but it will take on the form similar to that of a roller coaster ride. However, ups and downs are not out of the ordinary when it comes to life's experiences. Although you may encounter some troubles at work throughout the initial stages of this month, everything will eventually fall into place in the end.

農曆六月 (July 6th - August 6th) 癸未

Don't be surprised if your connection to the opposite sex seems average this month. It's due to the weak energy and fortune. Unfortunately, this is the reason behind your difficulties. While it may be a struggle to please or win his or her heart this month, refrain from making negative assumptions or accusations. Be patient and approach matters of the heart with love and sincerity. It's also wise for you to refrain from participating in any dangerous activities plus it is not a good month to kick start a new project.

農曆七月 (August 7th - September 6th) 甲申

While it's good to strike up a good conversation, mindless chatter may cause you unwanted trouble. You should be careful what you say as you won't know what type of information may come out of your mouth. Although you mean well, other people might misunderstand it and take it in a negative way. The worst part is when they pass it on to other people. This is not good for your reputation. It's also better if you refrain from provoking conflicts with superiors in your workplace and students should avoid contradicting their teachers to succeed academically.

農曆八月 (September 7th - October 7th) 乙酉

This month is a rewarding month for students. If you are a student or attending classes to gain additional knowledge in any area, this month's good energy will make it easier for you to achieve success. With a sharp mind and consistent focus, you'll get to the top in no time. It is advisable, however, to be careful. You should be mindful of every step you take while weighing the pros and cons wisely. Minor monetary losses may happen too which will lead to a change of direction in terms of wealth luck. Don't take it too lightly because although it is a small shift, the outcome will not be a pleasant one.

農曆九月 (October 8th - November 6th) 丙戌

Unexpected events are common in one's everyday life, but this month, the cycle may not be as pleasing as your previous experiences if you don't fixate your mind on positive aspects. Although various areas of your life might be affected, unexpected events will be more prevalent in your workplace this month. In terms of health, there is high potential for minor health issues to creep in and bother you. To prevent this from happening, it's best to be consciously aware of your overall health and take steps to improve it. It is also advisable for you to keep your body active through moderate physical activities on a consistent basis.

農曆十月 (November 7th - December 6th) 丁亥

Although you can be thankful that this month will anchor your position at work with so much stability, you should not let the good news get to your head. A focused and clear mind is needed to steer away from negativity. If you get a proposal to be someone's guarantor, it's best to turn him or her down nicely because if you say yes, you might regret your decision later on. This month is also a month for you to beware of frauds and deceivers. Instead of thinking you have to say yes all of the time, ponder on the reasons and figure out all of the possible implications behind that action.

農曆十一月 (December 7th 2020 - January 4th 2021) 戊子

Be receptive to positive situations as good energy is so pervasive this month. There is high possibility for you to get rewards in the form of gifts or praises, and although these won't be the ultimate cause of your joy or satisfaction, the meaning behind these rewards will definitely cause you to be exceptionally happy. Expect a stable month of career luck and since this month is also a month that is linked to a strong Peach Blossom luck, it means you should go ahead and ask your crush out on a date. He or she might say yes.

農曆十二月 (January 5th - February 2nd 2021) 己丑

Tip toe your way to success at your workplace this month. And although you may feel more inclined to splurge when it comes to shopping, try to save your money for a rainy day. Be prepared for any monetary losses that you may encounter this month. While it's good to take swift action when approaching your tasks, it's best to think twice when making any decisions. It will put you in a position of power and will enable you to see the bigger picture more clearly.

Personalised Forecast For 2020 Based on Day of Birth

(Assessment based on the 60 Jia Zi 甲子 Day Pillars)

甲子 Jia Zi Day

Overview

It might be a year full of uncertainties and chaos for you. It will be a bumpy road ahead of you and with all the confusion, you're more prone to stress whenever there's a problem. Try not to attract unnecessary attention as your focus is severely limited. Being aware that there is a challenging year ahead, you should try to prepare yourself for it as much as possible. Acquire new skills, explore new options and improve your capabilities.

 Wealth

Travelling will bring you wealth-related opportunities so capitalize on them as they appear. If nothing else, fresh experience gives you better perspective as well. If you are in a relationship, make sure to keep track of your bank statement as there might be communication and misunderstanding issues related to it.

 Relationships

This year will be straining to those who are already committed. There's a risk that your relationship might be over if you don't fix the core problem. Whatever arguments you might have with your partner, don't make it any worse. As it takes two to clap, both sides have to put in effort if you are to keep the relationship going. Instead of problems, see these as challenges you need to overcome in order to strengthen your bond. For those not in a relationship, focus on other aspects of your life as there is no romance luck for you this year.

Health

Even if you think your health is fine, don't take it for granted. Go for check-ups. Something minor could be a sign of more serious illnesses; you'll never know. Schedule a regular check up to prevent any nasty surprises.

Career

If you're travelling for work, you might find opportunities to enhance your financial situation. Whatever opportunities you get, big or small, you take it and make the best out of it. If you find no opportunity to even travel, it means your advancement in career is going slow.

農曆正月

(February 4th - March 4th) 戊寅
If you were born during autumn, this month you'll be able to enjoy excellent luck for wealth.

農曆二月

(March 5th - April 3rd) 己卯
This month, your wealth luck is still favourable and going strong. The same does not apply to other aspects of your life.

農曆三月

(April 4th - May 4th) 庚辰
There are obstructions standing between you and your ambitions. You have the choice of letting this annoy you or accept it as it is. At least for the latter, you are more likely to find the solution.

農曆四月

(May 5th - June 4th) 辛巳
Your relationship outlook is currently shaky and a betrayal might transpire. This is especially so for married women.

農曆五月

(June 5th - July 5th) 壬午
The environment in your workplace is quite tense at the moment. When you have the opportunity to perform, it might lead you to be prideful. As such, always remember to have humility in everything that you do.

農曆六月

(July 6th - August 6th) 癸未
In life, you can't have the good without the bad. As long as you have this mentality, you'll be able to handle disappointments around you. Being down-to-earth and at the same time open to any possibility is the right choice to make.

農曆七月

(August 7th - September 6th) 甲申
It is a favourable time for you to be looking for partners in terms of career or business. They would be able to be an effective middle man.

農曆八月

(September 7th - October 7th) 乙酉
If you wish to travel this month, you would be enjoying good luck ahead. Though travelling luck is on your side, it doesn't mean you should let your guard down. Keep an eye on your health and safety, particularly in regards to what you eat. You might be susceptible to food poisoning or stomach flu at the moment.

農曆九月

(October 8th - November 6th) 丙戌
Be careful with your property as well as any legal documentations this month. There may be some trouble ahead involving paperwork.

農曆十月

(November 7th - December 6th) 丁亥
If you were born in autumn, you'll be able to enjoy excellent fortune this month. Whatever plans you have in store will proceed smoothly and you'll enjoy good returns for your efforts.

農曆十一月

(December 7th 2020 - January 4th 2021) 戊子
This month, you might be dealing with legal documents that involves property. Pay attention to the details and take your time. Acting impulsively will lead to unfavourable results.

農曆十二月

(January 5th - February 2nd 2021) 己丑
This month, auspicious travelling luck comes by again. As it was before, despite the favourability you still have to remain vigilant. If you are in in a foreign country, pay attention to the local laws and customs just to be on the safe side.

乙丑 Yi Chou Day

Overview

This year, success could be yours provided you stay determined to reach your goals. What you do for work might lead you to far-off places. You will find favourable results should you travel. It's an ideal time to take the initiative as you'll be able to be recognized and respected easily. While you might feel like slowing down or taking it easy, always remember to pick up your pace afterwards. If you wish to obtain great success, put in a great deal of effort that is deserving of a reward.

 ## Wealth

Your financial outlook for the year is not so stable. You should look into investments that would take a while to produce results as opposed to spending your money on things of little to no value. Be more frugal with your finances, come up with a budget and stick with it so that you'll make the best out of your money.

 ## Relationships

It doesn't look good this year in terms of your relationship. Problems might escalate out of control if the root cause of it is not nipped in the bud. In fact, you should even try to prioritize and allocate some time to solve the issue with your relationship this year. Other aspects of your life might try to get in the way but try to do whatever you can to keep your relationship afloat.

 ## Health

In terms of health, you should be relatively okay. You might be susceptible to issues related to the stomach and blood pressure, but nothing serious beyond that. You might develop more severe health issues later on due to your weight so you might want to keep it in check.

 ## Career

You might feel like procrastinating this year but don't give in to the feeling. Focus on your career. Keep giving your best and if you have the opportunity to travel, you should go for it. In the long run, it would help advance in your career and it's another step closer to achieving your goals. If you choose to do nothing instead, then nothing would happen.

農曆正月

(February 4th - March 4th) 戊寅
Although you would be dealing with additional work this month, consider it to be an opportunity to show how capable you are.

農曆二月

(March 5th - April 3rd) 己卯
Work-related stress and pressure are building up, possibly from the additional tasks. If you must, take a break once in a while so that you'll have the energy to persevere.

農曆三月

(April 4th - May 4th) 庚辰
Your might be susceptible to negative thoughts in your head that gets in the way of your decisions. Think twice before making any choices.

農曆四月

(May 5th - June 4th) 辛巳
There are petty people around you who would distract you with gossips and drama. Their negativity won't do you any good and as such, you should not associate yourself with them.

農曆五月

(June 5th - July 5th) 壬午
If there's anything you find too hard to handle alone, it's not wrong to be asking for help. In fact, you might discover great new connections as a result.

農曆六月

(July 6th - August 6th) 癸未
When you take the initiative to do your work, you will find efficiency in anything you do. Try not to be lazy.

農曆七月

(August 7th - September 6th) 甲申
This month might make you more temperamental than usual. Whatever you are feeling, don't take it out on other people.

農曆八月

(September 7th - October 7th) 乙酉
There is someone in your life who will be there for you in your time of need. As long as you are receptive of their help, they will be there for you.

農曆九月

(October 8th - November 6th) 丙戌
This month, you'll be enjoying fantastic wealth luck. This is especially true if you are working with others or in a team.

農曆十月

(November 7th - December 6th) 丁亥
The market seems to be against you this month, so it would be advisable for you to stay away from investments for the time being.

農曆十一月

(December 7th 2020 - January 4th 2021) 戊子
This month, you might be able to see advancements in your career in one way or another.

農曆十二月

(January 5th - February 2nd 2021) 己丑
You might find yourself paying expensive medical bills especially if you were born during the summer season.

丙寅 Bing Yin Day

Overview
It will be a fast and furious year for those that are working as full-time employees or those who are born in the summer. One is expected to have a tight and busy schedule ahead which might require one to travel to another country. This might demotivates you, but you should take this as an opportunity to further enrich yourself.

 Wealth

You must resist the temptations of spending your hard-earned cash over costly and deluxe things. These luxurious belongings will only provide you with short-term happiness after spending big amount of money. As one is able to handle one's own finance well, one will smoothen one's wealth fortune approaching the end of the year.

 Relationships

Couples will be going through a tempestuous and shaky year of emotion. In order to be devoted into a long term relationship, coupled individuals must be frank to each other. That being said, think long and hard about the required process and effort to fix your relationship. Take charge of your own emotion and endeavour to compromise for better communication.

 Health

Be on watch for your cholesterol level by going for frequent medical check-ups. As the saying goes, "An ounce of prevention is worth a pound of cure", one should plan for frequent medical check-ups at least twice a year to avoid health issues such as high cholesterol level. Food and skin allergies might give you some tough time too. Having said that, try to find the equivalence between work and leisure time to prevent yourself from getting too stressed which will negatively affects your health.

Career
Brace yourself to encounter various hurdles to be leap over in your career. Perseverance and persistence are you best friends to overcome these problems and to edge closer towards your goals. Treat the troubles as chance to build your character.

農曆正月

(February 4th - March 4th) 戊寅
In order to accomplish your targets more efficiently, you are advised to dive yourself into building team spirit as the team will provide you timely assistance at work.

農曆二月

(March 5th - April 3rd) 己卯
It is the time when you should utilize the great networking and communication skill of yours to gain help and connections while progressing towards your goals. You might even draw the assistance from Noble People as a result.

農曆三月

(April 4th - May 4th) 庚辰
Procrastination and laziness are your worst enemies while executing your arrangements. One shall always brace oneself and stick to one's plans.

農曆四月

(May 5th - June 4th) 辛巳
Your discipline and personal virtues are keys to overcome the upcoming financial issues this month.

農曆五月

(June 5th - July 5th) 壬午
Those who born in the summer may encounter strong sense of jealously over the others this month. Get rid of it by being optimistic and hardworking to avoid any career distraction.

農曆六月

(July 6th - August 6th) 癸未
Your travel expenses will be filled by a great idea that can gain you significant income this month.

農曆七月

(August 7th - September 6th) 甲申
Those who work as full-time employees will particularly enjoy career advancement in the form of promotion and salary increment.

農曆八月

(September 7th - October 7th) 乙酉
Never let others to persuade you to break the existing law at all costs and all times. Petty and unscrupulous people don't deserve your time and effort.

農曆九月

(October 8th - November 6th) 丙戌
You might experience the feeling of going unnoticed this month. Nevertheless, this is not the case in reality, thus do not take this to heart and focus more on the important matters in life.

農曆十月

(November 7th - December 6th) 丁亥
An auspicious turn of wealth fortune is in store for you! Besides, one will make the most of life's opportunities by grabbing them at the right time, especially one who born in the autumn.

農曆十一月

(December 7th 2020 - January 4th 2021) 戊子
Serious food allergies may lead to severe health concerns. Therefore, be extra cautious of what you cannot eat to avoid unnecessary issues regarding your wellbeing. In other words, be more attentive of your diet.

農曆十二月

(January 5th - February 2nd 2021) 己丑
Your opinions may differ to that of your partner more than usual this month. Having said that, it is advisable that you should try to avoid these disputes.

丁卯 Ding Mao Day

Overview

Great positivity will be coming your way, thanks to the blessing of some good stars coming your way. Thinking outside of the box will certainly bring you much success this year. Be more productive at work and you will be rewarded for your efforts. Financially you may see a little lack of inflow of money into your account. It will be to your favour to make rational choices in any potential investment while avoiding short term opportunities. Find new ways to reinvent yourself and your ideas so you progress towards your goals are unhindered.

 ## Wealth

When it comes to wealth, you have favourable wealth luck this year. How well you garner wealth would also greatly depend on your resourcefulness. Steer clear of risky setups of the likes of venture capitals and high yielding bonds and your finances will be stable. Prove yourself worthy of your capabilities this year and consider every opportunity that may yield greater returns for you.

 ## Relationships

There may be some small chances for love in your life this year if you happen to be single. Spend less time at home or at work and try to make yourself available for as many events or gatherings as you can make time and energy for. This will certainly increase your chances of meeting someone who has the potential of being your romantic partner.

 ## Health

The many responsibilities you have this year would result in anxiety and in turn, stress. Be cautious about what you eat and take time off work if you are feeling overwhelmed which may greatly contribute to your stomach issues.

 ## Career

You need to take the amount of effort you put in your work to the next level. Work expectations might see you a little frazzled so pay special heed to your needs and take time off when you need it. Remain calm, pleasant and have an open communication with your work mates – this will see you come out of any possible tensions.

農曆正月

(February 4th - March 4th) 戊寅
This month will see new projects on the horizon so be prepared to take things to a whole new level this month in terms of ideas and potential. Remember to ask for help when you need it.

農曆二月

(March 5th - April 3rd) 己卯
There's a possibility this month for women to experience gynaecological issues. Therefore make a doctor's appointment and eat healthy. It is always better to be safe than sorry.

農曆三月

(April 4th - May 4th) 庚辰
Boredom might sink in this month so grow your social network. Attend social gatherings that you've been invited to as this could be a chance to meet people and better stagnant relationships.

農曆四月

(May 5th - June 4th) 辛巳
An unexpected event might crop up this month which could potentially derail the work you have put in. In the process of trying to get what you want, you may be tempted to throw your ethics out the window. Hold on to your values.

農曆五月

(June 5th - July 5th) 壬午
If you were born in spring, things are likely to be a little more fulfilling this month. Seeing as things are progressing well, perhaps full advantage should be taken to get as much work done.

農曆六月

(July 6th - August 6th) 癸未
This month, your health is likely to take a small hit. Don't neglect yourself whilst in full pursuit of your career goals.

農曆七月

(August 7th - September 6th) 甲申
Take time to hone your skills this month regardless of whether you are still a student or a working adult. The month will certainly bring out the best in your motivation and aptitude.

農曆八月

(September 7th - October 7th) 乙酉
Before you do or decide on anything this month, think it through carefully. Reflect on what you have learnt and what you could do to improve your personal and professional life.

農曆九月

(October 8th - November 6th) 丙戌
There will be some ups and downs, this month. Be cautious and vigilant in who you confide in as there are malevolent people all around you.

農曆十月

(November 7th - December 6th) 丁亥
This month is going to be quite favourable both personally and professionally. Make some travel plans and see what's on the other side of the horizon.

農曆十一月

(December 7th 2020 - January 4th 2021) 戊子
You will likely encounter some issues with work or at home this month. Be patient and communicate your feelings to the other party in aspects of the relationship that may not sit well with you.

農曆十二月

(January 5th - February 2nd 2021) 己丑
Everyone deserves a break every now and then and right now it would be ideal for you to do so. Relax and enjoy yourself, take the time to catch your breath and get yourself back on track.

戊辰 Wu Chen Day

Overview

This year will see a boost to your social life which in turn will see a lasting positive effect on your life. You might be a little overwhelmed this year with the appearance of major projects. Try not to be hero and ask for the aid of your colleagues, as their help will certainly ensure that everything runs smoothly. You are likely to be given the opportunity to be the star of your own show. Handle this opportunity carefully as it has been placed before you as a test of your character and ability.

 ### Wealth

With some added wealth stars in your corner, the year will give you the edge that you need to enjoy better wealth prospects this year. There will be a spike in improvement to your financial management skills which in turn will see you save more.

 ### Relationships

For those who are in a long-term relationship, consider popping the question this year as this year stars will guide you in the right direction for a happy and prosperous marriage. Married couples on the other hand, will see better ease in their relationships with their spouses and this will allow for better bonding and growth as united unit.

 ### Health

A reasonable year for health. A more concerted effort needs to be made on health matters. Exercise and strive to live a better, more well-adjusted lifestyle which will help better other areas of your life as well. Be extra cautious about what you eat and drink.

 ### Career

This year will see a boost to your social life which in turn will see a lasting positive effect on your life. Use this year to strengthen and deepen your bonds with your close friends and acquaintances. The year will give you the opportunity to form new friendships and widen your social circle.

農曆正月

(February 4th - March 4th) 戊寅
Wealth will bode well this month but be cautious of potential extravagant spending or investments that could lead to some monetary loss.

農曆二月

(March 5th - April 3rd) 己卯
Considering that money is likely to fall in favour with you this year, keeping close tabs on your cash flow as well as utilizing the money wisely is pertinent.

農曆三月

(April 4th - May 4th) 庚辰
This is the time to buck up and put your best foot forward and present yourself for that promotion you have had your eyes on.

農曆四月

(May 5th - June 4th) 辛巳
Play it safe this month as you're more prone to be entangled with legal issues.

農曆五月

(June 5th - July 5th) 壬午
Best to curtail high spending habits that may deplete gained wealth. Increase work productivity which will in turn guide you to better savings with higher returns.

農曆六月

(July 6th - August 6th) 癸未
Practice a little patience in your marriage. Be mindful in allowing subtle flirtations to gain traction – it may likely lead you astray.

農曆七月

(August 7th - September 6th) 甲申
This is the month where you're likely to advance in your career. For single women, it's a great month as well because you are likely to find a great match around this time.

農曆八月

(September 7th - October 7th) 乙酉
As a reward for all your endeavours, your fortune in career, wealth and relationship will see positive outcomes this month.

農曆九月

(October 8th - November 6th) 丙戌
Be tactful with your words as a little slip up may leave you open to malicious gossips and rumours which could affect your wealth outcome. This is especially so for women.

農曆十月

(November 7th - December 6th) 丁亥
In this month, you seriously need to get some rest. Give yourself a break and take good care of yourself more.

農曆十一月

(December 7th 2020 - January 4th 2021) 戊子
To make this a good month - exercise, eat and rest well – these will aid you in putting your best foot forward in all areas of your life.

農曆十二月

(January 5th - February 2nd 2021) 己丑
Pay attention to possible issues with your digestive track – avoid excesses of oil and fat in your diet.

己巳 Ji Si Day

Overview

In terms of wealth, a prosperous year awaits you. Focus on expanding your social network and learn how to make the best use of it to achieve your goals. In your endeavours, you might be hampered by false accusations and baseless rumours especially for those born in spring. Stay true to your goals and ignore these petty issues.

 ## Wealth

The opportunities that you find this year would originate from your social circles. By being more proactive in socialising, you may increase your professional standing. While you're looking to make a considerable amount of money, do practice caution when it comes to investments and go for more reliable avenues such as property.

 ## Relationships

For men, it will be an auspicious Peach Blossom Luck this year which may translate to marriage. Women on the other hand would not experience the same luck. If your love life is not as you hope it to be, there are other aspects of your life that you can work on to improve your overall happiness.

 ## Health

Be careful with your heart and eyes for the next two years. For this year, you may be afflicted by fever frequently so do take care of yourself to make sure your health is uncompromised. You might also find yourself easily tired this year.

 ## Career

Travelling for work-related reasons would help you in your career advancement. An example would be taking on outstation assignments. You might be feeling that you are being taken advantage of by your superior and burdened by work. But, these frustrations are merely temporary as the rewards that you would eventually gain are long-lasting.

農曆正月

(February 4th - March 4th) 戊寅

You can expect some good news this month especially for those born during autumn or winter. There's a possibility for you to gain some wealth too.

農曆二月

(March 5th - April 3rd) 己卯

In this month, travelling would be beneficial to your wealth so get yourself out there. You can also take this opportunity to relax from the work-related stress.

農曆三月

(April 4th - May 4th) 庚辰

In this month, there's a chance to find a new job. Before deciding anything, think your options through carefully as this change would affect your life adversely.

農曆四月

(May 5th - June 4th) 辛巳

Extra focus and effort is needed this month when it comes to work. Practice discipline especially if you were born during winter.

農曆五月

(June 5th - July 5th) 壬午

This month you would not be in short of inspiration. The catch is you need to organise these new ideas well in order to fully utilise them.

農曆六月

(July 6th - August 6th) 癸未

You might find yourself being envious of others but that's just how things are. Be more appreciative of what you have instead.

農曆七月

(August 7th - September 6th) 甲申

Be mindful of your diet this month or you might run into some health problems such as stomach flu or food poisoning.

農曆八月

(September 7th - October 7th) 乙酉

You might be affected by heart-related troubles this month and this is particularly true if you are older. Make the necessary preparations and make sure you try to minimise this trouble.

農曆九月

(October 8th - November 6th) 丙戌

For those who own a business or supervising anyone, there may be problems concerning your staff that needs your attention. This includes household staff.

農曆十月

(November 7th - December 6th) 丁亥

You might be quite careless with the words you use this month. Keep that in mind and your head cool to avoid making any cutting remarks that would cause offence.

農曆十一月

(December 7th 2020 - January 4th 2021) 戊子

It will be beneficial for you to travel southwards this month. You also shouldn't be working alone for your wealth can be greatly improved through collaborations.

農曆十二月

(January 5th - February 2nd 2021) 己丑

Take the time to spend with your family as much as possible because they may have felt neglected.

庚午 **Geng Wu Day**

Overview

Overall, this year would be good for you particularly regarding your wealth luck. Things are likely to be a little more fulfilling this year. This will give you a chance to sit back and relax and watch your plans fall in line. Aim to maintain a balanced life of work and play, as rest and relaxation is essential in preparing yourself for the week and weeks to come. There may be some unexpected change to your finances or perhaps even some interference of a third party. Don't let these events and circumstances faze you as you are likely to come up with an appropriate solution to your dilemma.

 ## Wealth

Wealth will bode well in 2020 but be cautious of potential extravagant spending or investments that could lead to some monetary loss. Considering that money is likely to fall in favour with you this year – keeping close tabs on your cash flow as well as utilizing the money wisely is pertinent. Keep some money aside for a rainy day, for any eventuality.

 ## Relationships

When it comes to relationships, men in particular would have to deal with meddling from their mothers this year. Some lucky stars will lend a helping hand if you are single. Therefore, this is the year to find that perfect companion. The year opens up opportunities to meet interesting people while those already in a long term relationship, should, for their interest, avoid temptation.

 ## Health

This year you can expect to have good health in general. Avoid involving too heavily in extreme and dangerous activities of the likes of hiking or diving. Opt instead for some lighter exercise such as yoga, bicycling, or walking – these will still give you the exercise you need.

 ## Career

The year needs you to focus on your career as this is where much of your luck will be residing. This luck cycle would be in your greatest favour where your talent is finally showcased and your capabilities could be put to good use. Work expectations might see you a little frazzled – so pay special heed to your needs and take time off when you need it.

農曆正月

(February 4th - March 4th) 戊寅
The month will give you the opportunity to form new friendships and widen your social circle.

農曆二月

(March 5th - April 3rd) 己卯
There might be risks of complication for pregnant women this month so they ought to take good care of their physical wellbeing.

農曆三月

(April 4th - May 4th) 庚辰
Remain calm, pleasant and have an open communication with your work mates. Avoid procrastination.

農曆四月

(May 5th - June 4th) 辛巳
There will be some stumbling blocks will be in your way this month, but they are nothing to frown over. Avoid engaging in gossips an drama.

農曆五月

(June 5th - July 5th) 壬午
Peach Blossom is gracing you with its presence this month and therefore head on out and put yourself out there.

農曆六月

(July 6th - August 6th) 癸未
Be cautious about what you eat and take time off work if you are feeling overwhelmed which may greatly contribute to your stomach issues.

農曆七月

(August 7th - September 6th) 甲申
It will be quite a troubling month for you. It is best to prepare an umbrella before the rain, as then you are prepared to weather the storm.

農曆八月

(September 7th - October 7th) 乙酉
This month, don't let impulse dictate your choices and decision. Your pride might demand irrational things from you but try to put it aside and see things as they truly are.

農曆九月

(October 8th - November 6th) 丙戌
You will see positive guidance and support at work. Be thankful for your colleagues as you may need these people's help someday.

農曆十月

(November 7th - December 6th) 丁亥
You have favourable wealth luck this month and how well you garner wealth would also greatly depend on your resourcefulness.

農曆十一月

(December 7th 2020 - January 4th 2021) 戊子
Social obligations might shackle you this month. It is a good time for strengthening your social bonds with the people in your organization.

農曆十二月

(January 5th - February 2nd 2021) 己丑
If you're a single woman looking for love, this month brings better luck in finding your ideal partner. Place yourself in the right place at the right time for that cosmic encounter.

辛未 Xin Wei Day

Overview

A challenging year awaits you. You will see the year progressing a lot slower than the previous year. And sometimes slow is good as all good things take time to manifest. As the saying goes 'The longer the wait, the better the results'. Take your time in devising a good plan of outcome and be persistent in the changes you want to see in the relevant areas of your life.

 ## Wealth

Keep a close watch on your wallet as you may be susceptible to pick pockets and thieves – this might in turn cause you to lose substantial amounts of money. Keep some money aside for a rainy day, for any eventuality. In any event, you will have the love and support of your family and friends to help you out of any sticky situation that may arise.

 ## Relationships

Married couples will need to be strong in their relationships with their spouses and this will allow for better bonding and growth as united unit. For those who are single, it's better to focus on other aspects of their life besides relationship as it is not the right time for romance.

 ## Health

The year might leave you a little open to stress related illnesses which will disrupt your life cycle if preventive measures are not taken. A more concerted effort needs to be made on health matters – exercise and strive to live a better, more well-adjusted lifestyle which will help better other areas of your life as well.

 ## Career

You might be given a significant work commitment this week. It is entirely up to you to decide the level of commitment you wish to put into the work. You might be given a significant work commitment this week. It is entirely up to you to decide the level of commitment you wish to put into the work. Your time has come to shine at work and the year is looking bright for you to gain the recognition you want in your work.

農曆正月

(February 4th - March 4th) 戊寅
Be wary of arrogance as this could pose a threat to your career development. Opportunities are rare and when they do knock, remember to give it your best shot.

農曆二月

(March 5th - April 3rd) 己卯
For those born during summer, expect some minor disputes stemming from misunderstandings with superiors and colleagues. Exercise tolerance and patience.

農曆三月

(April 4th - May 4th) 庚辰
The month is ripe for you to do a little introspection and put in a little more hard work. Reflect on what you have learnt and what you could do to improve your personal and professional life.

農曆四月

(May 5th - June 4th) 辛巳
Try not to rush into things or perhaps even rush to try and finish things this month. Slow and steady is the way to go.

農曆五月

(June 5th - July 5th) 壬午
Give proper care and time to the work you are doing to avoid mistakes. Be thorough with your work, review your plans and execute them with care.

農曆六月

(July 6th - August 6th) 癸未
Take some time off work and studies to pursue something you like or perhaps indulge in hobbies. While you're at it, take good care of your health as you may injure your right leg.

農曆七月

(August 7th - September 6th) 甲申
As a reward for all your endeavours, your fortune in career, wealth and relationship will see positive outcomes this month. The roller-coaster ride has reached its station and you can finally let that sigh of relief.

農曆八月

(September 7th - October 7th) 乙酉
Expect some minor disputes stemming from your own emotions. Exercise tolerance and patience.

農曆九月

(October 8th - November 6th) 丙戌
In contrast to previous months, you will find yourself more fatigued than usual. But, as the saying goes, "Nothing worth having, comes easy".

農曆十月

(November 7th - December 6th) 丁亥
If you were born in winter, avoid any water activities which may lead to injuries.

農曆十一月

(December 7th 2020 - January 4th 2021) 戊子
There is possibility in you incurring monetary losses potentially due to failed investments and overspending. Watch your spending habits wisely and try to function on a workable budget.

農曆十二月

(January 5th - February 2nd 2021) 己丑
You are likely to see better personal luck this month. Work is likely to flow better with continued support from your Nobleman.

壬申 **Ren Shen Day**

Overview

When it comes to career and wealth, some tough times are ahead of you this year. You will find that your abilities will be tested this year by those you wish to impress. Be focused on what you wish to achieve and refrain from becoming overconfident. This would certainly shed better light to your character and how well you tackle challenges.

 ## Wealth

The doors to wealth opportunities may a little closed year. There may be some small lack of movement in terms of monetary growth this year. Best to curtail high spending habits that may deplete gained wealth. You may see yourself receiving a lot of help in achieving your desires in wealth accumulation. Before embarking on any possible investment opportunities, research the area you wish to delve into well.

 ## Relationships

It's a good year to find romance this year if you are still single. This is a great time for you to head out, socialise and meet people while expanding your social circle. You may need to be observant and start moving around your social circle, as there is good chance of meeting that one person who is meant for you, so start asking people out for coffee!

 ## Health

Your health should be your priority this week as you could be facing some hits with some minor ailments. Watch what you eat and be wary of consuming food from dodgy restaurants with questionable hygiene practices.

 ## Career

In terms of career, this is going to be a less than momentous year in terms of movement and progress. Staying calm and focused is key to getting the attention of your superiors. You are surrounded by strong people who will help guide you in your career quest.

農曆正月

(February 4th - March 4th) 戊寅
This month will see you skating on thin ice. You will be bogged down by stressful work constraints that you might need to take special heed to.

農曆二月

(March 5th - April 3rd) 己卯
You will be faced with a posiblity of a new job offer this month, so take this as an opportunity to learn. Prepare yourself with various capabilities.

農曆三月

(April 4th - May 4th) 庚辰
You will still be encountering some setbacks this month. Set aside time to deal with any unfinished business.

農曆四月

(May 5th - June 4th) 辛巳
Your fortune will take a better auspicious turn from the previous month. So relax a little and enjoy the finer developments that your career and wealth plans will provide.

農曆五月

(June 5th - July 5th) 壬午
You may encounter some trouble with your eyes this month. Also, refrain from lending money to anyone for the time being or go out of your way for others.

農曆六月

(July 6th - August 6th) 癸未
Watch out for opportunist who may want to use you as means to an end. Don't let yourself be swept away by their charms.

農曆七月

(August 7th - September 6th) 甲申
This month will see average movement in most areas of your life. Keep your emotions in check and try not to stress out on things you cannot control.

農曆八月

(September 7th - October 7th) 乙酉
You will see this month progressing a lot slower than the previous months. Do not allow yourself to become a guarantor for anyone as tides indicate that it will not go down well.

農曆九月

(October 8th - November 6th) 丙戌
There is some uncertainty in your financial wealth. There is possibility in you incurring monetary losses potentially due to failed investments and overspending.

農曆十月

(November 7th - December 6th) 丁亥
Things will progress slow this month. Sometimes slow is good as all good things take time to manifest.

農曆十一月

(December 7th 2020 - January 4th 2021) 戊子
Take your time in devising a good plan of outcome this month and be persistent in the changes you want to see in the relevant areas of your life.

農曆十二月

(January 5th - February 2nd 2021) 己丑
The month needs you to focus on your career. Your superiors will notice all the effort and hard work and this will help you to ascend the career ladder.

癸酉 Gui You Day

Overview

The positive energies of the year will certainly help with your social life as well as your career. You will be happy to note that this year will see you bond with your friends and your loved ones. There may even be chances to end your singledom if you wish. Financially you may see better inflow of money into your account. It will be to your favour to make rational choices in any potential investment while avoiding short term opportunities.

Wealth

Financially speaking, your wealth is average. There will be some ups and downs, however, relief will come from a Nobleman. By potentially sharing insights with you, you will discover that the aid given to you by your Nobleman will help you get much of the things you need to get done, done. While you're looking to make a considerable amount of money, practice caution when it comes to investments and go for more reliable avenues such as property.

Relationships

For single women who's looking for love, you need to get yourself out there and actually look. This is a lucky year that will see plenty of opportunities for you to enjoy the good food with good friend and family. There will be some struggles for single roosters this year in the romance department. Place yourself in the right place at the right time for that cosmic encounter – as despite the lack of opportune stars, you can still cast your own chances.

Health

This year, be careful with your upper torso area as it's prone to injury. Seek immediate medical attention if there are negative signs in the area before it gets worse. You might find yourself susceptible to bone-related injuries as well so try to be more careful wherever applicable.

Career

Career-wise, you're moving up the ladder this year; especially for those born in spring or winter. You are known to be highly intelligent and adaptable, thus with some help from the people around, you will be able to further develop their careers this year, gradually receiving more opportunities.

農曆正月

(February 4th - March 4th) 戊寅
Opportunities are abound if you keep your eyes and ears avoid risky and speculative investments this year as the outlook might not be in your favour.

農曆二月

(March 5th - April 3rd) 己卯
It is critical that you remain patient this month as there is likelihood of encountering work related issues that stem from some jealousy.

農曆三月

(April 4th - May 4th) 庚辰
It's time for your investment to pay off this month. Prove yourself worthy of your capabilities this year and consider every opportunity that may yield greater returns for you.

農曆四月

(May 5th - June 4th) 辛巳
You might be feeling stressed from work. Remember that worrying never gets you anywhere and you should not let your emotions add to your stress.

農曆五月

(June 5th - July 5th) 壬午
Health issues, including physical injuries, may arise this month linked to headaches or migraines.

農曆六月

(July 6th - August 6th) 癸未
Your successes this month will become even more meaningful when you earn them through your blood, sweat and tears. Try to be innovative and take fresh new approaches in how you go about things.

農曆七月

(August 7th - September 6th) 甲申
"Nothing worth having, comes easy", in order to reach your goals and achieve greater things, you will have to place more effort and time into your endeavours.

農曆八月

(September 7th - October 7th) 乙酉
A month where you will need to certainly tap into that reserve patience you have stored up. Patience and tactfulness will be required to navigate the month successfully.

農曆九月

(October 8th - November 6th) 丙戌
Try to keep a low profile this month at your workplace. This is to avoid you from getting caught in some petty drama that would distract you from your work.

農曆十月

(November 7th - December 6th) 丁亥
The month's energies suggests that you may need to take special care of your well-being.

農曆十一月

(December 7th 2020 - January 4th 2021) 戊子
This is a good month to be prudent with your spending and keep as much spare cash as possible to prepare a robust financial buffer for unforeseen circumstances.

農曆十二月

(January 5th - February 2nd 2021) 己丑
Starting a new business or going for a new investment would not be favourable this month. The results gained for the time being would not being positive.

甲戌 Jia Xu Day

Overview

This year, you will be met with many pleasant surprises. Time to introspect and retrospect and see what brings you internal happiness this year. The pursuit of wealth and success may witness you being stressed and bogged down and this is the year to try and get your life back in traction and focus on yourself. Be proactive in your endeavours and do what it takes to succeed. Use the positive energies coming your way to your best advantage.

 ## Wealth

Prepare for some bumpiness in terms of wealth. Wise to place little expectations on aspects of monetary gain. Business owners should consider looking into investing in innovative technologies to amplify their business and stock assets.

 ## Relationships

It's a good year for those in relationships to strengthen the bond they have with each other. This is a lucky year that will see plenty of opportunities for you to enjoy the good food with good friend and family. Catch up on some lost time with them from the toils of work. Aside from relationships, your other luck aspects will fare out moderately.

Health

Pay attention to the amount of sugar you consume. For further optimum performance, exercise, eat and rest well – these will aid you in putting your best foot forward in all areas of your life.

Career

When looking for inspiration related to your work, consider traveling. Opportunities are abound and you need to be brave in capitalising the chances that present themselves to you to make a shift. Exercise calm and patience when treading through work issues as these are likely not going to last very long.

農曆正月

(February 4th - March 4th) 戊寅
If you were born in summer, you might find some trouble in getting recognition from your boss. Handle this situation carefully as it has been placed before you as a test of your character and ability.

農曆二月

(March 5th - April 3rd) 己卯
This month, an offer for you to change jobs might appear. Consider seeking the help and advices of the professionals who can aid you into making ideal investments which can aligned to your financial goals.

農曆三月

(April 4th - May 4th) 庚辰
It is critical that you remain patient this month as there is likelihood of encountering some issues. The best way to solve any arising issues is to keep positive and exploit the resources given to you.

農曆四月

(May 5th - June 4th) 辛巳
Thisi month might see your work life balance compromised by stressful work constraints that may hold you back. Exercise calm and patience when treading through work issues.

農曆五月

(June 5th - July 5th) 壬午
Responsibilities at work will hardly be a problem as every assigned task will be completed to perfection with little to no delay.

農曆六月

(July 6th - August 6th) 癸未
It is perhaps best for you to lie low this month and concentrate on your own plan. Mind your temper this month as your emotions run wild.

農曆七月

(August 7th - September 6th) 甲申
Considering that money is likely to fall in favour with you this month, keep close tabs on your cash flow as well as utilizing the money wisely is pertinent.

農曆八月

(September 7th - October 7th) 乙酉
You may want to hold your tongue this month as there is likelihood of miscommunication on the horizon. It is important for you to keep calm and accept the opinions of others in order to prevent miscommunication.

農曆九月

(October 8th - November 6th) 丙戌
Stress at work is to be expected. You are encouraged to take things slow this month and work at your own pace.

農曆十月

(November 7th - December 6th) 丁亥
There's a chance this month for your stomach to cause you problems, especially if you're travelling north. Watch what you eat and practice good hygiene.

農曆十一月

(December 7th 2020 - January 4th 2021) 戊子
Be aware of opportunities to meet varying people as things have a way of presenting themselves — so keep your eyes peeled.

農曆十二月

(January 5th - February 2nd 2021) 己丑
The secret to a happy marriage would be trust and honesty. Those who are married should practice this when they disagree with one another. Have open communication between both parties to dispel any distrust that might harm the relationships.

乙亥 Yi Hai Day

Overview

You will enjoy a rather smooth sailing year where you will see your superior and colleagues agree with your innovative ideas. Furthermore, those that are in school will see more dedication and responsibility flowing within them. Your health will be at its peak and the only thing you may need to worry about is making sure that you give yourself time for some rest and relaxation.

Wealth

There may be some positive growth in your wealth and career sector owing to the year's auspicious energy. You will experience better communication with clients and co-workers. This year, long-term investments are favouring you compared to the short-term ones. Long term investments may require high patience and slower process, but it works multiple times better than investments with low and unstable returns.

Relationships

Use this year to scout for potential love mates. He or she could be right around the block or possibly even under your very nose. Watch out for third party interference and ensure that your relationship is good and solid. Singles should sign up for a singles event, or a meet up session in your local area that will expand your social circle and put you on the right path to meeting the one!.

Health

Your eyes and heart are the health concerns that you watch out of this year. Seniors need to pay closer attention to their diet and perhaps vary their exercise plan. Avoid overindulging in late night snacks and food as this may prevent the appearance of digestive problems. Set boundaries for healthier diets and coupled these routines with appropriate exercise habit that sustain your wellbeing throughout the year.

Career

Great developments in career this year with developments happening closer to the post autumn season. The month needs you to focus on your career as this is where much of your luck will be residing. This luck cycle would be in your greatest favour where your talent is finally showcased and your capabilities could be put to good use.

農曆正月

(February 4th - March 4th) 戊寅
Small stumbling blocks might be placed before you but you will barrel down the obstacles. Avoid spending too much money on unnecessary things.

農曆二月

(March 5th - April 3rd) 己卯
Pay attention to your task and refrain trom letting yourself get distracted by things as this might result in errors that could have been easily avoided.

農曆三月

(April 4th - May 4th) 庚辰
Your advice for the month is to pay more attention to tasks at hand and side stepping issues that will derail you.

農曆四月

(May 5th - June 4th) 辛巳
Fierce competition are heating up between you and your colleagues this month. This will be a good month to take part in team sports and work and also collaborate with your colleagues at work.

農曆五月

(June 5th - July 5th) 壬午
Besides having good career luck this month, you will also experience considerable good luck in other aspects of your life as well.

農曆六月

(July 6th - August 6th) 癸未
There will be cooperation and collaboration opportunities with the others this month. You will receive recognition from your superiors or other half for the contribution you have given.

農曆七月

(August 7th - September 6th) 甲申
Your health this month is likely to take a small hit. Be careful of leg injuries and be extra cautious and careful whether you're driving on the road or walking down the street.

農曆八月

(September 7th - October 7th) 乙酉
Choose your words carefully as some small miscommunication may put a damper on an otherwise great career prospect. It is best to watch what you say to avert any possible outburst.

農曆九月

(October 8th - November 6th) 丙戌
This month will take you on a fortune rollercoaster, and like a rollercoaster you will experience some ups and downs. Be more detailed and attentive when dealing with your plans and day to day tasks.

農曆十月

(November 7th - December 6th) 丁亥
Avoid risky and speculative investments this month as the outlook might not be in your favour. Seek out good advice when discussing and making potential investments choices before committing to them.

農曆十一月

(December 7th 2020 - January 4th 2021) 戊子
Pay attention while driving or walking on the street. Employing better driving etiquette is crucial in avoiding possible accidents on the road.

農曆十二月

(January 5th - February 2nd 2021) 己丑
You will receive recognition from your superiors or other half for the contribution you have given.

丙子 **Bing Zi Day**

Overview
You will be front and centre this year with three auspicious stars residing in your sign giving you the edge you have been needing. With auspicious stars lined up, your career and wealth will bode well with ample growth and successes on both fronts. It would be imperative for you to juggle your responsibilities with balance.

 ## Wealth
There is a strong possibility this year that you will gain financial wealth. At the same time, don't put all your eggs in one basket as there may be hidden opportunities coming your way. In the process of making money, don't take any shortcuts or obtain it illicitly. Breaking the law is never worth it. Play it safe and keep yourself clean.
.

 ## Relationships
2020 is not looking to be the year for great romance especially for men as it is void of the Peach Blossom Luck that is needed. However, single people should still socialise as things may turn in their favour during the months where the Peach Blossom star is present. Be wise and brave in seeking what you want and do not let setbacks and personal self-esteem hold you back.

 ## Health
Your liver would be your main concern this year in regards to your health. Practice moderation when it comes to alcohol and take good care of your health. Be on a lookout for tumours and growths as well.

Career
If you were born in spring, then you may expect this year to be good for your career. You need to remember that you don't have to take everything on by yourself. Allow others to help you out so that your burden would be reduced. The people around you are more than willy to lend a hand.

農曆正月

(February 4th - March 4th) 戊寅
You may run into some additional income this month. However, make sure your means are legitimate and ethical.

農曆二月

(March 5th - April 3rd) 己卯
There's a chance you might say or do something offensive this month so be careful with your behaviour.

農曆三月

(April 4th - May 4th) 庚辰
Stay on your path towards achieving your goals and contribute to your own cause by obtaining new skills or experiences.

農曆四月

(May 5th - June 4th) 辛巳
Minor health issues might plague you this month. Consider taking the necessary choices to improve your overall health, perhaps by taking care of your diet better.

農曆五月

(June 5th - July 5th) 壬午
This month, you are susceptible to mood swings. Your state of mind could be further affected negatively by arguments at home. Give yourself a break and do some introspection and learn to control your emotions better.

農曆六月

(July 6th - August 6th) 癸未
Those close to you might approach you and ask for aid. Offer only what you can afford to give and decline politely if you are unable to help.

農曆七月

(August 7th - September 6th) 甲申
In the process of getting your tasks done, remain focused. Ensure that your emotions won't compromise your work and you are able to make full use of your talents.

農曆八月

(September 7th - October 7th) 乙酉
Alcohol should be taken with caution this month, particularly if you are in a social setting. Make sure your behaviour and words in public remain proper.

農曆九月

(October 8th - November 6th) 丙戌
This month you can expect to gain returns from side projects and minor investments as you will be experiencing strong Indirect Wealth Luck.

農曆十月

(November 7th - December 6th) 丁亥
This would not be a good month for you to decide on any financially related matters and you should postpone your decisions to a much more auspicious time.

農曆十一月

(December 7th 2020 - January 4th 2021) 戊子
If you're driving this month, there's a chance you might get speeding tickets. Drive carefully and obey the law.

農曆十二月

(January 5th - February 2nd 2021) 己丑
Your hard work and contribution will be acknowledged. If you stay on this path without slowing down, you may eventually advance in your career.

六十甲子 Forecast for 2020 based on Day of Birth

丁丑 Ding Chou Day

Ding

Chou

Overview
In this year, the plans you wish to accomplish will able to be done without much problem. This momentum will contribute to building your confidence in yourself. What's more is that your Wealth Luck is looking great as well so your finances are secured. Since you are in a position where you are stable and steadily rising, it would be imperative for you to avoid any financial pitfalls such as risky investments or gambling. Your best bet at the moment would be to strategize for the future and handle your budget tightly.

Wealth
Throughout the year, your Wealth Luck would remain strong. Perhaps you would find an increment in your salary. For entrepreneurs and business owners, consider stepping up your game by expanding your market beyond the borders. Try and see if you can find the opportunities in foreign lands. As you will receive help from many parties that are interested, it shouldn't be a problem.

Relationships
For those who are already in a long-term relationship, consider making it official this year. If you are a single woman, you might have a couple of individuals who are interested in you at the moment. For married women, there are possible temptations that might harm your marriage and arguments regarding money is to be expected.

Health
Overall, your physical health should be okay this year without much issue. But, it's important to practice a healthy living style. Practice moderation when it comes to what you eat, exercise regularly, go for a medical check-up every now and then and you'll be fine. Good health is something almost everyone takes for granted and it's better to prevent than it is to cure any ailment.

Career
In terms of career, this year seems to be quite promising. You may get the chance to travel and along with it are opportunities for you to advance in your career. The rewards that can be gain will come in both financial and reputation boon. Don't hesitate when the opportunities present themselves as the results would be positive.

農曆正月

(February 4th - March 4th) 戊寅
This month, you'll find yourself with good Financial Luck. You might even be surprised with some financial reward that you didn't expect.

農曆二月

(March 5th - April 3rd) 己卯
The Financial Luck from the previous month continues. You may want to consider asking your superior for a pay raise.

農曆三月

(April 4th - May 4th) 庚辰
You're really on a roll with this good luck of yours as it spans into this month as well. Looks like you might get promoted or advance in your career.

農曆四月

(May 5th - June 4th) 辛巳
Positive romance luck is in the air for the single ladies this month. If you're looking for love, take the initiative and make the first step to make it happen.

農曆五月

(June 5th - July 5th) 壬午
There may be problems at home as you find yourself dealing with a lot of disagreements. Practice patience and try to be understanding when you handle them.

農曆六月

(July 6th - August 6th) 癸未
At times, you will be tempted to impulsively spend beyond your budget. Try to curb this habit and be stricter when it comes to your wealth management.

農曆七月

(August 7th - September 6th) 甲申
If ever you feel like travelling, now's a good month. Consider going to places where you've always wanted to see with your own eyes.

農曆八月

(September 7th - October 7th) 乙酉
Your social life will experience a boom this month. Your network will grow larger and you will be swept up in parties and gatherings. However, you should refrain overindulging in alcohol.

農曆九月

(October 8th - November 6th) 丙戌
For those who were born in summer, they'll be plagued with stress this month. On the other hand, those born in spring will have their talents recognized and enjoy good fortune.

農曆十月

(November 7th - December 6th) 丁亥
This month unlocks your creative talents to its full potential, allowing you to breath in new life to old projects. Give a brand-new twist to an old concept.

農曆十一月

(December 7th 2020 - January 4th 2021) 戊子
There may be an increase in profit for you coming from good business prospects. Make your preparations now so that when the time comes, you will be ready for it.

農曆十二月

(January 5th - February 2nd 2021) 己丑
As your Financial Luck is looking good this month, consider doing some investments.

戊寅 Wu Yin Day

Overview

A prosperous year can be expected if you were born in spring. You may look forward to financial growth as well as self-improvement in terms of your knowledge and know-how. There will be many valuable lessons that you can learn from this year. As it is a good time to learn, make full use of this opportunity by adding new skills that may prove to be useful in the future.

 ## Wealth

Your financial situation is not quite stable early on this year. Fortunately, the situation is looking to improve as you progress through the year. You might have to innovate or come up with creative use of your capabilities as the wealth might have to come in a way you may not expect. Whatever strategy you wish to implement, think it through carefully and you'll be able to accomplish a lot of things.

 ## Relationships

If you are a woman who is looking for love, this year you might be able to find the right match. In order to meet the right person, however, you have to be receptive in meeting them. Try to be more social, meet new people and say yes to be more outgoing. If you are a single man, you might be able to find someone as well through your mother's help.

 ## Health

This year, you might experience some health issues related to your kidneys and bladder. It may potentially be caused by an unhealthy diet. In order to mitigate this negative effect, always go for the healthier option when it comes to meal time. Not only would you be able to avoid the problem if you were to eat healthy, in general your overall health would improve as well.

 ## Career

This is a good year for you to learn and pick up new skills. Be smart with the opportunities you are given. Each of them is a door that would lead you to more success for as long as you are able to take the first step. If you were to show eagerness, your boss might even provide you training or education that would tremendously boost your capabilities.

農曆正月

(February 4th - March 4th) 戊寅
This month, there are plenty of chances for you to make money. Before these opportunities even appear, make ample preparations for them.

農曆二月

(March 5th - April 3rd) 己卯
If you are a man in a committed relationship, your partner might want some extra attention. Balance your responsibilities in your personal and professional life well as it can be very taxing on your wellbeing.

農曆三月

(April 4th - May 4th) 庚辰
You need to have some strategy or a plan if you wish to get some work done. Arguments and conflicts might get in the way if you don't learn to ignore them and only focus on what's important.

農曆四月

(May 5th - June 4th) 辛巳
It's not recommended for you to be handling any legal documentations, particularly ones involving land or property. It's best that you postpone such plans to another time.

農曆五月

(June 5th - July 5th) 壬午
Get ready for a productive month as there are many opportunities to increase your financial spending. Don't let it go to waste, make the necessary preparations to capitalize on them.

農曆六月

(July 6th - August 6th) 癸未
It would be a month of confusion and uncertainty for those born in the winter or autumn season. If this applies to you, you should set some time to clear your thoughts and think objectively. Try not to make judgement based on your immediate perception.

農曆七月

(August 7th - September 6th) 甲申
There might be petty people around you seeking to bring you down. As long as you ignore them, they won't be able to do anything that could jeopardise your positions.

農曆八月

(September 7th - October 7th) 乙酉
It is likely there is an issue with your family, particularly your mother, that could be the biggest problem you're facing this month. Try to be diplomatic in order to solve this problem.

農曆九月

(October 8th - November 6th) 丙戌
You might be taking on new responsibilities this month. Take this as an opportunity to show what you are capable of and let your true value shine.

農曆十月

(November 7th - December 6th) 丁亥
For those born during the winter or autumn seasons, it's a good time to travel. It's advisable for you to go southwards.

農曆十一月

(December 7th 2020 - January 4th 2021) 戊子
This month, there's no shortage of petty people. Don't let them distract you from achieving the success that you seek.

農曆十二月

(January 5th - February 2nd 2021) 己丑
You will be recognized for your hard work this month. Perhaps it would be your side projects finally showing profitable results.

六十甲子 Forecast for 2020 based on Day of Birth

己卯 Ji Mao Day

Overview

This year, you might feel like you're facing an obstruction with no way around it. For you to overcome this, you need to learn to rely on others. With teamwork, you'll be able to achieve whatever you've set out to do with ease. As such, maintain your connection to the helpful people in your life. Be open-minded to whatever that comes this year and adapt yourself accordingly.

Wealth

Your wealth luck is largely positive this year. For your luck to show you tangible results however requires you to take action. It is recommended that you go travelling after you done the necessary planning and research. If you're thinking of investments, be cautious. You have to possess some degree of financial security before you invest in anything.

Relationships

At the moment, you might be pining for a certain someone. However, this person might have their eyes elsewhere and as a result, you would be green with envy. Try not to be so self-critical about it as there is always someone out there who will accept you the way you are. For those who are committed, don't let the shady rumours you hear from your friends to negatively influence your relationship.

Health

If you are years old or above, your cholesterol level might be rising this year so be mindful of your sugar consumption. As prevention is better than cure, take necessary measures. Cut down on sugary drinks and food, go for a medical check-up often; live healthily.

Career

If you wish for promotions or increments, it will come eventually if you're willing to wait. For those who are in the line of sales or any work that involves frequent travelling, this year will be a good one. It would be competitive but it's nothing you can't handle. Along the way, you might even turn your enemies into friends.

農曆正月

(February 4th - March 4th) 戊寅
With the coming of the new year, opportunities are all around your career might even advance. With good wealth luck also in store, it is a positive start for you.

農曆二月

(March 5th - April 3rd) 己卯
Keep your eyes peeled for any opportunities in your vicinity. You might be able to earn some extra cash this month if you do.

農曆三月

(April 4th - May 4th) 庚辰
You can't expect to get a different result if you keep doing the same thing. For you to change the outcome, you must change the activity. Nonetheless, be practical and have some wisdom when you do this.

農曆四月

(May 5th - June 4th) 辛巳
This month, you might not be thinking when you make any decision. You might even procrastinate before you can make your choice. Pay no attention to these bad habits and keep your eyes on the prize.

農曆五月

(June 5th - July 5th) 壬午
If you were to be presented with a choice, take the time to deliberate on it. Deciding hastily may get you in trouble. Think about it thoroughly before you commit to your decision.

農曆六月

(July 6th - August 6th) 癸未
There is a likelihood that you would be on the road this month because of work. Along the way, you might find opportunities that could potentially increase your standing and wealth.

農曆七月

(August 7th - September 6th) 甲申
Pay extra attention to your dietary habits this month as you might succumb to problems related to the stomach. If any signs of the problem surfaces, get medical attention as soon as possible.

農曆八月

(September 7th - October 7th) 乙酉
If you are able to find any short-term investments, give it a go. It's possible that you might be able to benefit from it.

農曆九月

(October 8th - November 6th) 丙戌
Your wealth luck seems to be on the rise this month. This could translate to you enjoying the fruits of your previous labour.

農曆十月

(November 7th - December 6th) 丁亥
At work, it might be getting extra competitive this month. For those who are in a partnership, make sure that you two are taking on the workload equally.

農曆十一月

(December 7th 2020 - January 4th 2021) 戊子
It is a challenging month for married couples. Past issues between the two of you might be the cause.

農曆十二月

(January 5th - February 2nd 2021) 己丑
There might be opportunities for you to increase your wealth this month. When you are given the chance to do so, do your best.

庚辰 Geng Chen Day

Overview

This year, you will be inspired to be more creative than usual. This would be a valuable boon to have if you're in the arts and entertainment industry. For you to fully capitalize on the opportunities given, you have to make preparations. While you won't be short of inspiration and ideas this year, your wealth is looking to be rather unstable. As such, manage your finances well.

 ## Wealth

The first half of the year would be where you can make the most out of your wealth luck for the year. After that, it's all about maintaining what you've obtained by managing it with intelligence. If you squander your extra wealth, you'll just be back to square one.

 ## Relationships

Love luck and romantic encounters are mostly likely to elude you this year. If you want to give it a try anyway, be prepared for negative outcomes such as rejections or meeting people who aren't a good match to you. Try not to think of this as a negative thing. The less time you spent on love, the more time you can spend working on other aspects of your life. Love will come eventually so don't worry too much about it.

 ## Health

Be mindful of your mental health as you might be under a lot of stress this year. It is advisable for you to find a healthy way to regulate your emotional strain. If you simply let it be, it may affect eventually affect your physical well-being. Whatever happens at work, leave it at work and whatever happens at home, leave it at home. Managing your stress level would be key in having good health this year.

 ## Career

Take the initiative to find and create opportunities instead of waiting for it to be handed to you. There are plenty of chances for you to advance in career if you simply make yourself receptive of them. For example, you could pick up a new skill and subsequently increase your own self-value. Always remember that you have the potential to offer much more than your current skillset.

農曆正月

(February 4th - March 4th) 戊寅
There might be changes happening in your office this month. These changes are favourable; perhaps you'll be getting a new superior or even a salary increment.

農曆二月

(March 5th - April 3rd) 己卯
There might be some added responsibility this month at work which contributes to an increased stress level; if you were born in summer, this is quite likely to take place. Manage your schedule wisely so you can pace your work and handle your deadlines accordingly.

農曆三月

(April 4th - May 4th) 庚辰
Whatever you're planning to do, you would be able to accomplish it provided you're focused on your goals. Have faith in what you can do and you'll be able to create results.

農曆四月

(May 5th - June 4th) 辛巳
You may be plagued with a series of choices that you have to make. In order for you to come to a decision, you could consider what others have to say on the matter.

農曆五月

(June 5th - July 5th) 壬午
Overall, it would be quite a competitive month for you. In order to gain the upper hand over your rivals, you should come up with a solid plan and strategy. Instead of something undesirable, try to see this as a learning experience on how to handle competitors.

農曆六月

(July 6th - August 6th) 癸未
There might be a lot of arguments in your office this month. Before these disputes get out of hand, try to play the peacemaker. Handle each issue with patience and compromise and don't let your feelings do the talking.

農曆七月

(August 7th - September 6th) 甲申
This month, your life might change for the better. This change might not necessarily be comfortable but as long as you are able to go with the flow, you'll be able to enjoy it.

農曆八月

(September 7th - October 7th) 乙酉
Your personal belongings might be robbed this month if you're not careful. At the same time, you are also prone to be temperamental for no particular reason.

農曆九月

(October 8th - November 6th) 丙戌
Your respiratory system might be weak this month that may result in health issues related to it. Avoid things that might worsen your condition such as smoking. As soon as there are any signs of trouble, go for a check-up.

農曆十月

(November 7th - December 6th) 丁亥
This month, you should go travelling especially if it's related to work. It's a good learning experience and a change of scenery is favourable.

農曆十一月

(December 7th 2020 - January 4th 2021) 戊子
You might be promoted or receive a salary increment this month. While you're enjoying your career advancement, certain colleagues might be envious of you. Try not to associate yourself with petty people who can't stand to see you happy.

農曆十二月

(January 5th - February 2nd 2021) 己丑
As a result of having too much work, it's possible that you might be feeling lonely this month. When you're experiencing this feeling, try to remember the people in your life that you care about and simply give them a call.

六十甲子 Forecast for 2020 based on Day of Birth

辛巳 Xin Si Day

Overview

You might be able to make leaps and bounds in terms of your career this year. There will be plenty of opportunities that would bring you closer to your ambition. If you're thinking of changing jobs to another company that you've been keen on joining, now would be a good time for you to apply.

 ## Wealth

There will be opportunities to make a lot of financial gains during the first half of the year. As long as you put effort in the right places, you'll be able to grow your wealth. Make sure you handle the fruits of your labour wisely and not let it be squandered or wasted.

 ## Relationships

If you are single, you may find a right match this year. If you already have a significant other, it might be an argumentative year that may turn the relationship toxic. Whatever it is you are unhappy about your partner, discuss about it with honesty and maturity.

 ## Health

You can expect your health outlook to be good this year if you have been taking good care of it. However, there's a chance you might suffer minor issues such as food poisoning towards the end of the year if you aren't mindful of your diet. This is particularly true for those born in the winter season.

Career

This is the year where you reach new heights in your career. With new position comes new responsibilities where you are able to let yourself shine. As everyone is paying attention to you right now, you might even get better career opportunities elsewhere if you wish to change jobs.

農曆正月

(February 4th - March 4th) 戊寅
Your Wealth Luck is going great this month. Take advantage of this by monetizing your creative ideas.

農曆二月

(March 5th - April 3rd) 己卯
Your luck for wealth continues to be favourable this month. When you're undergoing good luck, it is the time where you should be doing as much as you can.

農曆三月

(April 4th - May 4th) 庚辰
Get on good terms with your boss. Being friendly with your superior grants you access to their help in your times of need.

農曆四月

(May 5th - June 4th) 辛巳
This month, you're susceptible to being distracted by frivolous things and be unproductive as a result. Don't procrastinate as you'll only trouble yourself in the future.

農曆五月

(June 5th - July 5th) 壬午
You may find progression in your career this month. It could come in the form of a job offer or a promotion.

農曆六月

(July 6th - August 6th) 癸未
This month, you'll find yourself to be more openminded towards new activities. It's a good time to put your talents to good use or learn new skills to increase your self-value.

農曆七月

(August 7th - September 6th) 甲申
You may be travelling a lot this month on the pretence of work. For those who are married, this might put a strain on your marriage.

農曆八月

(September 7th - October 7th) 乙酉
This month, it is likely there are petty rumours in your immediate environment. Don't get yourself involved in them and simply focus on your goals.

農曆九月

(October 8th - November 6th) 丙戌
You'll be blessed with positive energy this month and it is recommended you channel it into something productive. At the same time, don't overdo it and end up offending your boss.

農曆十月

(November 7th - December 6th) 丁亥
It is possible that someone might offer you a partnership this month. If this happens, don't say yes just yet as it is current inauspicious to do so. Postpone your decision to another time.

農曆十一月

(December 7th 2020 - January 4th 2021) 戊子
Some people might be looking to take credit for your ideas. Choose who you trust carefully and make sure you take the necessary steps to safeguard important information.

農曆十二月

(January 5th - February 2nd 2021) 己丑
Even if you're busy with work, don't neglect your health. The stress you accumulate might eventually affect your physical well-being. Before this happen, take some time off so it won't come to that.

六十甲子 Forecast for 2020 based on Day of Birth

壬午 **Ren Wu Day**

Overview

You might be overwhelmed with extra work this year. To handle these new responsibilities, it is recommended that you manage it wisely. Create a schedule and realistic deadlines you can follow to keep up a productive pace. If you put effort in the right direction, you'll be able to attain success. With success however comes petty people. When others are trying to bring you down, you focus on your ambition. Maintain your work ethics and you will become more accomplished in the future.

Wealth

It's a good year to be making money. Having said that, you still have to plan your finances carefully. Have some strategy in your spending and set aside for investments. Practice discipline when it comes to your wealth and you'll be able to make full use of your favourable wealth luck.

Relationships

For any argument that you encounter this year, think before you speak. Whenever possible, try to compromise with your partner. If you don't choose what you say with tact, it is likely you'll come off as offensive. If you are a married woman, your marriage requires extra attention this year. Single men might be able to find love provided they are more outgoing and meet new people.

Health

In terms of health, this year is looking to be generally pleasant. Even so, you are still susceptible to minor injuries that could come from overstraining yourself such as sprains. If you don't do something about it, it could potentially worsen. Even in good health, you should still go for regular check-ups just in case. There's also a possibility for you to put some strain on your heart.

Career

During midyear, you might have an opportunity to switch jobs. If you're thinking of leaving, you should wait until then. Before the time comes, be cordial to the people in your current office. In the future, they might be of help to you even after you move on in your career. Keep in touch with them, perhaps in the future they might be crucial for you to find opportunities.

農曆正月

(February 4th - March 4th) 戊寅
This month, things get competitive in the office. Be prepared for competition if you don't want to get left behind. At the same time, be careful with your shoulders as it is prone to injury.

農曆二月

(March 5th - April 3rd) 己卯
You might have a feeling that your boss is treating you unfairly. Perhaps you find that you are being treated worse than your colleagues. Don't let this get to you, focus on carrying out the responsibilities that were given to you well.

農曆三月

(April 4th - May 4th) 庚辰
It's possible that you are able to travel this month. Make the necessary preparations. You might also feel like procrastinating this month; try not to give into this feeling.

農曆四月

(May 5th - June 4th) 辛巳
It would be a financially rewarding month if you are working with others as a team. If you wish to make more money, simply rely on your social network.

農曆五月

(June 5th - July 5th) 壬午
This time of the year is where you are likely to receive a job offer. Think of the pros and cons before you come to a conclusive decision.

農曆六月

(July 6th - August 6th) 癸未
If you are a man, it is likely that different aspects of your life will affect one another this month. Draw a clear line between your professional life and personal life so that neither of them would compromise the other.

農曆七月

(August 7th - September 6th) 甲申
This month, you might find yourself entangled with litigation while on the road. When travelling, pay attention to your documentations and action so that nothing can be used against you.

農曆八月

(September 7th - October 7th) 乙酉
It's possible that you're feeling rather negative this month. This feeling might lead you to alcohol consumption but it's not really the solution to your worries.

農曆九月

(October 8th - November 6th) 丙戌
It's a good time to unleash your creativity and explore new ideas. Don't be afraid to experiment with different concepts or be innovative with established methods.

農曆十月

(November 7th - December 6th) 丁亥
This month, there is a possibility for you to travel. Travels are good opportunity for you to learn something new and increase your personal value.

農曆十一月

(December 7th 2020 - January 4th 2021) 戊子
There might be some problems at home plaguing you. Should it happen, try to address the problem immediately and don't let the situation worsen.

農曆十二月

(January 5th - February 2nd 2021) 己丑
You might be tempted to take shortcuts or resort to unethical behaviour this month. These things would lead to negative outcome in the long run and ultimately won't be worth it.

癸未 Gui Wei Day

Overview

Overall, it would be an average year for you that's leaning towards the positive side. If you were to travel, you might get the chance to increase your wealth through the new connections you'll be making. For those who were born in the seasons of autumn or winter, it is crucial for you to be paying attention to your health.

 ## Wealth

If you been working hard towards expanding your wealth, you might begin to see the results of your effort this year. This includes whatever investments you might had in the years prior. Remember to stay humble even if you now have some extra wealth. If you own a business, it's a good time for you to go for an expansion. As such, consider introducing your business to new countries.

Relationships

If you're a man and you're still single, you're in luck this year. With Peach Blossom Luck in your corner, you'll be able to meet the right match. If you're already attached, this luck may backfire as you might attract attention from other people who might threaten your relationship. For the opposite sex, single woman would also have some degree of the Peach Blossom luck.

 ## Health

For those born in the seasons of autumn or winter, pay extra attention to your health. Your gastrointestinal organs such as your liver might run into some issues. It's nothing serious, but you should still look into it just in case. There's a chance you might also get your limbs injured, particularly on the right side of your body.

Career

Big changes are in store for you in terms of your career this year in the form of advancement. Travelling for work purposes might bring about these changes. If you're thinking of changing jobs, there are plenty of opportunities for you to find. Nonetheless, you should still think through any choice you might be making.

農曆正月

(February 4th - March 4th) 戊寅
This month, work gets competitive. It's not comfortable, but it's a chance for you to rise to the challenge. Look for trusted allies in the office and find arrangements that are mutually beneficial.

農曆二月

(March 5th - April 3rd) 己卯
This month, you can expect an increase in your wealth at the cost of your health. If you had to pick between the two, give your attention to your health issues first before you sort your financial matters.

農曆三月

(April 4th - May 4th) 庚辰
For those born in the seasons of autumn and summer, it would be highly favourable for you to be collaborating with others to get the job done.

農曆四月

(May 5th - June 4th) 辛巳
You might be prone to overspend this month so be mindful of your expenditure. If you were born in autumn, stay away from short-term investments that sounds too good to be true.

農曆五月

(June 5th - July 5th) 壬午
Whenever you travel this month on the road, practice extra caution. You might run into accidents or trouble with the law if you're careless.

農曆六月

(July 6th - August 6th) 癸未
You might receive a form of career advancement this month. Go ahead and celebrate, you're going to need a clear head to tackle on the new responsibilities that comes with it.

農曆七月

(August 7th - September 6th) 甲申
It's a good month for you to acquire new skills and hone your talent. Make the most out of it.

農曆八月

(September 7th - October 7th) 乙酉
If you're still single, you'll have good Peach Blossom Luck so why don't you give love a try. Right now, it is actually favourable for you to take the first step as the results would be in your favour.

農曆九月

(October 8th - November 6th) 丙戌
Your work can be done more efficiently if you can get others to help you out so don't be afraid to ask the people around you.

農曆十月

(November 7th - December 6th) 丁亥
You might undergo some mood swings this month and as a result, you might become argumentative. No matter what your pride tells you, prioritize other people and try to look from their point of view to find a compromise.

農曆十一月

(December 7th 2020 - January 4th 2021) 戊子
Whatever you have planned, make sure you have every detail covered thoroughly. Any loopholes that you might've missed out could jeopardize the entire operation. Nonetheless, be prepared for any unexpected changes and don't be afraid to get criticized.

農曆十二月

(January 5th - February 2nd 2021) 己丑
If you're in a relationship, you might be arguing with your partner this month over money matters. Try not to make things worse than it already is by keeping your emotions in check.

甲申 Jia Shen Day

Overview

Your career is looking favourable this year as you will see significant progress. This progress could be many things; perhaps you would be tasked with new responsibilities, given more opportunities to travel or get yourself promoted. As long as you are receptive to opportunities, you can make the best out of them when they come. It is likely however that your domestic life is not going to fare so well. At home, there might be an air of confusion and it's up to your own effort to make sense of things.

 ## Wealth

For those who are itching to take a vacation or travel, this year might be the year it finally happens. The prospects here are largely positive; there's a lot to gain when you travel. From the people you'll meet to the fresh new sceneries you'll see, all of these would enrich your experience. Overall, this year's theme should be that of self-improvement.

 ## Relationships

If you have been committed to your partner for quite a while now and want to make it official, this would be a good year to do so. Before you tie the knot, make sure you two are clear with each other especially in terms of expectations. When you are able to establish a strong foundation for your relationship, it will be able to stand the test of time.

 ## Health

In terms of health, you should keep an eye out for issues that affect your blood and stomach. These health problems might manifest itself in the form of indigestion or blood poisoning. If you spot any symptom related to these ailments, it's recommended that you seek immediate medical attention to mitigate the negative effects.

 ## Career

Your career is looking to soar and progress far this year. While this opportunity might hold most of your attention, don't forget to leave some for your health. Remember, you need to be in your best shape to be doing your best. Learn to balance different aspects of your life so that you are able to enjoy all of them to the fullest.

農曆正月

(February 4th - March 4th) 戊寅
This month, all the effort you have put in your work would be recognized and monetary reward might be in store. Make sure your success won't slow down your momentum.

農曆二月

(March 5th - April 3rd) 己卯
The added Wealth luck you enjoyed so far continues into this month. Keep up the good work and you'll be able to capitalize on this luck. If you're a guy, it's a good month to be looking for love.

農曆三月

(April 4th - May 4th) 庚辰
For women, it is a favourable month if you're looking for a potential partner. To make full use of this month's luck, keep an open mind. Whatever expectations you might have for a partner, try not to use it as standard. You might find a happy surprise if you let things happen.

農曆四月

(May 5th - June 4th) 辛巳
While you may find favourable love luck in the previous months, this month would be rather problematic in that department. Keep calm and look at the situation objectively if you're looking for a peaceful resolution. One aspect of your life might be stressful, but don't let it get to you personally.

農曆五月

(June 5th - July 5th) 壬午
This month, ideas and inspiration comes to you seamlessly. As creativity flows through you smoothly, you would be able to gain some wealth if you are able to monetize your ideas.

農曆六月

(July 6th - August 6th) 癸未
This month, it is likely that you would have the opportunity to travel. While on the road, watch what you eat. There is also a possibility that you might suffer ailment related to the stomach this month and as such, pay attention to your diet.

農曆七月

(August 7th - September 6th) 甲申
You might experience some major mood swings this month. However temperamental you are right now, don't let your feelings cloud your judgement. The internal problems you have might translate into external problems if you were to take it out on other people.

農曆八月

(September 7th - October 7th) 乙酉
Remember, you're not responsible for everyone's problem even if you are their leader. Instead of trying to help others with their trouble, it's better for you to stay away from them altogether.

農曆九月

(October 8th - November 6th) 丙戌
This month, those who are married might experience some domestic turbulence. While trouble is likely to happen, it can be mitigated through compromise. Have some patience when you're trying to settle your differences.

農曆十月

(November 7th - December 6th) 丁亥
It will be a competitive month in the office this month. Even if you don't like how things are, you should try to keep up in order to stay relevant.

農曆十一月

(December 7th 2020 - January 4th 2021) 戊子
Your workplace environment continues to be competitive this month. The extra stress from your current circumstances might test your limits, but don't do anything drastic. If you are tempted to do anything that is morally ambiguous in order to remedy the situation, don't do it. Everything that you have experienced will be beneficial for you in the end.

農曆十二月

(January 5th - February 2nd 2021) 己丑
While you have been working hard, don't forget the other people in your life. Take some time to work on your personal relationships. One way to do so would be to try new things together. The moments you share with others would strengthen your ties with them.

乙酉 Yi You Day

Overview

Your overall luck would be quite favourable this year. You may expect your financial standing to increase if you have invested in real estate or property. In fact, you might be able to acquire a new property or house by the year's end. Even if you're not in the capacity to invest in land or property, it's still a good year to invest and allow your wealth to grow.

 ## Wealth

It's an excellent year for you to be investing. Make the best out of every opportunity that you are given. Despite the fact that it's auspicious to invest, you still have to handle your money with wisdom. Make plans, do ample research and have a solid foundation before you invest. When you are able to establish extra income, it will give you the freedom to pursuit more things in life.

 ## Relationships

If you are a man who is looking for love, you might find the right match some time this year. If you are already married, trouble can be expected. Before your problems get out of hand, you should try to resolve it as soon as possible. If you are a single woman, you'll have better luck in love and relationship sometime during the autumn season.

 ## Health

It can be quite an emotional year for you. Rather than letting it fester in your mind, you should mitigate the negative feelings you might have through calming methods such as meditation or relaxing activities. You can also gain some clarity of mind if you were to do some self-reflection. For those who are forty years old and above, there's a chance that you might develop heart problems.

 ## Career

Your career is looking great this year provided you are working with other people. Whether it's colleagues or partners, they will prove to be instrumental in getting ahead in your road to success. For any challenges or obstacles you might face, it's good to have reliable allies to depend on. If nothing else, having support is good for your morale.

農曆正月

(February 4th - March 4th) 戊寅
This month, you might experience some mood swings. For any arguments or conflicts you get yourself into as a result, try your best to be cordial about it.

農曆二月

(March 5th - April 3rd) 己卯
Your office or workplace might get competitive this month. Make necessary preparations before that happens to overcome this circumstance better. Additionally, in terms of health, you might also be susceptible to sore throats and fever.

農曆三月

(April 4th - May 4th) 庚辰
This month might be quite tiring and you may end up feeling demotivated. You can still maintain a good level of productivity if you were to keep your eyes on your goals.

農曆四月

(May 5th - June 4th) 辛巳
Your friends are there for you if you need them. It would be advisable for you to get a second opinion from them before you make any decision.

農曆五月

(June 5th - July 5th) 壬午
You may require some extra financial support if you have any side-projects you'd like to work on. The good news is that you'll be able to ask for funding. Plan ahead and schedule with that in mind.

農曆六月

(July 6th - August 6th) 癸未
At work, you might receive a financial boon this month.

農曆七月

(August 7th - September 6th) 甲申
There's a potential for you to climb up your career ladder this month that would bring you new responsibilities as well as financial gains. While the opportunity is there, it would only happen if you are truly deserving of the position.

農曆八月

(September 7th - October 7th) 乙酉
This month, you might be feeling impatient and thus lead you to act impulsively. However, shortcuts would prove to be more harmful than it is beneficial so it's best you avoid them. Have patience and just soldier through your current situation. In time, you will see how this is the better way.

農曆九月

(October 8th - November 6th) 丙戌
Ideas and creativity will be abundant this month as there will be no shortage of inspiration for you. Of course, you still require to put in effort to turn these ideas into reality. It would be a waste if you simply let them be pipedreams.

農曆十月

(November 7th - December 6th) 丁亥
This month, you will be recognized by your boss for the value you give. As a result, you may find yourself praised and others would begin to see your talents.

農曆十一月

(December 7th 2020 - January 4th 2021) 戊子
For those in relationships, this would be an argumentative month with your significant other. If the conflict persists, it might threaten your relationship with them. Take the high road, be more understanding and forgiving even if they refuse to budge. Find a resolution or compromise before it gets out of hand.

農曆十二月

(January 5th - February 2nd 2021) 己丑
This month, watch what you say. There is nothing good for you to gain from insulting or offending others.

丙戌 Bing Xu Day

Overview
Your career might feel like it's obstructed this year with little progress to be made. The cause of this issue could be internal or external; it could be that you're not efficient in your workflow or you have teammates who aren't carrying the same weight and thus bring the overall performance of your group down. Either way, your focus should be on carrying out your responsibilities.

 ## Wealth
If you have the opportunity to get out of the country, that's where you'll find your wealth this year. If you own a business, consider expanding it somewhere in the north. Another way you could improve your business would be to collaborate with others. Spend cautiously; make sure for every penny you spend, you save two.

 ## Relationships
If you're in a relationship, it's not going to be a good year. You might develop some resentment towards your significant other because you feel ignored. At the very least, be honest to your partner on how you feel. If you're not in a relationship, it's advisable to stay clear of it this year. For the time being, it's more trouble than it's worth.

 ## Health
Your weight will see an increase this year and it may bring additional problems such as your blood cholesterol level rising. With that in mind, try to go for a healthier diet and take food that contains less sugar. It will be beneficial for your overall wellbeing for you to be taking better care of your health.

 ## Career
Your career can be your silver lining this year provided that you are able to travel. Going to new places would broaden your horizon. If it is not within your means, try to make an effort to change departments or climb the corporate ladder. If you wish to improve and advance in your career, you have to get out of your comfort zone.

農曆正月

(February 4th - March 4th) 戊寅
You will be tasked with new responsibilities by your boss this month. If you need help, don't be afraid to reach out to your colleagues.

農曆二月

(March 5th - April 3rd) 己卯
You may find some valuable insights and advice from the people around you this month. As such, be receptive to their opinion and listen.

農曆三月

(April 4th - May 4th) 庚辰
When dealing with a lot of work, procrastinating is a temporary relief at the cost of your future self. While you still have the time, finish your work.

農曆四月

(May 5th - June 4th) 辛巳
This month, you might suffer from health issues related to your stomach. As soon as the first symptom appears, it would be wise for you to seek medical treatment.

農曆五月

(June 5th - July 5th) 壬午
There might be people around you at your workplace who are looking to take credit for your ideas. If you're inclined to share valuable information with other people, make sure they are trustworthy.

農曆六月

(July 6th - August 6th) 癸未
You might be experiencing some stagnation at work. It's possible that you might react to this situation by being frustrated and demotivated. To get yourself out, shift your focus elsewhere. Consider that you're doing well in other aspects of your life.

農曆七月

(August 7th - September 6th) 甲申
This month, your Wealth Luck is looking favourable. It's a good time for you to be making money as you'll earn extra.

農曆八月

(September 7th - October 7th) 乙酉
Your workload may overwhelm you this month so it's imperative for you to manage it. Come up with a schedule that's achievable and deadlines that are realistic. With some discipline, you'll be able to complete all your work.

農曆九月

(October 8th - November 6th) 丙戌
As last month has been stressful, you should take some time off; perhaps you should go on a vacation to refresh and reenergize yourself.

農曆十月

(November 7th - December 6th) 丁亥
If you wish to travel this month, consider going northwards. Be open to new opportunities, new places and new people.

農曆十一月

(December 7th 2020 - January 4th 2021) 戊子
If you are in a partnership, you should be looking at the fine print. Some funny business may be happening behind your back. To avoid trouble, your business should be practicing accountability and transparency.

農曆十二月

(January 5th - February 2nd 2021) 己丑
This month, allocate some time for those you hold dear in your heart. It takes effort to have a meaningful relationship with others. Be more honest to them.

丁亥 Ding Hai Day

Overview

For the first few months of this year, you might feel that it will be rather uneventful and boring. If you wish to change this monotony, it is up to your own effort. Make plans to change your circumstances. This year can also be quite stressful and tiring, more so than usual. But, if you can keep your chin up and continue to push forward, you'll find that it will all be worth it in the end.

 ## Wealth

Your Wealth Luck affords you to realize all your goals and ambition with little to no hindrance. If you want to make something happen, you have to do it yourself and take the initiative. Positive wealth luck happens when you are able to match what you have to offer with the demands of the market. Having said that, either adapt to the market or find one that suits you.

 ## Relationships

This year, luck in romance would elude you for the first half of the year. When the second half comes along, you will see some improvements in the opportunities you are given. Nonetheless, it's not really a year for you to be pursuing romance. Instead, you should shift your attention to other areas in your life such as career or health. Love will come when it comes, it's not necessary for you to be forcing it to happen.

 ## Health

Pay extra attention to any health issues pertaining your eyes, heart and kidney, particularly in the second half of the year. Good health is not only maintained through a healthy lifestyle but also with regular check-ups. As they say, prevention is better than cure.

 ## Career

You career will progress at a frustratingly slow pace this year and you may feel tired as a result. Even so, you shouldn't give in to the fatigue and maintain your momentum because every step you take is a step forward. Utilize the time that you have to the best of your ability; pick up a new skill or learn something that might be of use in the future. If you were to increase your own self-worth, it will open many doors in your journey ahead.

農曆正月

(February 4th - March 4th) 戊寅
Success is much easier to achieve when you collaborate with others. If you were born in winter, your luck in networking will be boosted for the duration of this month so make use of it.

農曆二月

(March 5th - April 3rd) 己卯
If you are an expectant mother, beware of possible health issues. For any symptom that might appear, you should go for a check-up.

農曆三月

(April 4th - May 4th) 庚辰
When you're doing your work, maintain your energy level and keep going. If you were to slow down, it's easy for you to be tempted into procrastination. Stay determined and focus on your goals.

農曆四月

(May 5th - June 4th) 辛巳
You might be undergoing some mental stress this month as it has been tiring. There's a likelihood that the stress will only be getting worse. It is possible for you to mitigate the negative effects of this month by taking good care of both your physical and mental wellbeing.

農曆五月

(June 5th - July 5th) 壬午
If you're in a relationship, pay attention to your partner's health this month. It's possible that they might be having some undetected issue. There's no harm for you to bring them for a check-up just to be on the safe side.

農曆六月

(July 6th - August 6th) 癸未
In any endeavour you might have, be mindful of the rules or regulations. Don't push yourself too hard. At work, uphold integrity and honesty.

農曆七月

(August 7th - September 6th) 甲申
If you were born in winter or autumn, you should be careful of health issues affecting your digestive system. Naturally, practice good hygiene when it comes to eating.

農曆八月

(September 7th - October 7th) 乙酉
At your workplace, there might be some people who are gunning for your position through unscrupulous means. Mind your actions and your words as to not create enemies among your co-workers.

農曆九月

(October 8th - November 6th) 丙戌
It is possible that your current view of things is negative and pessimistic this month. Don't lock it up inside. Instead, talk it out, find someone who can listen. In time, everything will be okay.

農曆十月

(November 7th - December 6th) 丁亥
Pay attention to what you eat this month because there's a chance that you might have health issues concerning the stomach. If you remain careless, you might suffer from ailments such as food poisoning or stomach flu.

農曆十一月

(December 7th 2020 - January 4th 2021) 戊子
To build a better social network for yourself, you have to practice teamwork. With the help of those around you, you would be able to overcome any challenges you might face from your boss.

農曆十二月

(January 5th - February 2nd 2021) 己丑
Be professional in your career. Don't let your personal problems to affect your work. Draw a definitive line between the two and keep these two aspects of your life separate from one another.

戊子 Wu Zi Day

Overview

You might feel like this year is too much for you to handle and find the challenges to be overwhelming. In your endeavours, set aside some break time in order to manage your tasks better. While it might seem like a good idea to multi-task, it's actually better for you to get things done one at a time. Sometimes it's not about how much effort you give in, but how you efficiently you manage your resources.

 ## Wealth

This year, you are at risk of losing some of your wealth so be cautious with where you put your money. Try to mitigate overspending by being in control of your expenditure. If this is something you're not used to doing, the first half the year would be a good time to practice. From the second half onwards, that's when you really have to keep your budget in check.

 ## Relationships

It's a good year for women in relationships to make their ties official. On the other hand, women who are already married will have to deal with a stressful and emotional year. Arguments are inevitable, but not something you can't handle. Practice diplomacy and compromise to mitigate the negativity. If you're a guy, appreciate what you have. Don't jeopardise what you have for something that might not be for you in the long run.

 ## Health

Pay extra attention to your health this year as you might have experience some minor health issues. This would be more obvious during the second half of the year, particularly for those born in the seasons of autumn or winter. Eat healthily and exercise regularly to avoid complications to your health. If you were to participate in any activity near bodies of water, practice extra caution.

 ## Career

This year, you might get into disagreements with your boss. Your differences can be politely discussed and settle so always go for the diplomatic route. Make sure you communicate your opinion clearly and carefully. Maintain good ties with your fellow co-workers so you'll have dependable allies you can rely on.

農曆正月

(February 4th - March 4th) 戊寅
Don't let your pride get in the way of your work. Perhaps other people's ideas are objectively better than yours. If that is the case, give them your support.

農曆二月

(March 5th - April 3rd) 己卯
While you might consider changing jobs this month, don't jump to conclusions just yet. Weight in the pros and cons as well as have your assumptions grounded in reality before you make any decision.

農曆三月

(April 4th - May 4th) 庚辰
Take the initiative in your office this month. There are opportunities at every corner that would allow you to show what you capable of.

農曆四月

(May 5th - June 4th) 辛巳
When it comes to work, set your priorities straight. When you reflect on your own abilities, you would be able to find a way to work more efficiently.

農曆五月

(June 5th - July 5th) 壬午
Try not to be impulsive and think before you act. You'll be able to save yourself a lot of trouble in the future if you were to do so.

農曆六月

(July 6th - August 6th) 癸未
You might not realize the impact you have with what you say or what you do but some people might take it the wrong way. Pay attention to how you appear to them from their perspective.

農曆七月

(August 7th - September 6th) 甲申
Your Wealth Luck is on the rise this month. If you are a man looking for love, you might find a good match this month.

農曆八月

(September 7th - October 7th) 乙酉
This month, your efforts are beginning to show results. Take this as a sign that you should keep up the good work.

農曆九月

(October 8th - November 6th) 丙戌
There's a possibility that you begin a new relationship this month. If you are a woman, you may want to keep this relationship on low profile for the time being.

農曆十月

(November 7th - December 6th) 丁亥
While you may enjoy good Wealth Luck this month, your health may be declining. Even if you're engrossed in work, be sure not to sacrifice your health for it.

農曆十一月

(December 7th 2020 - January 4th 2021) 戊子
It's possible that you're experiencing some negative feelings towards your significant other. However, it's advisable that you don't act on these feelings. Instead, try to communicate calmly with them and achieve a resolution that both of you could agree with.

農曆十二月

(January 5th - February 2nd 2021) 己丑
This month, your mind might be clouded with confusion and negatively affect your decision-making skills. Perhaps you should ask your friends for their opinions to achieve some clarity on your situation.

甲子
六十甲子

Forecast for 2020 based on Day of Birth

己丑 Ji Chou Day

Overview

There will be many challenges for you to face this year that might require the aid of others to overcome. As such, you should maintain cordial relationships with your friends and family in case you need their help. Your financial outlook this year is not so positive either. Nonetheless, this won't be permanent. In time, it will all come to pass. Until then, you should plan well for the future.

 ## Wealth

This year, your wealth luck is borderline average. It could be better if you were to manage your finances wisely. Otherwise, it's very easy for you to be overspending your expenditures to the point where it would be hard to remedy. If you want to spend your money anyway, you should put it where it may grow such as investments or assets that would increase in value over time.

 ## Relationships

Your luck in love and romance is not looking so well this year. For those in relationships, expect frequent arguments with your partner. For those who are single, it would be the better option to remain on your own. Take the time to focus on other aspects of your life instead until better luck comes along.

 ## Health

There's a possibility that your kidneys might cause you issues or your blood pressure going up. To mitigate this, consider going for regular check-ups or adopt healthy living habits. In the event that you experience any symptoms related to these issues, get medical attention immediately. You may also encounter other health issues such as skin problems and allergies; particular if you were born in summer.

 ## Career

This year, there might be some changes when it comes to your career. Whatever it may be, make preparations and be as adaptable as possible. If you are able to secure a partner, it would afford you some extra security and stability in your work. If you possess these factors, you can expect great success and accomplishment ahead.

農曆正月

(February 4th - March 4th) 戊寅
For every opportunity that comes your way, you should be the one to take the initiative. If you don't see any, be creative and create one.

農曆二月

(March 5th - April 3rd) 己卯
If you're looking to earn some extra money, you're in luck this month. There are opportunities for you to do so and your friends may help you to find out how.

農曆三月

(April 4th - May 4th) 庚辰
Take care of your legs this month, particularly your ankles and knees, as you may get them injured. With that in mind, exercise caution when it comes to physical activities.

農曆四月

(May 5th - June 4th) 辛巳
Your finances might take a hit this month because of your health. This may be avoidable if you are extra cautious this month. Keep an eye out on sharp objects around you.

農曆五月

(June 5th - July 5th) 壬午
For employees who believe they are deserving of more benefits or salary increment, right now is a good opportunity to be asking for it.

農曆六月

(July 6th - August 6th) 癸未
This month, you might unintentionally offend those around you. If you have nothing nice to say, then it's better not to say anything at all.

農曆七月

(August 7th - September 6th) 甲申
You are prone to overthinking this month about things beyond your control. If you dwell on it, this may obstruct your progress.

農曆八月

(September 7th - October 7th) 乙酉
There might be some problems on the domestic front that may affect your professional life. Address the issue while it's still manageable.

農曆九月

(October 8th - November 6th) 丙戌
This month, safeguard whatever your ideas you have as it might get stolen by certain people near you. Choose who to trust carefully.

農曆十月

(November 7th - December 6th) 丁亥
When it comes to decision-making, make your choices with your head instead of your heart. Acting impulsively would lead to regret.

農曆十一月

(December 7th 2020 - January 4th 2021) 戊子
Give yourself a breather from the hectic work life you've been having and take some time off.

農曆十二月

(January 5th - February 2nd 2021) 己丑
When you encounter any problems, nip them in the bud. If you don't take immediate action, these problems could spiral out of control.

庚寅 **Geng Yin Day**

庚 Geng
寅 Yin

Overview

This year make time to expand your social circle with new people and acquaintance as your Peach Blossom luck is blooming this month. This is the year to attend any or all networking functions that may be in the works and get to know more people in these 365 days. Be sure to pace yourself to avoid over exhaustion. Look sharp and keep a focused eye out as together with the possibility of forging new friendships, you may even meet your soulmate.

 ### Wealth

Options and opportunities are abound this year. However, in order to seize the opportunities, you need to work harder than the rest. Undertake some market research and make unbiased judgement based on facts and figures instead of letting desires cloud your clarity. Any decisions you make needs to be done with conviction and perseverance for it to bear good fruits. Set your sights on what you want to achieve and make sure you keep a keen eye out for any eventualities.

 ### Relationships

In terms of love, your outlook for this year is average. Women may find that they are certainly not short of potential suitors, however, thread carefully. Be watchful of potential male suitors as not all are as they seem. Single males need to be observant and start moving around your social circle, as there is good chance of meeting that one person who is meant for you, so start asking people out for coffee!

 ### Health

This year will see you skating on thin ice. You will be bogged down by stressful work constraints that you might need to take special heed to. You will be faced with a higher workload, so take this as an opportunity to learn. Prepare yourself with various capabilities but be cautious of every move you make. Besides, always think before you act to avoid any costly decision. Take care of your digestive tract. Intestinal, liver and kidney issues may rear their ugly heads. Avoid over indulging in food laden with carbohydrates and sugar.

 ### Career

In terms of business and career, fortune is favouring you due to your traits and abilities. Take this time to share your rewards with the others to acknowledge their help and assistance in the past. Continue to practice the values that help shape your delightful life. You may need to do a little introspection in terms of career goals this year. Go on a self-improvement quest and learn new skills that you can bring to the table. You will gain the recognition and respect of your colleagues and superiors. Accept these accolades but do not place too much importance to them. Career advancement works best with humility.

農曆正月

(February 4th - March 4th) 戊寅
All is well for you this month, and henceforth you will find yourself executing plans with great ease and dexterity. As a reward for all your endeavours, your fortune in career, wealth and relationship will see positive outcomes this month.

農曆二月

(March 5th - April 3rd) 己卯
Carrying over the good fortune from the previous month, most of your tasks will have great progress and you will see benefit in return. Listen to people around you as some may have some good piece of advice that you can take as a life lesson.

農曆三月

(April 4th - May 4th) 庚辰
You may run into some argument with your superior. Understanding your strength and weakness is crucial particularly at work. Take time out to introspect from time to time and continue to move forward, putting one step in front of the other.

農曆四月

(May 5th - June 4th) 辛巳
You may have expectations about the way you want your subordinates or colleagues to interact with you. Just because you have been placed in an authoritative position – this does not automatically imply respect. Remember that everyone has a voice and a contribution to make.

農曆五月

(June 5th - July 5th) 壬午
As you pursue your endeavours this month, be prepared to put a twist to your usual routine. This is the time to pause and reflect on yourself instead of forcibly charging forward. You don't have to start big to succeed.

農曆六月

(July 6th - August 6th) 癸未
Try and practice some patience with your colleagues and avoid instigating bad communication. Ensure you look in before you look out and make judgements. In order to be a better person with someone else, you first need to be a better person yourself.

農曆七月

(August 7th - September 6th) 甲申
It is best to keep your eyes peeled out this month. Be particularly careful when participating in sports and outdoor activities. The month's stars bring the chance of being inflicted with a minor injury due to external circumstances.

農曆八月

(September 7th - October 7th) 乙酉
You will be blessed with great celestial energies of the month. You may see a good change of tidings of two particular aspects of your life namely your Wealth Luck and Career Luck. This is particularly true if you were born in summer.

農曆九月

(October 8th - November 6th) 丙戌
You are likely to be given the opportunity to be the star of your own show. Handle this opportunity carefully as it has been placed before you as a test of your character and ability. Avoid conflict and jealous work colleagues by fostering mutual understanding.

農曆十月

(November 7th - December 6th) 丁亥
This is not a good time to make life, or business altering decisions that has a lot riding on it. Pause, and pay attention to details and smaller matters. Now is not the time for rash decisions, but rather refining existing abilities or developing new talents.

農曆十一月

(December 7th 2020 - January 4th 2021) 戊子
Try not to lend money or give in to possible risky investments. If you intend to purchase securities it is important that you understand what you are getting yourself into before you start putting your money in.

農曆十二月

(January 5th - February 2nd 2021) 己丑
Be wary of potential third party interference this month. Expend a little more effort and time to strengthen your relationship and to listen to each other's needs and wants in order to avoid conflicts.

辛卯 Xin Mao Day

Overview

The coming year might initially be a little frustrating in both life and work, with a little less blessings from auspicious stars and harder impact from inauspicious stars. Patience and perseverance are definitely words to live by this year as they will certainly help you reign things into perspective individuals. The focus this year is enhancing your social life. Your efforts will be of much use to you in the months to come. The year will also see numerous tasks and assignments coming your way at the workplace. This is where your patience and tactfulness will be required to navigate the week successfully.

 ## Wealth

Opt for long-term over short-term to investments this year. Short-term investments might seem to produce quick results but, in this case, it will not be a favourable one. Consider seeking the help and advices of the professionals who can aid you into making ideal investments which can aligned to your financial goals. There are great avenues to make a little money in if you can seize the right opportunities. Take a conservative attitude with money management matters and avoid high-risk investments.

 ## Relationships

If you are male and single and want to change that, this year will see ample opportunities coming your way to participate in different social events and to possibly meet new people. Love sometimes comes at a time when we are not looking but rather just enjoying the company of others and more importantly being ourselves. The year is also perfect for you to expand your social circle better by attending social events proactively trying to meet new people.

 ## Health

In general, you would have good health this year. Still, you need to be on your toes while travelling as you may be susceptible to feet and head injuries. Guard against acquiring gastroenteritis as well as stomach related ailments. Avoid over indulging in food laden with fats and sugar as well as the consumption of comfort foods no matter how tasty and tempting they may be.

Career

Things will most likely go smoothly this year with regards to your career advancement plans. There will be ease in carrying out plans and projects with little hassle. You will be surrounded by people willing to help you should you be humble enough to ask for it when you need it. There will be possible opportunities for promotion and career advancements, so keep your mind sharp and ready for any potential appraisals and interviews.

農曆正月

(February 4th - March 4th) 戊寅

There will be some minor hiccups in terms of finances this month. Take the time to be wary and perhaps be a little more vigilant to your surroundings, in particular when engaged in travel or driving for work related purposes.

農曆二月

(March 5th - April 3rd) 己卯

Things are likely to be a little more fulfilling this month. This will give you a chance to sit back and relax and watch your monetary plans fall in line. Consider every opportunity that may yield greater returns for you.

農曆三月

(April 4th - May 4th) 庚辰

Watch your communication with others as you may unknowingly offend someone by saying something wrong which would put you in an awkward position. Any slip ups you make this month will leave a lasting impact on you.

農曆四月

(May 5th - June 4th) 辛巳

There may be some changes that you will need to adapt to at work this month, be it a new project or simply a change of place. You will be surrounded by people willing to help you should you be humble enough to ask for it when you need it.

農曆五月

(June 5th - July 5th) 壬午

It is recommended that you focus on your work and uphold your morals and try to avoid temptations. Distance yourself from workplace politics as well as office gossip to keep your sanity throughout the month.

農曆六月

(July 6th - August 6th) 癸未

Focus on fostering strong relationships with your better halves this month as this will certainly aid your work productivity inadvertedly. Stable couples may find their relationship tested – tolerance needs to be exercised in these trying periods.

農曆七月

(August 7th - September 6th) 甲申

Life might is likely to trouble you this month. The best approach to things is with a calm and patient demeanour. Put your best foot forward in dealing with whatever comes your way. Your luck cycle will improve eventually.

農曆八月

(September 7th - October 7th) 乙酉

You might find yourself travelling somewhere far this month either due to business or a vacation that is long overdue. In this regard, it is therefore important for you to ensure that you get the rest you need. It would be favourable for you to travel south.

農曆九月

(October 8th - November 6th) 丙戌

Look out for gossips and rumours that may come your way. These rumours may have a direct and indirect impact on your finances that may need to watch out for. Stay out of interfering into the business of people this month as your good intentions may be abused by others.

農曆十月

(November 7th - December 6th) 丁亥

You are likely to experience happy events this month. It is recommended that you focus on your work and uphold your morals. Understanding your strengths and weaknesses are crucial particularly at work. Refrain from short cuts, make sure that you develop a firm foundation.

農曆十一月

(December 7th 2020 - January 4th 2021) 戊子

Pay attention to legal documents. Make sure that you keep all your legal documents in a safe place. Avoid becoming anyone's guarantor as this responsibility as there may be likely legal repercussions down the road.

農曆十二月

(January 5th - February 2nd 2021) 己丑

Make your health your priority this month. Start by making healthier choices in terms of food and committing to an exercise regime that you can manage within your monthly schedule.

壬辰 **Ren Chen Day**

Overview

This would be a rather lacklustre year for you in some areas of your life. Be wary of legal issues if you are an autumn child as this could bode for legal woes. Work hard, but also remember to play hard this year. You are likely to gain the recognition and the respect of co-workers in your organisation and this will in turn put you in the limelight. It is a good time for strengthening your social bonds with the people in your organization.

 Wealth

You will certainly be financially blessed this year with the inflow of money into your accounts exceeding its outflow. It will be to your favour to make rational choices in any potential investment while avoiding short term opportunities. This is a good year to be prudent with your spending and keep as much spare cash as possible to prepare a robust financial buffer for unforeseen circumstances. Hopefully, this will encourage you towards strengthening your financial position.

 Relationships

Cupid is armed and ready to strike for all singles in 2020. The year will also present you with countless opportunities to expand your social circle and attend some mixers. If you are single, you may even meet your future partner in one of these occasions. This might be the right time for you guys to expand your social circle and perhaps ask to be introduced to more people. Those thinking of tying the knot this year – go right ahead. The year sees bright opportunities for a wonderful and lasting unions.

 Health

This is year to take control of your health and well-being. The year might leave you a little open to illnesses which may require surgical attention. However, this will be relatively minor and there is nothing to be overly concerned about. Avoid involving too heavily in extreme and dangerous activities of the likes of hiking or diving. Opt instead for some lighter exercise such as yoga, bicycling, or walking – these will still give you the exercise you need.

 Career

A seemingly good year ahead in terms of career. You will see flourishing profits from the different areas of investment and for those on a fixed income – this will probably be a good year to ask for that raise that you have been meaning to. Relationships with your superiors will see better ascension, prompting better promotion opportunities. Do not push yourself too hard with work commitments and falling into the trap of stress related illnesses.

農曆正月

(February 4th - March 4th) 戊寅
The month asks that you learn some patience and resilience as the stars indicate that you will on the losing end of competition or race. Don't let these events and circumstances faze you as you are likely to come up with an appropriate solution to your dilemma.

農曆二月

(March 5th - April 3rd) 己卯
This month you will be trying to meet the demands of your rising financials and work commitments while making bigger ends meet with income and spending. Any arising obstacles can be managed by seeking out your Nobleman who will certainly be your guiding saviour.

農曆三月

(April 4th - May 4th) 庚辰
This month, positivity and wealth blessings will be coming your way, thanks to the blessing of the some great stars, which denotes professional and financial success. Opportunities are abound if you keep your eyes and ears open.

農曆四月

(May 5th - June 4th) 辛巳
Remember to let go of your hurt and pain this month. Let the month be a time for closure. There will be those who seek to distract you and cause trouble, but they are none of your concern. Be wary in getting to excited and giving in to impulsive decisions that may lead to monetary loss.

農曆五月

(June 5th - July 5th) 壬午
Your career cards may see some light this month. You might see more increase in earnings in terms of income and investments. It is prudent that you spend your money wisely and refrain from counting your chickens before they hatch.

農曆六月

(July 6th - August 6th) 癸未
This month you will need a clean and orderly environment. You'll find having an organised desk and living space help keep your mind clear. You might find some minor hurdles or hiccups, but they won't set you back on your goals.

農曆七月

(August 7th - September 6th) 甲申
Married couples should refrain from engaging to unwanted and unwarranted arguments – instead aim for a balanced relationship that fosters better communication. It would be good start to spend the month with your family and loved ones to foster stronger bonds.

農曆八月

(September 7th - October 7th) 乙酉
As you pursue your endeavours this month, be prepared to encounter some unforeseen circumstances. There may be some unexpected change to your finances or perhaps even some interference of a third party.

農曆九月

(October 8th - November 6th) 丙戌
Invest your time with people who are worthwhile, as you will find contentment in your relationships this month. Have positive people around you for support and advice. People will look at you and there will be those who will judge you.

農曆十月

(November 7th - December 6th) 丁亥
This month will see weaker love prospects due to the weak Peach Blossom Luck. Singles might consider perhaps taking themselves out on a date and treating themselves to a luxurious massage. Sometimes in order for people to invest in us, we need to first invest in ourselves.

農曆十一月

(December 7th 2020 - January 4th 2021) 戊子
The month might see your work life balance compromised by stressful work constraints that may hold you back. Exercise calm and patience when treading through work issues as these are likely not going to last very long.

農曆十二月

(January 5th - February 2nd 2021) 己丑
Some injuries and illness may be prevalent this month – be wise to partaking in risky activities that may be to your detriment. Be cautious with sharp and hot objects as well as operating heavy machinery.

六十甲子 Forecast for 2020 based on Day of Birth

癸巳 Gui Si Day

Overview

Be ready for change in 2020! The ball is in your court this year so how the it plays out depends on you. Rewards will come to you this year if you work hard enough. You may encounter little shortcuts that you can take to pursue and complete your tasks faster but a note of caution should be exercised. This is the perfect year to start your climb up the corporate ladder. Great stars ahead that will aid your work performance and put you in the talent limelight. Be proactive in your endeavours and do what it takes to succeed - use the positive energies coming your way to your best advantage.

 ## Wealth

You have favourable wealth luck this year and how well you garner wealth would also greatly depend on your resourcefulness. Fair fortunes in money matters will see you being besieged by beer parties and good food. Good monetary qi flow in terms of earnings and investments would greatly induce the potential of monetary gain in other new areas with good proper prior research.

 ## Relationships

Your social life is likely to take an upward swing this year and you might even find it difficult to catch up with the invites flooding your social calendar. There are a lot of opportunities to meet a romantic partner this year, as a single female. Be clear with your intent in the pursue in romance so that you won't waste anyone's time.

 ## Health

Pay extra attention to your health as some minor threats are likely to emerge. Take prudent care of your health – exercise and watch your consumption of fatty and oily food. Wear masks and take vigilant precautions particularly around viral epidemics that may rear its ugly head.

 ## Career

There will be possible opportunities for promotion and career advancements, so keep your mind sharp and ready for any potential appraisals and interviews. Keep your earnings from your work well documented. Evaluate your choices and options. Spend your money wisely on things that would increase in value and pay no attention to those who seek to bring you down.

農曆正月

(February 4th - March 4th) 戊寅

A month of inspiration will allow you to generate many good ideas. Become a superstar and take advantage of all the attention you're getting. Don't mind the naysayers and keep on charging forward. Be proactive in your endeavours and do what it takes to succeed.

農曆二月

(March 5th - April 3rd) 巳卯

The month will go smoothly if you can conquer the obstacles and frustrations that in brewing in your workplace. Don't be afraid to take on new projects and roles as helping hands are ready to give you the lift you need.

農曆三月

(April 4th - May 4th) 庚辰

You'll connect with the right people to realize your ambitions of a possible promotion or advancement. Trash the dimming passion when it surfaces. Set your sights on that whale of a dream and harpoon your way into achieving it.

農曆四月

(May 5th - June 4th) 辛巳

There will be opportunities to expand your business. This will further add responsibilities at work but will bring better income. Prepare for some work related travel engagements. This is the moment to prove your effort and resolution.

農曆五月

(June 5th - July 5th) 壬午

Another interesting month all round with plenty of chances to enjoy great food and interesting conversations at social venues. You are likely to have very little frustrations at work and you may even see your wealth grow.

農曆六月

(July 6th - August 6th) 癸未

Frustrations at work will get the better of you. With work commitments and expectations piling on, you might feel the nagging stresses of these nipping at you from the sidelines. Take prudent care of your health. Watch your consumption of fatty and oily food.

農曆七月

(August 7th - September 6th) 甲申

This month is shaping up to be one of the luckier months. Be ready to take on challenges with the ferocity and tenacity of the king of the jungle! Keep a clear head, stay focused, and follow through. Your planning, patience, and perseverance will pay off.

農曆八月

(September 7th - October 7th) 乙酉

Be tactful with your words as a little slip up may leave you open to malicious gossips and rumours which could affect your wealth outcome. It is important for you to keep calm and accept the opinions of others in order to prevent miscommunication.

農曆九月

(October 8th - November 6th) 丙戌

Your mental, emotional and physical health requires attention as well so don't leave them neglected. Go on a journey that would nourish your both heart and soul. Exercise is crucial as well as eating a healthier, more balanced diet.

農曆十月

(November 7th - December 6th) 丁亥

There might be a slow decline in your progress at work. You might need to be patient in your efforts of righting the course of things. Show loyalty and steadfastness toward your superiors, heed their advice and this will be the stepping stone for future successes.

農曆十一月

(December 7th 2020 - January 4th 2021) 戊子

You are encouraged to take things slow this month and work at your own pace. Even if you feel as if your actions do not seem to be producing the results you desire, you should not simply throw in the towel and stop trying.

農曆十二月

(January 5th - February 2nd 2021) 己丑

There will be some minor hiccups in terms of finances this month. These financial pitfalls may pose a potential delay in your projects. You may feel powerless in finding answers to your situation but be patient, you will find the light.

甲午 Jia Wu Day

Overview

This year, positivity and wealth blessings will be coming your way. The year sees professional and financial success. Support and assistance will be available if you ask this year with the activation of the Nobleman Star. With this you will be surrounded by people willing to help you. Bear in mind that asking for help will do you good this year and does not make you weak. Stabilise your work life and start making grander plans for the year ahead and you'll slowly but surely get to execute them – your fortune lies within the industry you are based at, so persevere.

Wealth

There is good chance of your wealth sector and monetary gains proceeding without a hitch this year. Time to introspect and retrospect and see what brings you internal happiness this year. The pursuit of wealth and success may witness you being stressed and bogged down and this is the year to try and get your life back in traction and focus on yourself. Time to revaluate your spending habits and look into saving a little more this year – material pursuits are only temporary.

Relationships

There will be some struggles for singles this year in the romance department. The year's stars may not be aligned to those trying to find their better half but fret not – life is mostly about putting yourself in the right place at the right time for that cosmic encounter. Love sometimes comes at a time when we are not looking but rather just enjoying the company of others and more importantly being ourselves. Meet people and remember to have fun.

Health

This year will be quite emotionally taxing for you. Do not push yourself too hard with work commitments and falling into the trap of stress related illnesses. A more concerted effort needs to be made on health matters – exercise and strive to live a better, more well-adjusted lifestyle which will help better other areas of your life as well. Follow healthy nutritional and dietary practices – as you are what you eat.

Career

This year will see new projects on the horizon so be prepared to take things to a whole new level this year in terms of ideas and potential. Take opportunities to task when they present themselves. Your career front is likely to see smooth progression with most things turning in your favour. Opportunities to work on new exciting projects will also likely crop up as well as new roles in the office.

農曆正月

(February 4th - March 4th) 戊寅

The month will certainly see you sail through, particularly more if you have made good plans towards all your endeavours. You are likely up in your game which will see you meet your timelines, despite your swamped workload.

農曆二月

(March 5th - April 3rd) 己卯

This is looking to be a hectic month so the best thing you can do is keep your head down and stay focused on your work this month. There is good chance that the outcomes you seek will be met. Look into maintaining and keeping track of your priorities as the hectic schedule is likely to make your head spin.

農曆三月

(April 4th - May 4th) 庚辰

Remember that no man is an island and that we sometimes need to receive as much as we give. Try not to be hero and ask for the aid of your colleagues, as their help will certainly ensure that everything runs smoothly.

農曆四月

(May 5th - June 4th) 辛巳

This month you will also come into contact with well-meaning individuals who will prove to bring good tidings and support in certain rough patches where the waters will be slightly murkier. Know that your talent is finally showcased and your capabilities could be put to good use.

農曆五月

(June 5th - July 5th) 壬午

The month is expected to be less than stellar and unexciting. Stay strong and try not to feel disheartened. With the best of your effort, you will have a fair chance to win the appreciation of people around you, particularly yourself.

農曆六月

(July 6th - August 6th) 癸未

The month is ripe for you to do a little introspection and put in a little more hard work. Ignore the negativity at your workplace and reflect instead on what you have learnt and what you could do to improve your personal and professional life.

農曆七月

(August 7th - September 6th) 甲申

You are likely to see better personal luck this month. Work is likely to flow better with continued support from your Nobleman. Use the month's energy to put your heart and soul into your academics if you are a student.

農曆八月

(September 7th - October 7th) 乙酉

As there is a risk of robbery this month, make sure you keep your personal items as well as yourself safe. Seeming random mood swings can also be expected.

農曆九月

(October 8th - November 6th) 丙戌

Pay wise attention to your health and overall wellbeing. Look into boosting your immunity this month as all this running around is likely to impact your health. If you do come across the unfortunate luck of falling sick take this time to rest and recuperate.

農曆十月

(November 7th - December 6th) 丁亥

The month may see you be swamped with both social engagements and work activities. Look into maintaining and keeping track of your priorities as the hectic schedule is likely to make your head spin. It would be favourable for you to travel for work-related reasons this month.

農曆十一月

(December 7th 2020 - January 4th 2021) 戊子

This month, you may expect a form of career advancement at work. However, your colleagues might be jealous of your success. Keep a healthy distance between yourself and the petty people who are unable to be happy for you.

農曆十二月

(January 5th - February 2nd 2021) 己丑

Loneliness would be upon you this month and this may be caused by focusing too much on work and not enough on your relationships. Remember those who are close to you and give them more of your attention.

乙未 Yi Wei Day

Overview

You are headed for a slightly bumpy ride this year in terms of work and life. Try not to feel so defeated if your plans fail to materialise even after all your efforts to gain really wanted to achieve this week. Things may get rough but you will still reach your goal. Try not to rush into things or perhaps even rush to try and finish things. Slow and steady is the way to go. Give proper care and time to the work you are doing to avoid mistakes that will undermine your credibility.

 ## Wealth

This year, balance your finances outflow and inflow and check your approach towards spending on what is unnecessary and perhaps seek out financial planning advice. Keep some money aside for a rainy day, for any eventuality. In any event, you will have the love and support of your family and friends to help you out of any sticky situation that may arise. In an attempt to increase monetary gain, increase work productivity which will in turn guide you to better savings with higher returns.

 ## Relationships

Your love and social life for the year is likely looking to be a little uneventful and uninspiring. There be some issues brewing in where relationships are concerned. Practice a little patience if love is what you seeking this year your time will come in the specific months ahead. Use the quieter time to rediscover the simple joys of life and strengthen your bonds with those close to you. Spend time on yourself, and perhaps do a little introspecting to better understand your wants and desires.

 ## Health

If you thought medical check-ups are unnecessary, think again. As the saying goes, "Prevention works better than cure". Place caution on what you consume this year as there will be risks of you contracting a tummy upset or some minor gastrointestinal issue. Start by making healthier choices in terms of food and committing to an exercise regime that you can manage within your weekly schedule.

Career

The year will likely yield positive results in work agendas which may perhaps even exceed your expectations. If you are intending to embark on personal projects or perhaps are hoping for a career advancement with travel engagements this is a good year to set things in motion. You may find that you feel more motivated to complete your tasks and work and this might get you the attention of your superiors. Be diligent and practice the values that have helped you to achieve the success you have enjoyed so far and to safeguard your career.

農曆正月
(February 4th - March 4th) 戊寅
This month there will be a good in terms of wealth. Follow up on everything down to the last detail and be meticulous in terms of job details. This will not only ensure the quality of your work but also gives you credibility and respectability.

農曆二月
(March 5th - April 3rd) 己卯
This is a good month to pay closer attention to your finances and also look into opportunities to expand your current wealth. Consider exploring alternative avenues for investment by expanding your current investment portfolio.

農曆三月
(April 4th - May 4th) 庚辰
Your stress levels are likely to increase this month with a whirlwind of work likely coming your way. This will not be a problem if you prioritize the workload calmly and correctly. Remember to also pay attention to your overall wellbeing while chasing your goals.

農曆四月
(May 5th - June 4th) 辛巳
You may want to be mindful this month particularly in aspects of relationship. Monitor for any third party interference. This will certainly test the loyalty of your partner. Think carefully on what you want.

農曆五月
(June 5th - July 5th) 壬午
Tension is building among colleagues at workplace this month. Approach things with a calm and patient demeanour. Focus on fostering strong relationship with your colleagues this month as this will certainly aid your work productivity.

農曆六月
(July 6th - August 6th) 癸未
Try not to feel so defeated if your plans fail to materialise even after all your efforts to gain really wanted to achieve this month. Things may get rough but you will still reach your goal. Be wise and cautious as you cannot afford to be careless at work.

農曆七月
(August 7th - September 6th) 甲申
The month is likely to be great particularly where work is concerned. You will find that your energy and creative efforts will be at its optimum level, allowing you to do your best and produce great results.

農曆八月
(September 7th - October 7th) 乙酉
An auspicious travelling month for you ahead! Prioritise your physical safety while taking the necessary safety precautions to avoid undesirable situations. Watch your food intake as chances are you will have risk of stomach flu or food poisoning.

農曆九月
(October 8th - November 6th) 丙戌
This will be a fast paced month for you so take precautions. You are likely to feel that you are finally achieving something in your life. Take some time off from work to enjoy the many festivities coming your way.

農曆十月
(November 7th - December 6th) 丁亥
Autumn babies are graced with excellent fortune this month. Good tidings are on the horizon this month with regards to your wealth and professional life. The energy that flows through you allows you to perform your duties at work or at home with confidence.

農曆十一月
(December 7th 2020 - January 4th 2021) 戊子
This month with the aid of some patience, you may complete your work with ease. Be sensible and careful in your approach to the many issues coming before you and not try and make hasty decisions. Problematic Issues will be resolved and turn out even better than the initial outcome.

農曆十二月
(January 5th - February 2nd 2021) 己丑
Be careful while travelling this month. Although a good month to travel scrutinize surroundings before embarking on anything. Remember, be careful and watchful at all costs especially when you're in another country or state to obey the laws and traditions there.

丙申 Bing Shen Day

Overview

The doors to wealth opportunities may open this year. There will be some stumbling blocks will be in your way this year, but they are nothing to frown over. You may feel a little bored at work which would greatly affect your motivation to contribute much. Not the best idea to move jobs as of yet as the stars will not be in your favour for a big leap. Be patient and make the best of the situation at hand. Proactive in your endeavours and do what it takes to succeed - use the positive energies coming your way to your best advantage.

 ## Wealth

2020 will see a less than ideal fiscal movement. However, they need not be overly concerned as there will aid to buffer and keep that financial loss to a minimum. When there is an element of inadequate financial gain, it is always good practice, to cushion that loss by purchasing something will prove useful to you. Do not hesitate in getting the aid of others to improve your financial standing.

 ## Relationships

A good year to end your singlehood for couples who wish to unite and tie the knot. Be wise and brave in seeking what you want and do not let setbacks and personal self-esteem hold you back. Through your network of friends, you might be able to find your ideal partner.

 ## Health

Prioritize your health this year as the stress of work and family responsibilities would probably leave you little time to take care of your health. If you do come across the unfortunate luck of falling sick take this time to rest and recuperate. Therefore, make that daily effort of maintaining a healthy lifestyle with a balance diet and regular exercise.

 ## Career

Positive changes in both your career and wealth prospects can be expected this year. With these positive changes comes the chance to prove your worth and sidestep issues and be the possible envy of those not as privileged to be in your shoes. Wise to be reminded that everyone has differing opinions on matters and issues and it is best to be respectful of that, particularly in the workplace.

農曆正月

(February 4th - March 4th) 戊寅
There's an air of jealousy at work this month as there are people who feel like your superior favours you over them. Regardless of how these petty people perceive you, ultimately, they don't matter in the bigger picture and you shouldn't let yourself be affected by what they think or say. What matters is the work that you deliver.

農曆二月

(March 5th - April 3rd) 己卯
This month, let your ideas flourish by sharing it with others. Have confidence in what you come up with as it will be well-received and beneficial for your work in the future.

農曆三月

(April 4th - May 4th) 庚辰
Trouble is brewing at work as you find yourself in disagreements with your colleagues. These problems can be resolved diplomatically through compromise and empathy. They should be settled as soon as possible before it grows into something worse.

農曆四月

(May 5th - June 4th) 辛巳
You may expect a financial boon this month for the efforts you have invested in a side project. By working hard, you will see the fruits of your labour soon enough.

農曆五月

(June 5th - July 5th) 壬午
It will be a busy month for you which can contribute to an increase in your stress level. This in turn may manifest itself as poor physical health. The symptoms of stress and illness can be lessened or avoided altogether should you alleviate the root cause of the problem that is stress. Take some time to relax.

農曆六月

(July 6th - August 6th) 癸未
You may offend the people around you unknowingly with your words and actions if you're not careful with them. Be more sensitive to others and how they react to you.

農曆七月

(August 7th - September 6th) 甲申
An increase in Financial Luck is to be expected this month along with financial gains. This is particularly true if you were born in summer season.

農曆八月

(September 7th - October 7th) 乙酉
Through business travels, you would be able to find new opportunities. It can only be beneficial for you should you make yourself aware of these.

農曆九月

(October 8th - November 6th) 丙戌
You might be feeling unsatisfied and tired this month and not being content with how things are. Rather than waiting for this spell of ennui to disappear eventually, try to find out what made you feel this way. At the same time, don't do anything that would aggravate the matter.

農曆十月

(November 7th - December 6th) 丁亥
There will be a lot of distractions all around you that are mostly trivial in nature. You should remain focus on your goals and the things that matter. Keep a distance from everything else so your vision can remain clear.

農曆十一月

(December 7th 2020 - January 4th 2021) 戊子
This month, it will be rewarding for your career should you travel south. It will bring more opportunities that can be translated into more gains.

農曆十二月

(January 5th - February 2nd 2021) 己丑
Your colleagues might be able to share very useful information to you that you can utilise for your own benefit. It may not seem to be applicable now, but you might find it handy when you're undertaking a new project in the future.

丁酉 Ding You Day

Overview

This year will likely hectic, as you may have a lot to deal with at work and at home. With this increased level of personal commitment you could be faced with the task of having to make decisions regarding the importance of certain duties and prioritising some over others. Be bold enough to nurture your career and business, and make those financial plans a reality. They are likely to produce formidable outcomes. One good idea is aiming to put together a schedule of things that need to be prioritised. This should help you get through the year.

Wealth

There will be some stumbling blocks will be in your way this year in terms of career, but they are nothing to frown over. There will be some rather slow or career development but this proves that you need to dedicate yourself to strive harder and persevere through challenging times. Be wary and practical with your moves and never take any shortcuts in new beginnings. Success will certainly be within sight when you have both humility and capabilities. Remember to leverage on the support from your team members when help is needed.

Relationships

This year, single ladies should endeavour themselves to other interesting areas in life. Spend time with yourself and give yourself some self-love. Those in established relationships should spend quality time with your partner and family to strengthen your bond, keep the love alive, as well as make the relationship itself grow. Try new things together, go on a date and spend some time doing fun activities whether it's a trip to the beach or a fun day at the park.

Health

Your health should be your priority this year. Watch what you eat and be wary of consuming food from dodgy restaurants with questionable hygiene practices. It is crucial that you strike a balance between being successful in life as well as maintaining a healthy body. Strive to fit in regular exercise and have a balanced diet in your daily routine. Exercise for better mental health because it is just as important as your physical health.

Career

This years' luck cycle is in your career. Your talent is finally showcased and your capabilities could be put to good use. Your superiors will notice all the effort and hard work and this will help you to ascend the career ladder. Remember, while you can't always control your problems, you can control how you react to them. Remind yourself why you want to accomplish your goals or overcome your problems. Carry out your responsibilities without the need to show off and make sure that you follow the rules.

農曆正月

(February 4th - March 4th) 戊寅
There may be some positive growth in your wealth and career sector owing to the month's auspicious energy. As you've what it takes to lead your colleagues, they too will be happy with their progress at work.

農曆二月

(March 5th - April 3rd) 己卯
If you were born during summer, your health should be your priority this month as you could be facing some hits with some minor ailments. Refrain from participating in high intensity exercises and practice better eating habits.

農曆三月

(April 4th - May 4th) 庚辰
If you were born during winter, there is good chance of work and life proceeding without a hitch this month and you will get the much needed reprieve. You will need to be a little more patience at work. Recognition will come in due course.

農曆四月

(May 5th - June 4th) 辛巳
Work life will be filled with highs and lows this month and this will test your resilience and push you to overcome challenges. Remember that the lessons you'll learn on your way to the top will only make you stronger.

農曆五月

(June 5th - July 5th) 壬午
There may be some positive growth in your wealth and career sector owing to the month's auspicious energy that may even see some chances to earn a side income. Use this energy boost to good effect in all areas of your life.

農曆六月

(July 6th - August 6th) 癸未
Your fortune takes another big step towards prosperity. Be bold enough to nurture your career and make those financial plans a reality. They are likely to produce formidable outcomes. Allow yourself to a have a better-relaxed mind and body to embrace all the excitement that is coming your way this month.

農曆七月

(August 7th - September 6th) 甲申
Be careful with your choice of words this month, as personal discords happens when one says something before they think. Keep your ideas on a tight lock and be wary with who you share it with. There is potential that these ideas and inspiration may be used by someone else.

農曆八月

(September 7th - October 7th) 乙酉
Stock up on some health supplements particularly if you are pregnant. Keep an eye out on your eating habits and diet and ensure that your meals provide you with all the nutrients and minerals that your body needs. Take precautions on injuries particularly on your right limbs.

農曆九月

(October 8th - November 6th) 丙戌
Life is filled with highs and lows that will test your resilience and push you to overcome challenges. Strive to maintain a positive attitude and uphold your professionalism to combat any negative situation that may crop up.

農曆十月

(November 7th - December 6th) 丁亥
It would best for you to take a more conservative approach when it comes to investments and steer clear of risky investments. Options and opportunities are all around you. Be sure to analyse all angles of any potential investment.

農曆十一月

(December 7th 2020 - January 4th 2021) 戊子
It's essential to spend quality time with your partner and family to strengthen your bond, keep the love alive, as well as make the relationship itself grow. When times are rough and you think that no one believes in you, your family will always be there to cheer you on.

農曆十二月

(January 5th - February 2nd 2021) 己丑
Your health should be your priority this month as you could be facing some hits with some minor ailments in relation to your stomach. To be on the safe side, you might also want to stick to food that is easy on the stomach such as brown rice, bananas and eggs.

戊戌 Wu Xu Day

Overview
Be ready to take on challenges with the ferocity and tenacity. Keep a clear head, stay focused, and follow through. Your planning, patience, and perseverance will pay off. Great year ahead in terms of wealth and therefore a good time to increase monetary gain. Ensure that you have positive people around you for support and advice. People will look at you and there will be those who will judge you and in times like these you will need the support and drive of a positive influence. Remember to spare some time for your loved ones and make some memories and make good use of the good tidings of the week.

 Wealth

The pursuit of wealth and success may witness you being stressed and bogged down and this is the year to try and get your life back in traction and focus on yourself. In looking for new avenues to make money pay more attention to branding and forming strong partnerships and collaborations. Your social life is likely to get a positive boost and this is also where you are likely to meet people that would better your wealth prospects.

 Relationships

If you are a single woman, you can expect to find love in the office this month which will leave you with many chances to start a relationship. This year you may find joy in having and maintaining a relationship. That said you should never rely on the others to make you happy. Make sure you are happy with yourself and give them all a chance to prove themselves worthy without discrimination. We are all unique individuals and what we find attractive certainly differs from the next person. Love comes in unlikely forms.

 Health

Although a generally good year in terms of health, you may be a little more vulnerable to viruses and illnesses and caution must be made. Spare time to look into your health. Take time to exercise and improve your diet with better food choices. Be vigilant when driving or undertaking high risk activities to avoid any potential mishaps.

 Career

It may not be the best year for your career. Understanding your strengths and weaknesses are crucial particularly at work. Practice the values and behaviours that have gotten you the success previously to safeguard your career. You might find some minor hurdles or hiccups, but they won't set you back on your goals. Think expansion in terms of your road to financial success. Invest in something meaningful and with purpose. The results to your year's efforts will likely bring about positive results and your accomplishments will likely earn you great recognition.

農曆正月

(February 4th - March 4th) 戊寅
Watch out for infidelity particularly if you are female in a committed relationship. To counter a potential crisis, compromise and tolerate your loved ones, restricted manner and action will wheel your relationship back to the right track.

農曆二月

(March 5th - April 3rd) 己卯
Watch your communication with other this month. Your words might be a little misconstrued, so it is best to watch what you say. Take all negative words out of your mental dictionary and focus on the solutions with utmost conviction and patience.

農曆三月

(April 4th - May 4th) 庚辰
You may feel a little demotivated at work which would greatly affect your motivation to contribute. This could further contributed by the fact that there will be some minor hiccups and disagreements at work. Your future career advancement will be better benefitted by a display of humility.

農曆四月

(May 5th - June 4th) 辛巳
This month make time to expand your social circle with new people and acquaintance as your Peach Blossom luck is blooming. Engage with people as this will not only help expand your networking links but the people you meet will also prove helpful in the coming months.

農曆五月

(June 5th - July 5th) 壬午
If you are in a toxic relationship, it is time to get out. It might be the harder short-term decision to make, but you will be saving yourself a lot of misery in the long-term. The sooner you end it, the sooner you can start getting over it.

農曆六月

(July 6th - August 6th) 癸未
You may be given more challenges this month. Stay strong and try not to feel disheartened. Don't be afraid to rise up to the challenge as you will be able to learn new things in the process. Practice patience and perseverance and you shall rise above the crowd.

農曆七月

(August 7th - September 6th) 甲申
Positive changes in your wealth prospects can be expected this month. With these positive changes comes the chance to prove your worth. This will certainly work in your favour and help you finalise side-lined projects with success, thus allowing for better monetary flow.

農曆八月

(September 7th - October 7th) 乙酉
Your priority this month should be your health. There is great need for you to maintain your energy in case of the rising potential of developing minor ailments.

農曆九月

(October 8th - November 6th) 丙戌
This month, your partner might find themselves entangled with the law. Should you wish to help them out with it, be careful with how you involve yourself with their legal issues. Be vigilant when driving or undertaking high risk activities. Always better to be safe than sorry.

農曆十月

(November 7th - December 6th) 丁亥
Be cautious about what you eat and take time off work if you are feeling overwhelmed which may greatly contribute to your stomach issues. Exercise and watch your consumption of fatty and oily food.

農曆十一月

(December 7th 2020 - January 4th 2021) 戊子
This month, be yourself and stay grounded and disciplined. Guard against lending people money as there is a possibility that you will not be seeing the money again. Set yourself achievable goals and work hard to get to where you need to be.

農曆十二月

(January 5th - February 2nd 2021) 己丑
Keep an eye on your expenses and try to curb your spending this month. Although treating yourself to nice things is a good way to be kind to yourself, you certainly do not want to go broke as a result.

六十甲子 Forecast for 2020 based on Day of Birth

己亥 Ji Hai Day

Ji

Hai

Overview

A good year with positive results can be expected ahead, particularly if you were born in spring. Your luck is likely to see a small surge this month which will alleviate you from troubles that may be plaguing you. Seek a financial planner's advice, draw up a plan, and follow through. At work, volunteer for additional responsibilities and projects. There will be naysayers; so, surround yourself with positive people. Your time has come to shine at work and the year is looking bright for you to gain the recognition you have wanting in your work.

 ## Wealth

Look out for valuable tips and seek out good advice when discussing and making potential investments choices before committing to them. Business owners should consider looking into investing in innovative technologies to amplify their business and stock assets. There may be a spike in improvement to your financial management skills which in turn will see you save more. When dealing with risky monetary matter, it is best to seek outside counsel, particularly from financial experts on matters of investment before putting your money in any potential opportunities.

 ## Relationships

Things are looking up if you are a single man this year. A good year to end your singlehood for couples who wish to unite and tie the knot. Be wise and brave in seeking what you want and do not let setbacks and personal self-esteem hold you back. Aside from having good love luck this year, you will also experience considerable good luck in other relationship aspects of your life as well. It would be good start to spend time with your family and loved ones to foster stronger bonds.

 ## Health

Pay extra attention to your health as some minor threats are likely to emerge particularly problems stemming from your stomach and the digestive system. If you manage your health wisely, the likelihood for your projects being disrupted can be minimized. Boost your overall well-being by making better diet choices and exercising sufficiently.

Career

For all your efforts at work, you are likely to receive the well-earned recognition and acknowledgement. The people around you at your workplace will shower you with praises. Having said that, shining bright at work also means your superior would assign you with more responsibilities. Dealing with a higher set of expectation may cause your stress level to rise. It's important that you manage this aspect of your life in relation to other factors in a balance.

農曆正月

(February 4th - March 4th) 戊寅
Lady luck will be smiling down on you in terms of work and career. You will see flourishing profits from the different areas of investment and for those on a fixed income – this will probably be a good year to ask for that raise that you have been meaning to.

農曆二月

(March 5th - April 3rd) 己卯
Take your time on working on an executable plan. Your plans will align and you will be at the forefront of success. You will receive recognition from your superiors or other half for the contribution you have given.

農曆三月

(April 4th - May 4th) 庚辰
The month brings the tides of good fortunes and a smooth sailing journey in almost all endeavours. You may see yourself gaining help and connections from people that can help you attain your aspirations which will subsequently lead you to where you want to go and be.

農曆四月

(May 5th - June 4th) 辛巳
As you pursue your endeavours this month, be prepared to encounter some unforeseen circumstances. There may be some unexpected change to your finances. Think twice before you make an investment and spend your money carefully.

農曆五月

(June 5th - July 5th) 壬午
This is looking to be a hectic month so the best thing you can do is keep your head down and stay focused on your work this month. Frustrations at work will get the better of you. With work commitments and expectations piling on, you might feel the nagging stresses of these nipping at you from the sidelines.

農曆六月

(July 6th - August 6th) 癸未
The month might see some possibility of minor surgery. A more concerted effort needs to be made on health matters – exercise and strive to live a better, more well-adjusted lifestyle which will help better other areas of your life as well.

農曆七月

(August 7th - September 6th) 甲申
There will be plenty of reasons for celebration and good cheer as in most areas of your life this month. You will see definite fulfilment as well as advancements in career and wealth. One word of caution is to take time to consider any decisions made.

農曆八月

(September 7th - October 7th) 乙酉
There may be some unexpected change to your finances with the arrival of some monetary gain from work. This may even translate in your career where you are likely to see fast progression towards that corporate ladder.

農曆九月

(October 8th - November 6th) 丙戌
The month would see you running around akin to a giddy goat valiantly trying to meet the demands of your rising financials and work commitments while making bigger ends meet with income and spending.

農曆十月

(November 7th - December 6th) 丁亥
This month will be an enjoyable and smooth month for you both in your career and personal life. You are likely to find that events or situations will move in your favour and expectations. Keep your eye of the prize and hard work hard if you want it to produce the results you desire.

農曆十一月

(December 7th 2020 - January 4th 2021) 戊子
There might be a change in your progress at work. You might need to be patient in your efforts of righting the course of things. Change is good as it allows you the opportunity to see new things and try on new endeavours for personal growth.

農曆十二月

(January 5th - February 2nd 2021) 己丑
2020 will leave you a little more relaxed and blessings will come in the form of auspicious stars gracing the year. You may see movement and improvement in previously stagnant areas of your life which would then lead you to attain the goals and dreams.

庚子 Geng Zi Day

Overview

If you have been living life on the fast lane and are looking for hard and fast success to something you have been meaning to accomplish, you need to step on the brakes, just a little. This is a good year in terms of career and growth. There are many things to pick up in order to gain better career advancement and business growth. Your competitors can be an excellent source of inspiration, information and industry insight. Capitalise things to your greatest favour - where your talent is finally showcased and your capabilities could be put to good use.

 ## Wealth

In terms of your finances, it's looking good. Given recent market events, you may be wondering whether you should make changes to your investment portfolio. Remember that if you work hard enough and want something badly enough, you can breakthrough limitations of your environment. You will see stronger buying power in terms of investment and returns. Beware of where you decide to place your money as well as the source of incoming wealth.

 ## Relationships

Peach Blossom Luck is present this year and single men would benefit more from it than women. For those in a long on-going relationship, it's a good time to make it official. For those already in marriage, beware of outside temptations.

 ## Health

For those born in winter or spring, you don't have to worry about your health too much. For those born in summer or autumn, there's a chance for injuries on your head and limbs as well as a possibility for tumours and growth. Go for medical check-ups as soon as the first symptom appear.

 ## Career

It's possible for you to advance in your career if you put your effort in it. Not doing anything or putting your work on hold would obstruct you from taking on the opportunities that come your way. Make sure you get all your work done so you would be in a position where you are able to adapt to any situation.

農曆正月

(February 4th - March 4th) 戊寅
Your ideas and position might be challenged by others this month. When that happens, prepare to defend yourself and continue with what you have planned.

農曆二月

(March 5th - April 3rd) 己卯
Expect fever or sore throat this month especially for those born during the summer season.

農曆三月

(April 4th - May 4th) 庚辰
You may expect great rewards from financial opportunities this month. Bear in mind that this is achievable only through the help of others and teamwork.

農曆四月

(May 5th - June 4th) 辛巳
Positive career luck awaits those born during spring. You may be able to receive a promotion or at least a pay raise.

農曆五月

(June 5th - July 5th) 壬午
You may be facing a considerable amount of stress during work this month because of an increase in the amount of responsibilities. Make sure your time is managed properly to avoid overworking yourself.

農曆六月

(July 6th - August 6th) 癸未
You may be going through surgery this month. Try not to panic and discuss the options and procedure carefully with your physician so that it would take some of the fear away.

農曆七月

(August 7th - September 6th) 甲申
At work, you might be finding yourself going through some battles all on your own. Don't be lazy or procrastinate as it won't help you in your cause.

農曆八月

(September 7th - October 7th) 乙酉
When handling tools or activities that are potentially harmful, practice caution as there's a chance for you to injure yourself.

農曆九月

(October 8th - November 6th) 丙戌
Learn how to spread out your responsibilities to other capable and willing people. In doing so, there will be less stress on your part and more productivity overall.

農曆十月

(November 7th - December 6th) 丁亥
Now's a good time to go for a holiday and take some time off. Consider it as a reward for your efforts and hard work.

農曆十一月

(December 7th 2020 - January 4th 2021) 戊子
This month, your ideas would provide you with favourable financial outcomes. Don't hesitate to initiate and realise what you have in mind.

農曆十二月

(January 5th - February 2nd 2021) 己丑
Keep your budget tight this month and spend only when you need to. Save up your money as spontaneous spending would have negative effects on your wealth for a long time.

辛丑 Xin Chou Day

Overview

This is looking to be a year with so many aligned stars that are going to work very much in your favour. There will be plenty of reasons for celebration and good cheer as in most areas of your life. You may also be travelling abroad for work if you should choose to accept the task given. This will help you gain the recognition and respect of your colleagues and superiors. You will be seen to have reaped the rewards of all your hard work. Accept these accolades but do not place too much importance on them. If you are a student, you may expect yourself to do well in your examinations.

 ## Wealth

If you own a business, remember to reward the people that work for you accordingly so that everyone feels that they are part of a team. Design a strategy and unite your people to keep step with you. A harmonious management style produces excellent wealth growth. There is possibility in you incurring monetary losses potentially due to failed investments and overspending, therefore it is prudent that you spend your money wisely.

 ## Relationships

If you have ever had someone meddle in your life you know how frustrating it can be! This year you might see some 'well meaning' people Interfering in aspects of your relationship that can cause serious problems in your life and relationship. If you encounter this, simply tune them out, busy yourself, and find an excuse to get off of the conversation. Establish yourself as someone who prefers to stay out of other people's business and you'll have an easier time when you ask them to stay out of yours.

 ## Health

Overall, this year your health would be mediocre. Some ear related issue can be expected so go for medical treatment when the symptom arises. Avoid overindulging in late night snacks and food as this may prevent the appearance of digestive problems. Late night snacking may also increase your blood sugar levels and blood pressure. Make that daily effort of maintaining a healthy lifestyle with a balance diet and regular exercise.

 ## Career

A good year is ahead of you. If you are in the academic line, utilize this chance to work on projects and assignments. Use the year's energy to put your heart and soul into your academics if you are a student. At work, you may find that your productivity has taken a huge leap, so utilise it to your benefit. Avoid taking shortcuts; good things will be given to you in due time. You will find strength to finally breakthrough that obstacle that stands in the way to your success.

農曆正月

(February 4th - March 4th) 戊寅
An excellent month is in store for you. You have opportunities to find helpful people to assist you in achieving your goals! You will cross path with them this month, provided you put yourself out there.

農曆二月

(March 5th - April 3rd) 己卯
Those born during autumn and winter will experience good luck in various partnerships and collaborative efforts. Stay humble in order to attract sincere collaboration and foster honest working relationships.

農曆三月

(April 4th - May 4th) 庚辰
Stand out from the crowd and show the people around you what you are made of. This is a good month for strengthening your social bonds with the people in your organization. The month will be auspicious on many fronts so step out of your comfort zone and start taking those reigns.

農曆四月

(May 5th - June 4th) 辛巳
This month work to put to good use your excellent communication and social network skills. Channel them into the right areas to boost your business and wealth endeavours. There will be possible opportunities for career advancements.

農曆五月

(June 5th - July 5th) 壬午
Untrustworthy co-workers can put a serious damper on any workplace and this month you may have to deal with this. Watch out for anyone displaying signs of envy or even those who seem overly keen on your life.

農曆六月

(July 6th - August 6th) 癸未
You will feel inspired this month. You will realise that nothing good comes from lying down so get up on your feet and start thinking about things you wish to change in your life. One good idea is aiming to put together a schedule of things that need to be prioritised.

農曆七月

(August 7th - September 6th) 甲申
The positive energies of the month will certainly help with your career. There will be great capacity for learning and chasing after some career goals and advancements you have meaning to gain under your belt.

農曆八月

(September 7th - October 7th) 乙酉
It is best in your interest for you to comply with the law and resist the urge to take shortcuts this month. Taking the easy way out of things may be tempting but it is wise to remember it always comes with a price and you should think of the consequences before you act.

農曆九月

(October 8th - November 6th) 丙戌
Be kind to yourself this month. Carve out some time for yourself and do something that brings you joy. Become aware of your own achievements and give yourself recognition that you deserve and be happy with the successes you receive.

農曆十月

(November 7th - December 6th) 丁亥
This month, pause before speaking or acting, giving yourself time to think. If you are angry, count to ten first, or walk away. Be diplomatic and avoids being too harsh. Build lasting connections in 2020 and earn the respect of the people around you.

農曆十一月

(December 7th 2020 - January 4th 2021) 戊子
People will look at you and there will be those who will judge you. Remember, critics are those who cannot be where you are. Know that you cannot control everything and always simply strive to be the best you can be with what you have.

農曆十二月

(January 5th - February 2nd 2021) 己丑
Social life is likely looking to be a little uneventful. Practice a little patience if love is what you seeking – your time will come at some point. The month will present you with countless opportunities to expand your social circle.

六十甲子 Forecast for 2020 based on Day of Birth

壬寅 Ren Yin Day

Overview

Family matters may be your focus for this year, which would likely lead to stress and leave you feeling emotionally drained. It is vital at times to take a step back, unwind and relax to get yourself back on your feet. Once things are sorted out, you can make great progress in your life.

 ## Wealth

Be mindful of your financial spending this year as your wealth luck is not on your side. It is best to keep track of your budget and plan ahead to avoid over-spending. Those of you born in the summer may however be less affected by this.

 ## Relationships

This is an ideal year for you to settle down and start a family. However, before you take on new commitments, you have to be certain that you are ready for marriage. You should also consider the concerns and needs of others. There may be potential problems for married women.

 ## Health

Pay extra attention to the food you are putting into your mouth this year, as you are more susceptible to stomach-related illnesses, especially if you were born in the winter. It is advisable to adopt a healthier lifestyle and start exercising regularly.

 ## Career

Your efforts in your career will likely be rewarded this year. As long as you remain focused on your objectives and maintain a high standard of productivity and efficiency, you will be able to step up the corporate ladder soon enough.

農曆正月

(February 4th - March 4th) 戊寅

Your financial outlook is strong this month, so it is a good time to look for new opportunities to make more money. Alternatively, you may receive offers to improve your financial standing. Either way, take care not to get yourself burned out too soon.

農曆二月

(March 5th - April 3rd) 己卯

Your positive outlook in the previous month will likely continue. Therefore, it is recommended to make full use of any opportunities that come your way. Be sure to maintain a work-life balance so you also have time for self-improvements.

農曆三月

(April 4th - May 4th) 庚辰

There may be communication breakdown in both your professional and personal relationships this month. At work, you may be frustrated with unclear instructions from your superiors. It is advisable to clarify whenever you have doubts.

農曆四月

(May 5th - June 4th) 辛巳

Watch out for any legal problems that may arise this month. You should try to solve these problems immediately before they escalate and cause you worse problems in the future. If necessary, get professional advice from a lawyer.

農曆五月

(June 5th - July 5th) 壬午

If you are willing to be open to different opinions and ideas, you will find supportive people who can offer you great insights this month. You will also receive assistance if you ask for it, so don't be afraid to reach out for help.

農曆六月

(July 6th - August 6th) 癸未

Be wary of what and where you eat, as this month you are more susceptible to food poisoning. If you eat out, make sure to eat in sanitary places. If you cook your own meals, take note not to store raw meat with cooked meat to prevent transfer of pathogens.

農曆七月

(August 7th - September 6th) 甲申

There may be issues in your romantic relationship this month where your partner is likely to do something that would upset you. You should however keep cool and try to understand your partner better. It could have been merely misunderstandings.

農曆八月

(September 7th - October 7th) 乙酉

It is advisable to read through any legal documents thoroughly before signing this month. There may be terms and clauses that you would want to amend or remove. Therefore, check the details to avoid regrets later.

農曆九月

(October 8th - November 6th) 丙戌

This month may appear to be slower than usual for you. You should make use of this time to restore your energy and outline plans for the months ahead. There may also be opportunities to join a meditation retreat, which you should consider taking.

農曆十月

(November 7th - December 6th) 丁亥

This is not a good month to be spontaneous, so avoid giving in to your impulses. Think carefully before you say or do anything, as every action has consequences. You may also hear good news about an old friend this month, which could be beneficial for you.

農曆十一月

(December 7th 2020 - January 4th 2021) 戊子

You may be tempted to cut corners to make some quick cash this month, but it is unlikely to be worth it. The consequences may be quite serious if you decide to ignore the rules; legal entanglements are likely.

農曆十二月

(January 5th - February 2nd 2021) 己丑

Married men may be met with temptations in the work place this month, but you are advised to reject any such advances to avoid destroying your marriage. Singles, though, should make use of this month to get out there and meet new people.

六十甲子 Forecast for 2020 based on Day of Birth

癸卯 **Gui Mao Day**

Overview

Career advancement will be your focus of the year as you take on new responsibilities at work. Although these responsibilities bring new challenges, you would have the capabilities to handle them effectively. Work on your leadership skill and stay focused on your objectives. Perseverance is the key to make this year the best year ever for you.

Wealth

There may be many obstacles in your way of obtaining wealth this year. However, you should maintain optimism and remain focused on your goals. There will be people who deliberately forget about returning the money you lend them, but it is advisable that you let go of past transgressions and look forward to better future endeavours.

Relationships

This year, your relationship may suffer due to negligence. You and your partner may be overwhelmed with other areas of your lives that you rarely have time to spend together. It would be best to make time for each other and lend an ear to your partner when needed.

Health

Overall, you shouldn't be concerned about health this year. However, there are still possibilities for minor annoyances with your kidneys or recurring skin irritations. This may be caused by an allergy, so try to identify the problem early on in order to avoid it.

Career

If you've been considering a career change, this is the time for it. Be proactive in looking for new prospects and strategise properly. With a change in the work environment, you could have your passion and purpose reignited. Keep the momentum going after the change to ensure you continue to deliver quality work in your new job.

農曆正月

(February 4th - March 4th) 戊寅
There may be troubles at home, but you shouldn't be overly-concerned as the situation will improve in due course. You are advised to focus at work or your businesses instead of overthinking the issues at home. Solutions will eventually come to you.

農曆二月

(March 5th - April 3rd) 己卯
You are able to find helpful people by your side this month especially in the workplace, so if you need help, don't hesitate to go out and ask for assistance. Even if you feel like you can complete everything solo, getting different opinions from others may offer new insights and inspirations.

農曆三月

(April 4th - May 4th) 庚辰
Delays may be expected this month for your work projects, possibly due to circumstances beyond your control such as a new policy taking place or the higher-ups having second thoughts. Nonetheless, when delays happen, you are advised to maintain your momentum and remain focused.

農曆四月

(May 5th - June 4th) 辛巳
Miscommunication is likely to happen this month. Ensure you give clear instructions if you are in a leadership role. If you are the one receiving orders, make sure you clarify if you have doubts. Also watch your words this month as what you say may unknowingly offend or hurt others.

農曆五月

(June 5th - July 5th) 壬午
Financial gains can be expected this month for those who have worked hard for the past few months. If there are people who have helped you in obtaining this financial gain, remember to share your rewards with them.

農曆六月

(July 6th - August 6th) 癸未
This month is favourable for taking an aggressive stance in your wealth pursuit as it would bring you profitable results. To ensure you achieve your desired goals, be well-prepared and do your research before making any investments.

農曆七月

(August 7th - September 6th) 甲申
There is a chance for you to travel this month. If you are required to travel for work or business, practice caution on the road as there is an increased risk for accidents to happen. If you travelling abroad, it would be best to have a travel insurance plan in place.

農曆八月

(September 7th - October 7th) 乙酉
You may find yourself taking on more responsibilities at work and with it, heavier workload as well. If you feel like you cannot do everything yourself, consider delegating your tasks and getting help. If that is not possible, you should consider expanding your team for more manpower.

農曆九月

(October 8th - November 6th) 丙戌
This month you will get a creative boost which will help you in presenting new ideas and new ways of doing things. If you are in the creative industry, this is a good time to get inspired and brainstorm for new projects. Be sure to write down your ideas before you forget!

農曆十月

(November 7th - December 6th) 丁亥
Carelessness is likely this month, so you are advised to keep an eye on your money and personal belongings during this period of time. That aside, you may also want to watch out for unexpected spending due to medical-related reasons.

農曆十一月

(December 7th 2020 - January 4th 2021) 戊子
There may be malicious rumours and gossip involving you in the workplace this month. It is imperative that you do not let these rumours bring you down and affect your work performance. More importantly, you need to be patient and not to react on them. Sooner or later, this too shall pass.

農曆十二月

(January 5th - February 2nd 2021) 己丑
Your relationship may need your attention this month. If you are in a committed relationship, your partner may be facing problems and it would be best you try to help him or her out. If you are single, try to avoid becoming too attached to people with emotional baggage.

甲辰 Jia Chen Day

Overview

There may unexpected opportunities in your career this year. You have to be well-prepared in order to make the best out of these opportunities. Make plans and act on them. Improve yourself by learning new skills and experimenting with new ideas. Business owners should consider changing their ways of operation to maximise profits.

 Wealth

Consider investing in some assets this year as this would likely produce favourable outcome. You are also advised to manage a budget to ensure your finances are on track. Avoid impulsive spending; only invest in things that you are confident that will be profitable.

 Relationships

This year, men will have better Peach Blossom Luck when compared to women. Women may need to be prepared for problems cropping up in their relationship. It is advisable to take this time for some introspection; ask yourself if these arguments are truly necessary.

 Health

Your health outlook is strong this year, but you should still keep your guard up for minor ailments. Be wary of food or skin-related allergies. Mind what you eat and try to adopt a healthier lifestyle such as exercising regularly.

 Career

This is a good year for a career change, so if you have been considering changing job, you should make full use of this year. No matter where you choose to work at, market your ideas strategically and your ideas can go far and wide this year. It would be best for you to improve your communication and presentation skills.

農曆正月

(February 4th - March 4th) 戊寅

This month, doing the same thing as before will not bring you expected results especially in terms of generating wealth. You should consider finding new ways to make money as the old ways seem to be outdated by now.

農曆二月

(March 5th - April 3rd) 己卯

Consider the unthinkable this month – try to collaborate with your worst rivals; you may be pleasantly surprised with the results. You could also find new insights and even learn new skills from this collaboration.

農曆三月

(April 4th - May 4th) 庚辰

You may be prone to procrastinating this month, but remember that will not do you any good. You should keep track of your work and how much time spent on each task daily. This way, you will find it easier to remind yourself to be more productive.

農曆四月

(May 5th - June 4th) 辛巳

Try to employ more patience this month as there will be multiple issues albeit minor in need of your attention. Instead of panicking, you will do well to prioritise things and tackle these problems one at a time.

農曆五月

(June 5th - July 5th) 壬午

This month you may be taking on more workload, which could result in you having less time to spend with your loved ones. If that happens, you should communicate and discuss with your loved ones on how to manage your time together better.

農曆六月

(July 6th - August 6th) 癸未

If you have been seeing someone for a while now, this is a good time to make things official. Your romantic partner is likely to respond with joy, while your friends and family will be supportive of this relationship as well.

農曆七月

(August 7th - September 6th) 甲申

If you believe you have worked hard enough to earn a pay raise or a job promotion, don't be afraid to ask for it from your superior. Your superior is likely to offer encouragement and support. This would likely result in a financial gain this month.

農曆八月

(September 7th - October 7th) 乙酉

Most often than not, it does not matter what you know, but who you know matters. This is particularly true if you are looking for a career change this month. Wherever possible, try to pull some strings to get the job you want.

農曆九月

(October 8th - November 6th) 丙戌

This month is a good time for you to experiment or try new things. It is also conducive for new relationships to flourish, so singles should make use of this time to go out and discover new places as well as new people!

農曆十月

(November 7th - December 6th) 丁亥

There is a high chance that you will be travelling this month. If you are required to travel, take note not to eat from unsanitary places as there is also a heightened risk of stomach flu or diarrhoea. It would be best to have a travel insurance in place as well.

農曆十一月

(December 7th 2020 - January 4th 2021) 戊子

You may be inclined to spend more than usual this month, but you will likely regret afterwards. Curb the impulse to spend on unnecessary items; only purchase things that you need to use frequently. Avoid making major investments at this time too.

農曆十二月

(January 5th - February 2nd 2021) 己丑

It would be beneficial for you to keep an open mind this month. This is because your colleagues at work may have good ideas that can inspire you. In addition, you should not participate in any extreme sports this month as there is an increased risk of injury.

乙巳 Yi Si Day

Overview

With plenty of hurdles ahead, you may find this a challenging year. There may be obstacles on your path towards your goals, leaving you demotivated or discouraged. Nevertheless, you should not be too harsh on yourself. Take time to relax and celebrate small success. That way, you can maintain your optimism in life to deal with problems this year.

 ## Wealth

In terms of wealth, this year is not the best time as investments are unlikely to bring favourable results. It would be wise to avoid high-risk investments this year. You should also beware of any get-rich-quick schemes as this may result in financial losses. It is recommended that you spend on self-improvement activities.

 ## Relationships

This year is particularly favourable for single men in terms of romance, as you would have high chances of meeting like-minded people with mutual attraction. On the other hand, single women may encounter a few minor problems on your way of finding love. Be sure to check if the man you are dating is truly single and available.

 ## Health

If you are forty and above this year, you need to pay extra attention to your heart and blood pressures as there may be problems in these areas this year. It would best to schedule yourself for frequent medical check-ups to tackle the early illness signs. Those of you under the age of 40 will experience a rather moderate health condition.

 ## Career

There will be many distractions at work this year. But if you remain focused on your goals, you can get what you want in your career with hard work and perseverance. Be mindful of your emotions and not let them get in your way of achieving your goals. When it comes to asking for what you want, you also need to be confident and firm.

農曆正月

(February 4th - March 4th) 戊寅
This month your career luck is improving, so if your projects in previous months have not been doing well, this month you will find the right resources and opportunities to make your projects run well.

農曆二月

(March 5th - April 3rd) 己卯
You may be required to make some important decisions this month while remaining discreet about it before announcing your decisions. Do your research, get as much information as you can about the subject matter before you make your decisions.

農曆三月

(April 4th - May 4th) 庚辰
This month is an ideal time for you to reach out to your friends and rekindle your friendships if you have not seen them for some time. If you have the time to, a short getaway with friends will help you to recharge and rejuvenate.

農曆四月

(May 5th - June 4th) 辛巳
When it comes to your investments, you are advised to be patient this month, as hasty decisions are likely to bring undesirable outcomes. Therefore, it is important that you take the time to carefully analyse any information you receive to prevent losing money.

農曆五月

(June 5th - July 5th) 壬午
Staying optimistic is important this month with whatever that's forthcoming. Many opportunities will present this month for you to challenge yourself and improve yourself in order to resolve issues and make progress with whatever you are undertaking.

農曆六月

(July 6th - August 6th) 癸未
This month you will be able to receive help from a Noble Person who will likely lead you towards new opportunities in your career or personal life. He or she can help you to open up new avenues that you have been wanting to explore.

農曆七月

(August 7th - September 6th) 甲申
There will be reasons to celebrate with people close to you this month, and you are encouraged to participate in these celebrations where you will be able to share the joy and improve relationships with people around you.

農曆八月

(September 7th - October 7th) 乙酉
The amount of work you have to complete this month may increase significantly and could cause you some stress. The best way to approach this would be to list down your priorities and then the most efficient ways to complete them.

農曆九月

(October 8th - November 6th) 丙戌
Your creativity receives a significant boost this month, so you are able to come up with original and innovative ideas and solutions seemingly without effort. Use this enhanced creativity to carry out your plans efficiently.

農曆十月

(November 7th - December 6th) 丁亥
This month you can expect good news at work as your superior is likely to acknowledge and appreciate your efforts and contributions. As such, you are likely to gain some financial rewards and respect that you deserve at work.

農曆十一月

(December 7th 2020 - January 4th 2021) 戊子
If you are thinking about investing in anything that promises fast return, this is not the ideal month to do so. The reason being there is a tendency of you over-looking details and making an ill-advised investment that can result in loss of wealth.

農曆十二月

(January 5th - February 2nd 2021) 己丑
This month is the ideal time for you to resolve some of your personal issues relating to work and finances. If you feel it is necessary, don't be shy to seek the guidance and help from more experienced individuals including your family members.

丙午 **Bing Wu Day**

Overview

This year is a fresh start for you. Let go of past mistakes and focus on doing better this year. Business owners will find this year a favourable time to go for partnerships or joint ventures. Career-wise, you will find plenty of opportunities in store for you. If you are in a committed relationship, this year you should try to be more understanding towards your partner as there is a high risk of miscommunications.

 ## Wealth

You should look towards partnerships and collaborations as these will bring favourable wealth opportunities for you this year. Teamwork is also important for achieving goals with desirable results. Even if the reward is divided between all the parties involved, it would be more than enough for you with the added benefit of a lighter burden. Make sure you are as socially affable as possible.

 ## Relationships

Single ladies can expect to find someone like-minded in the workplace this year. However, it is most likely to be short-lived. On the other hand, single men can expect to find love among friends. Married men though have to beware of getting too close with friends of opposite gender, causing unnecessary suspicion and jealousy.

 ## Health

Your health outlook is strong this year, but there may be minor issues with the eyes and heart if you don't take care of your diet and lifestyle. There is also risk of gaining more weight due to over-eating and a lack of exercise. Try adopting healthy habits such as eating right and routine exercises.

 ## Career

On the career front, you may not have the best year, but there are opportunities to be seized if you are persistent and patient enough. Getting to where you want may be a bumpy ride this year, but you will most likely learn valuable lessons and even skills throughout this process. Whatever opportunities that comes your way, make the best out of it.

六十甲子 Forecast for 2020 based on Day of Birth

農曆正月

(February 4th - March 4th) 戊寅

This month, women in relationships may find a third party threatening to sabotage your relationship. Therefore, you should be careful if your partner starts to act suspiciously. Open communication is key to understanding each other's needs in a relationship.

農曆二月

(March 5th - April 3rd) 己卯

Miscommunication is likely to happen this month. Therefore, you should watch your words when talking to people in your life, especially to your superior. Be mindful that you do not offend people unknowingly. Otherwise that could cause you unnecessary trouble.

農曆三月

(April 4th - May 4th) 庚辰

You may feel easily agitated this month at work, resulting in conflicts with your colleagues. However, it is advisable to be patient and remain professional. Be mindful of your emotions and keep your temper in check, so you don't create more enemies than you should at work.

農曆四月

(May 5th - June 4th) 辛巳

Be prepared for increased invites to social activities this month. While some of these social activities can be reenergising, some may leave you feel emotionally drained. Take care not to let others affect you negatively, as this could take a toll on your work performance.

農曆五月

(June 5th - July 5th) 壬午

Men may find their females close to them fighting with each other this month, causing a lot of troubles for them. It is advisable to stay out of it and let these problems solve themselves. If unavoidable, be as neutral as you can and try not to take sides.

農曆六月

(July 6th - August 6th) 癸未

Although this month may prove to be a challenging one especially at work, you have the willpower and capabilities to overcome them. Persevere with determination and grit, and you will overcome these challenges eventually.

農曆七月

(August 7th - September 6th) 甲申

There are opportunities to generate wealth this month, but you have to be quick to seize them when they arise, as competition is fierce. Remain focus on your goals and you will likely be the first to recognise an opportunity coming your way.

農曆八月

(September 7th - October 7th) 乙酉

Be careful of health issues related to the liver this month. If you consume alcohol regularly, you should pay extra attention to anything amiss. As prevention is better than cure, you should practise moderation in alcohol consumption and exercise more self-discipline.

農曆九月

(October 8th - November 6th) 丙戌

There is heightened risk of your partner being entangled with legal issues this month. You may try to find them better lawyers or help with legal fees, but it is advisable to not get yourself involved with their legal issues.

農曆十月

(November 7th - December 6th) 丁亥

Those of you who are travelling this month should beware of stomach-related health issues. There is an increased risk of food poisoning, so you should take care where you get your food from. It may be best to cook your meals, so you can ensure the food are prepared hygienically.

農曆十一月

(December 7th 2020 - January 4th 2021) 戊子

There is likelihood that your friends or relatives would approach you this month with the intention to borrow money. You should gauge your own capabilities before lending any money to them. If they are asking for anything beyond your capabilities, you must learn to say no.

農曆十二月

(January 5th - February 2nd 2021) 己丑

There is the tendency to over-spend this month, so you should watch your expenses to avoid going over your budget. Make use of mobile apps to keep track of your daily expenses, so you don't spend beyond reasonable limits.

丁未 **Ding Wei Day**

Overview

Expect much progress and rewards from all your hard work this year. There will also be chances to travel for your career. Take full advantage of this by expanding your circle of networks to open doors for future opportunities. However, remember not to let your ego get the best of you. This year will also see students attaining academic success provided they put in the effort.

 ## Wealth

There is tendency to overspend if you are not careful with your budget. Therefore, it is advisable to practise moderation this year. Spending money may bring temporary satisfaction, but its repercussion may bring long-term effects on your financial planning. It is also not a good year for making high-risk investments, so refrain from these.

 ## Relationships

This year your relationship may not be smooth sailing as problems are expected to arise. Though women will have better relationship luck than men. Even though others are inclined to help solve your problems, they will only worsen the matter. Married couples should not let rumours sabotage their relationships.

 ## Health

Overall, your health condition is positive this year. Although there may be minor issues with hearing and vision, you can easily get them sorted out in no time. Those in their mid-thirties or older might want to keep their blood pressure in check. It is advisable to exercise regularly and maintain a healthy lifestyle.

 ## Career

Those of you in the education field will find career progression likely this year. For others, strategic communication and positive relationships with people at work will ensure you get the job promotion you want. Although there is tendency to unknowingly offend others, you will do well by maintaining professionalism at all times in the workplace.

農曆正月

(February 4th - March 4th) 戊寅
This month holds strong financial prospects for you, so you should consider looking for new ways to generate wealth. However, if something is too good to be true, you should always do some background checks before investing.

農曆二月

(March 5th - April 3rd) 己卯
You should beware of health issues related to the respiratory system this month. Make sure you get enough rest and stay away from polluted environment as much as possible. Those with asthma should take extra care this month.

農曆三月

(April 4th - May 4th) 庚辰
If you have been eyeing for a job promotion or pay raise, this month sees likelihood of you getting what you want at work. Make sure your contributions are recognised by people who matter, and be prepared to present your work when asked to.

農曆四月

(May 5th - June 4th) 辛巳
There may be an increase in workload this month, so you need to be mindful not to let this overwhelm you or burn you out. Tackle the job one at a time and make sure you take breaks for yourself every now and then.

農曆五月

(June 5th - July 5th) 壬午
With a boost in creativity this month, you will be able to come up with new ideas easily. Put this creativity to good use by thinking of new ways to generate outcome or more efficient method of completing tasks at work.

農曆六月

(July 6th - August 6th) 癸未
Your colleagues will be able to help if you find yourself burdened by an increased workload this month. It is also advisable to communicate with your superior if you find yourself stressed out by the overwhelming workload. More efficient tasks delegation may be required.

農曆七月

(August 7th - September 6th) 甲申
Protect your work and ideas carefully this month, as there is the heightened risk of others looking to take credit for your work and steal your ideas. It is best not to speak or act prematurely as this could bring unnecessary attention and disturbances.

農曆八月

(September 7th - October 7th) 乙酉
Pregnant women should take extra care this month as there is a risk of health problems for them. Keep yourself safe and make sure you don't overwork yourself. For others, they should watch out for health issues related to the limbs.

農曆九月

(October 8th - November 6th) 丙戌
This month you may be inspired to break out of certain habits. Gather enough strength and determination and make that change happen. By doing so, you can change your life and transform yourself. This transformation is likely to bring positive results.

農曆十月

(November 7th - December 6th) 丁亥
There may be opportunities come knocking at your doorstep this month, but it is advisable to assess the risks involved before acting on these chances. Some risks are not worth it as you may have to deal with issues you didn't account for.

農曆十一月

(December 7th 2020 - January 4th 2021) 戊子
Try to maintain a work-life balance if you find yourself having less time to spend with your significant other due to your career. Make sure you don't ignore your loved ones. Try to manage your time efficiently so you can balance both your personal and professional life.

農曆十二月

(January 5th - February 2nd 2021) 己丑
This month there is a heightened chance of failing sick due to the intake of unhygienic food. Therefore, you are advised to pay extra attention to the food you eat and how the food is handled this month. Avoid eating at unsanitary places.

戊申 Wu Shen Day

Overview
Your energy level may be slightly lower this year compared with the last one, possibly due to added responsibilities in both personal and professional life. You may find yourself busy and tired most of the time as both work and family require your attention. Remember, it is important that you take care of yourself too, before you can take care of others.

 Wealth

This year your wealth luck does not look favourable, so you should be mindful of what you spend on. It is best to keep track of your spending using a mobile app. It would be wise to wait till there is a sales promotion before purchasing things to keep your expenses lower.

 Relationships

This is the ideal year for those of you who are ready to tie the knot. Friends and family will be supportive of your decision to start a family of your own. Those of you who are single can make use of this time to go out and meet new people; you may find someone you are attracted to.

 Health

Overall, your health condition has nothing to be worried about this year. Although you have to pay more attention to what you eat, as there is a chance of getting minor annoyance related to the digestive system. It also would not harm to take up a healthier lifestyle.

 Career

Career will be one of your main focus for the year as chances for you to be recognised in your career are aplenty, and together with it, you will find yourself taking on more responsibilities and workload. It would be wise to learn to delegate so you don't burn yourself out too soon.

農曆正月

(February 4th - March 4th) 戊寅
Financially, this month is a great time for you. If you are looking for a grant for your research or a course you intend to study, you will likely receive good news this month. At work, your abilities will be recognised and you may get a pay raise or bonus as a result.

農曆二月

(March 5th - April 3rd) 己卯
Although it's just the beginning of the year, you may feel like you need a break at this time. It would actually be beneficial for you to take a short break if possible, from work and family this month. If not possible, you should set some me-time every day to rejuvenate yourself.

農曆三月

(April 4th - May 4th) 庚辰
Those of you who are single should consider going to as many social events as you can this month. This is because the likelihood of you meeting someone you are attracted to, is at an all-time high. What's more, you will appear more charming and appealing than usual this month too.

農曆四月

(May 5th - June 4th) 辛巳
There may be offers to collaborate at work or business partnerships opportunities this month. No matter what you decide, it is always wise to assess the pros and cons of such collaborations and partnerships before agreeing to them.

農曆五月

(June 5th - July 5th) 壬午
This month you are advised against getting involved in any disputes. Refrain from playing "hero" and trying to mediate and resolve conflict during this time, as the chances of your reputation being tarnished due to reckless action will be high.

農曆六月

(July 6th - August 6th) 癸未
This month there may be an unexpected increase in your workload. As such, you should carefully plan how you would approach your work and how you can change it so that you can become more efficient at your job.

農曆七月

(August 7th - September 6th) 甲申
You may need to invest more effort this month than you usually do in order to achieve your goals. However, you are advised to treat this as a learning opportunity to challenge yourself and make self-improvements.

農曆八月

(September 7th - October 7th) 乙酉
If you plan your time and priorities well, you are likely to accomplish a lot during this month with the opportunities present. This is also a good time for you to begin new projects at work or personal pursuits that you are interested in.

農曆九月

(October 8th - November 6th) 丙戌
It would be good to make use of this month to engage in some self-reflection and even some self-improvements. If you have been meaning to end any behaviours or habits, this month is an ideal time to start doing something about it.

農曆十月

(November 7th - December 6th) 丁亥
Be mindful of your communication with your family this month, as there is the risk of miscommunications leading to conflicts with your family members. Be sure to be open to discussions and do not jump to conclusions before you have listened to all sides of a story.

農曆十一月

(December 7th 2020 - January 4th 2021) 戊子
Your wealth luck tends to fluctuate this month; therefore, it is possible that you incur some financial gains and losses during this time. However, you should not worry too much about it as the net of both will not be anything major.

農曆十二月

(January 5th - February 2nd 2021) 己丑
This month, your Peach Blossom luck is going strong, therefore you are encouraged to attend to as many social events as your energy level permits. If you are single, you are likely to meet someone that makes your heart beat faster, or someone that shares similar interests with you.

己酉 **Ji You Day**

Overview

Focus on improving your managing skills this year as this will ensure your success. For any endeavour you wish to partake, you should outline a plan of action in detail. Carefully consider all your options and make sure you take everything into account. In addition, be prepared to work with other people as there may be opportunities for a partnership this year.

 ## Wealth

If you want to make more money this year, you have to put in more effort than you did in previous years. Although you won't see immediate result from your hard work, you should be rest assured that your effort will set you up for future gains. Make a clear plan prior for the long run.

 ## Relationships

There are high chances for single men to meet a potential romantic partner this year. That said, you should also take care not to let a third party sabotage your relationship with the person you like. On the other hand, single women may be able to find love in spring.

 ## Health

Your health outlook will be average this year especially for those born in the autumn or winter. Be wary of health issues related to the stomach such as constipation and haemorrhoids. Do not take any symptoms lightly; you should immediately go for a medical check-up when symptoms appear.

 ## Career

There are opportunities that you can take full advantage of, provided you have what it takes to tackle the workload and manage your time efficiently. Even though you may feel burned out in the beginning, you need to stay determined as your hard work will be rewarded in the form of a pay raise and a job promotion in due course.

農曆正月

(February 4th - March 4th) 戊寅
If you have good ideas, don't be afraid to tell them to your bosses, as this month your superiors will be more open to your ideas and opinions. They will most likely be supportive as well. In personal life, you may also meet new friends who could offer you great inspirations.

農曆二月

(March 5th - April 3rd) 己卯
This month your efforts at work will likely be recognised by people who matter. This could mean a pay raise or a promotion is possible in the near future. If you have been working hard, this is the time to ramp up your efforts to be recognised.

農曆三月

(April 4th - May 4th) 庚辰
Collaboration will bring you forward this month, so you should make an effort to include others in your endeavours. Others may have great ideas that you can help them to develop and in the same time capitalise on.

農曆四月

(May 5th - June 4th) 辛巳
Watch what you put into your mouth and where you eat this month, as there is a heightened health risk of falling sick due to stomach-related illnesses. If you are travelling, it would be best to dine at places with better hygienic standard.

農曆五月

(June 5th - July 5th) 壬午
Elderly female member of the house may suffer from health issues, so you should pay extra attention to their health conditions this month. You should also be prepared to pay a sum for the medical bills that would ensue.

農曆六月

(July 6th - August 6th) 癸未
This month you will benefit from being more careful with what you say, as there is an increased possibility of you hurting or offending others around you unknowingly. Be mindful who you trust your secrets with, as some people may approach you with ulterior motives.

農曆七月

(August 7th - September 6th) 甲申
You will likely profit from collaborative endeavours this month, so you should continue engaging in teamwork and partnerships during this time. Business owners may find opportunities for partnerships during this time.

農曆八月

(September 7th - October 7th) 乙酉
Increased workload may leave you feeling burned out this month. If that is the case, you are advised to take some time off to rejuvenate and restore your energy. You could consider going for a short weekend getaway.

農曆九月

(October 8th - November 6th) 丙戌
A job promotion can be expected this month, provided you have worked hard enough to earn it. You should be bold enough to go and ask for it. Even if you fail to obtain what you want, your initiative will leave a positive impression.

農曆十月

(November 7th - December 6th) 丁亥
Avoid making major decisions that involve money this month, as your judgement may be clouded at this time. It is best to wait for another time that is more conducive. Do not let anyone rush you into making major investments during this time.

農曆十一月

(December 7th 2020 - January 4th 2021) 戊子
You are recommended to expand your social network this month as you will likely meet people who can offer you new ideas and useful insights. It's a good time to go out and socialise if you have been staying in most of the time.

農曆十二月

(January 5th - February 2nd 2021) 己丑
Financial opportunities may come to you in the form of a new acquaintance bearing unexpected news. Study and analyse the information; if it is potentially profitable, you are advised to take action as soon as possible to take full advantage.

六十甲子 Forecast for 2020 based on Day of Birth

庚戌 Geng Xu Day

Overview

This is an important year for you to improve in terms of career and achieving your goals. You may encounter unexpected problems such as rumours or gossip along the way, so you have to be mentally prepared for such challenges and stay focused on your goals instead of getting tangled in these petty problems. Find people you can trust to help you on your path to success.

 ## Wealth

Collaborative endeavours would likely bring fruitful outcome for you this year. Make the most out of these collaborations by solidifying your relationships and expanding your social network. In an unfavourable situation, you should take the time to think of new ways to turn the situation into a favaourable one and make substantial progress.

 ## Relationships

There may be competition for those in committed relationships this year. Instead of being paranoid whenever your partner does not reply your messages, you should focus on becoming a better you so your partner would find no one else better than you for them. If you are the one facing dilemmas with temptations, remember not to act lightly as this could affect your reputation in the long run.

 ## Health

In general, your health would be good this year, but you may want to keep your blood pressure and diet in check. Take care of your mental well-being as well this year; pent-up tension could manifest itself as a sickness. You should also pay attention to skin allergies and eye-related problems.

Career

Teamwork is imperative for advancing in your career this year. You are advised to learn to be a team player if you are not one. Uphold professionalism at work at all times and avoid letting your emotions affect your work performance. Stay focused on your goals and you will get what you want in due time.

農曆正月

(February 4th - March 4th) 戊寅
Be on the lookout this month as there will be opportunities coming your way in terms of business and career. You may receive news that you can act upon to reap benefits, or you may be offered an opportunity for business partnerships.

農曆二月

(March 5th - April 3rd) 己卯
You may find your creativity particularly enhanced this month, so it is recommended to make use of it to develop new ideas or new ways to solve problems at work. You should also share your ideas with others, so that others can add their input and improve your ideas.

農曆三月

(April 4th - May 4th) 庚辰
Perseverance is the key to getting what you want this month, especially if what you are looking for is a job promotion. There may be minor hurdles but you will eventually overcome them with determination. Your hard work will be rewarded in due course.

農曆四月

(May 5th - June 4th) 辛巳
You may encounter troubles related to romantic relationships this month. However, keep a level head and don't let this affect other aspects of your life especially your career. The key to solving these relationship issues is to be open for communication with your partner.

農曆五月

(June 5th - July 5th) 壬午
Be careful who you loan your money to this month. There may be people who approach you with ulterior motives; some may borrow money from you with no intention of returning the favour. If you insist on lending money this month, be prepared for it may never be repaid in full.

農曆六月

(July 6th - August 6th) 癸未
A friend may surprise you with information about your romantic relationship this month. Regardless how you feel receiving this news, you should always check the authenticity of the information and if your friend has any ulterior motive. Avoid jumping to conclusions.

農曆七月

(August 7th - September 6th) 甲申
You may easily feel emotionally drained this month, so steer clear of negative people as much as possible during this period of time. It is inadvisable to make any major decisions now because they will most likely be affected by your mood swings.

農曆八月

(September 7th - October 7th) 乙酉
Be careful with what you eat this month as there is an increased risk of food poisoning. Always keep your kitchen counter clean and properly sanitised. Do not store raw meat with cooked meat, as pathogens may transferr from the raw meat to the cooked meat, putting you in risk of infection.

農曆九月

(October 8th - November 6th) 丙戌
It is a good month to try out new activities as you will generally feel more energised at this time. It would be beneficial to take up new hobbies or kick-start an exercise regime. Start cycling or hiking; this could keep you in good shape if you persist.

農曆十月

(November 7th - December 6th) 丁亥
There is the possibility of things going wrong this month for you especially at work. You may want to check and ensure every step is done properly. Just because things have worked fine for the past few months, it doesn't mean things won't go wrong this time around.

農曆十一月

(December 7th 2020 - January 4th 2021) 戊子
This is the month to focus on teamwork and collaboration. The more manpower involved, the faster a project can be completed. Make sure you delegate tasks appropriately with your team members, and do not forget to acknowledge the team's efforts when the project is completed.

農曆十二月

(January 5th - February 2nd 2021) 己丑
Your loved ones may be frustrated that you spend too little time with them. Therefore, you should take care to manage your time better, so that you don't neglect your loved ones nor your career. Make time for your loved ones and they will appreciate your effort.

辛亥 Xin Hai Day

Overview

If you could learn to embrace changes, this year has the potential to become one of your best years to go through. There may be changes in many areas of your life during this time, but these changes also open up doors to new opportunities. Learn to seize these opportunities and make these changes work in your favour, and you will find yourself becoming a better person at the end of the year.

 ## Wealth

Your wealth luck this year depends on how much effort you are willing to put in to get the money you want. If you want easy money, this is not the time for it. However, if you are willing to work hard and also work smart, this year will see you earning a lot.

 ## Relationships

This year your Peach Blossom luck is strong, therefore it is a good time to be proactive in relationship matters; your efforts will likely bring favourable outcome. Those in a stable relationship may consider getting married; those single but with someone on mind may consider confessing.

 ## Health

You may find yourself weaker than usual this year, especially during the second half of the year. As your immune system tends to be weaker, you may be susceptible to ailments such as flu and cough. It would be best to do regular exercise and adopt a healthier diet.

 ## Career

There's a strong possibility of change to happen to you in terms of work this year. Besides getting well-prepared for any changes with back up plans ready at hand, you should also keep an open mind to find opportunities to be seized in these changes. If a certain movement in the workplace creates a vacancy that fits your capabilities, you should take the initiative to showcase your talents.

農曆正月

(February 4th - March 4th) 戊寅
You may be given new responsibilities in your workplace, making you busier than usual this month. In spite of the amount of work, you will be able to handle the stress well while maintaining the quality of your work, earning you well-deserved recognition by superiors.

農曆二月

(March 5th - April 3rd) 己卯
You may want to take advantage of your excellent luck in your social aspect this month by expanding your social circles and making new friends. You are likely to meet like-minded people and they will be beneficial to you in both professional and personal life.

農曆三月

(April 4th - May 4th) 庚辰
This month will provide a favourable environment for you to be productive and accomplish more. Therefore, it's best for you to go all out this month and get as many things done as you can. Start the month by properly priotising things you need to get done and you may charge forward with full speed.

農曆四月

(May 5th - June 4th) 辛巳
You may have to pay more attention to your physical wellbeing this month as your health luck is moderate. It is advisable that you maintain a healthy diet and exercise regimen to ensure that your good health is not compromised during this period of time.

農曆五月

(June 5th - July 5th) 壬午
Your Wealth Luck is doing quite well this month, so there will be plenty of opportunities for you to gain and accumulate wealth. Be attentive to information you receive, for there may be where you will find the ideas to earn more profits.

農曆六月

(July 6th - August 6th) 癸未
Be prepared for a rather dramatic month as your luck may be fluctuating this month, with a mix of happy and average situations. You will find opportunities to gain wealth or reputation, but there will also be challenges where you may lose what you gain this month.

農曆七月

(August 7th - September 6th) 甲申
You may need to pay attention to how you are communicating to your colleagues and subordinates this month, as there is the possibility of delays at work due to miscommunication. Get your message communicated clearly to ensure there is no room for confusion.

農曆八月

(September 7th - October 7th) 乙酉
There is an increased risk of you sustaining physical injuries this month. Therefore, you should refrain from all extreme sports and participating any dangerous activities this month if possible. If you have to, take extra precaution to take care of your personal safety.

農曆九月

(October 8th - November 6th) 丙戌
If you are single, this month is the ideal time to go out and meet new people, for you are more likely to find someone who is attractive for you. At the very least, you will find yourself enjoying friendly and pleasant conversations with people if you attend social gathering events this month.

農曆十月

(November 7th - December 6th) 丁亥
This month your colleagues will be of great help to you, so it is important to foster positive relationship with your co-workers. If you are in a leadership role, be sure to delegate your work well, so entire team can benefit from the best of outcomes.

農曆十一月

(December 7th 2020 - January 4th 2021) 戊子
There will be various opportunities for you to gain recognition this month. The opportunity may come in the form of a personal pursuit that proves to be handy at your work. When opportunities come knocking at your doorstep, remember to give your best shot and do not hold back.

農曆十二月

(January 5th - February 2nd 2021) 己丑
There may be issues you have to deal with at work or at home this month. Although individual issue is likely easy to handle, you will have to face a busy month with one issue coming after another. Steel yourself and be prepared to tackle problems one by one.

六十甲子 Forecast for 2020 based on Day of Birth

壬子 **Ren Zi Day**

Overview

Great changes are in store for your life this year. Therefore, you should get yourself prepared when the time comes. It would be wise to make use of this year to improve yourself and get out of your comfort zone. Take the initiative to ride the wave of change, as you will likely find favourable outcome. Be brave in adopting new methods for making better progress.

 ### Wealth

Your efforts may not immediately bring results in terms of wealth, but you are advised to stay determined. Consider taking this opportunity to plan ahead for the future. By getting well-prepared with back up plans, you will be ready for trials and tribulation that may come your way.

 ### Relationships

It would be quite challenging to manage your relationships this year. Men will have to invest more time in your relationship to avoid neglecting your partner. Women, on the other hand, may have chances to find love at the workplace. However, what you find is unlikely to last, so it is advisable to simply focus on your career instead.

 ### Health

Take extra care for your health this year as stomach flu and digestive problems could be expected, especially for those born in the autumn or winter. It would be best to exercise caution in food consumption and also adopt a healthier diet.

 ### Career

You can expect to have a smooth-sailing career path this year, though you still have to be careful of being at odds with your boss at times due to conflicting personalities. You should consider communicating in writing, as there are less chances for things to be misinterpreted.

農曆正月

(February 4th - March 4th) 戊寅
Office politics may be troubling you this month. Watch out for anyone trying to backstab you at work. They may try to sabotage your projects by taking credits for your contributions. You will do well to keep a positive relationship with your superior, so that your superior has more trust in you.

農曆二月

(March 5th - April 3rd) 己卯
Keep your temper in check this month as you may feel tempted to burst out in anger more easily than usual. It is advisable to stay calm and keep your cool, as if you let your emotions take control, especially in the workplace, there will be repercussions.

農曆三月

(April 4th - May 4th) 庚辰
Beware of tension in your marriage this month due to necessary changes. It is best to deal with this rationally and make proper adjustments. Instead of accusing each other for not doing enough, you should learn to appreciate what your partner has done for you.

農曆四月

(May 5th - June 4th) 辛巳
This is the month to reap the rewards of your hard work in the past few months, in the form of financial gains. With a positive wealth luck this month, you are also encouraged to look into long-term investments such as properties.

農曆五月

(June 5th - July 5th) 壬午
As your positive Wealth Luck continue this month, you would do well to take this opportunity to seize any available financial prospect, especially if you were born in the autumn or winter. Friends and family may offer you some useful insights too.

農曆六月

(July 6th - August 6th) 癸未
It would be best to take some time to make sure any project you're working on has no loose ends. If there are things you overlooked, you may suffer from its consequences. It is advisable to keep your emotions in check and make decisions with a clear mind.

農曆七月

(August 7th - September 6th) 甲申
Be careful of the appearance of a third party this month in your relationship with your significant other. It is best to practise honesty with your partner and be straightforward about your feelings. This way, misunderstanding can be avoided.

農曆八月

(September 7th - October 7th) 乙酉
This month, you should pay more attention to your health as you may struggle with coughs, weak lungs and other respiratory issues. On the other hand, this month is conducive for single men looking for a partner. However, they need to beware of unexpected complications.

農曆九月

(October 8th - November 6th) 丙戌
The amount of workload may double or even triple this month for you. However, you should stay focused and not let yourself be overwhelmed. Take this opportunity to show your capabilities instead of seeing this as an insurmountable challenge.

農曆十月

(November 7th - December 6th) 丁亥
Unexpected changes may disrupt your plans this month, especially if you are in the communication industry. Therefore, it is advisable to be prepared beforehand with additional backup plans. This way, you can be ready if anything happens.

農曆十一月

(December 7th 2020 - January 4th 2021) 戊子
You should learn to protect your original ideas particularly in this month, because there is a heightened risk of people out to steal your ideas and take credit for them. It would do you well to keep things to yourself until you have made solid progress to earn your credit.

農曆十二月

(January 5th - February 2nd 2021) 己丑
The workplace may be filled with gossips and rumours this month, but you are discouraged from participating in it. Of course, you should also watch your behaviour in the public to avoid being the subject of gossip this month,

癸丑 Gui Chou Day

Gui

Chou

Overview

You may benefit greatly from your professional connection with others this year. Those of you who are working in an office environment will be able to form positive relationships with colleagues. Those running businesses will find opportunities for partnerships and collaborations. You are advised to keep an open attitude when working with others, as this will bring you more opportunities.

 ## Wealth

This is an auspicious year for you in terms of wealth. When you celebrate success, remember to show your gratitude to those who have helped you in achieving your success. You may also consider expanding your social network to find potential business partners or people to collaborate in work.

 ## Relationships

It is recommended that you place your focus on other areas in life this year instead of looking for relationships. People you are attracted to are likely to become a different person once you enter a relationship with them. If you are already in a relationship, remember to pay attention to your partner as to not leave them feeling neglected.

 ## Health

On the health front, you should be more vigilant this year especially if you were born in winter. It is best to go for regular medical check-ups to ensure everything is okay. You should make sure you get enough rest as your immune system tends to be weaker and thus prone to falling sick this year.

 ## Career

Your career will get a boost from teamwork. Therefore, you should be open to your team members' ideas – you may find gems through these conversations. Those of you who work for others should make sure you are in your boss' good books as this is important for ensuring your success.

農曆正月

(February 4th - March 4th) 戊寅
This month you should pay more attention to your family as they may need your assistance with their problems. Make time for your family and understand what is going on in their lives. They will feel relieved to have someone to talk to about their problems.

農曆二月

(March 5th - April 3rd) 己卯
Beware of overthinking and overanalysing this month especially when it comes to relationships. Singles should try to be as straightforward as they can be in communication with people they are attracted to. Those in committed relationships should always ask and discuss openly with their partners.

農曆三月

(April 4th - May 4th) 庚辰
There may be unexpected issues with your projects at work this month causing delays. You are advised to stay calm and focus on solving the issues. Tackle the problems one at a time and you will eventually overcome all of them.

農曆四月

(May 5th - June 4th) 辛巳
Married couples may find themselves getting into heated arguments this month due to financial issues. It is best to keep your expenses in check and make sure neither of you overspend. It will also help if you could be more understanding towards your partner.

農曆五月

(June 5th - July 5th) 壬午
This is the time to set your plans in motion as your endeavours are likely to produce favourable outcome. However, if you do not feel confident or ready to kick-start a project, listen to your gut and do not let anyone else rush you into anything.

農曆六月

(July 6th - August 6th) 癸未
There may be third party influences that threaten to jeopardise your relationship this month. If you find yourself wondering if your significant other is cheating on you, it is best to ask them openly instead of trying to find clues on your own.

農曆七月

(August 7th - September 6th) 甲申
This month, you may be tempted to cut corners to obtain wealth. However, you should beware of any legal complications that may result should you take the risky path. Fortunately, you also have noble people on your side to give you valuable advice.

農曆八月

(September 7th - October 7th) 乙酉
If you make any impulsive purchase this month, you will likely regret it afterwards. Take into consideration how frequent and how long you would use this item, and also if its value would depreciate or appreciate in the long run.

農曆九月

(October 8th - November 6th) 丙戌
There is the possibility of you getting a job promotion this month, provided you have been working hard for the past few months. Your efforts will be recognised in due course. Keep doing what you are doing; do not slack off as this could jeopardise your chances of getting a promotion.

農曆十月

(November 7th - December 6th) 丁亥
This month, you could be required to travel for work or business. Take care of your belongings and be well-prepared for the trip to avoid unnecessary delays. Be mindful not to eat at unsanitary places as there is a heightened risk of food poisoning as well.

農曆十一月

(December 7th 2020 - January 4th 2021) 戊子
If an offer seems too good to be true, it may be a scam or fraud. Be careful not to fall into any of these traps this month. If necessary, seek others' opinions before making any investments or transfers of money, as your judgment tends to be clouded during this time.

農曆十二月

(January 5th - February 2nd 2021) 己丑
While some people are there to help you improve your ideas, some people are bent on exploiting your ideas and taking credit for your effort. Be wary of such petty people this month. Only share your ideas with trusted people who could offer you constructive feedback.

甲寅 Jia Yin Day

Overview

This is the perfect year for you spice your life up with positive changes. It's the perfect time to explore new options and ideas even if they are beyond your comfort zone. While you're doing so, pay attention to the details, especially when you're looking at it from a whole new angle. If you wish to have a better quality of life, creativity is the key and you can cultivate it through new experiences such as travelling.

 ## Wealth

As your career luck is looking to improve this year, your wealth would indirectly benefit as a result. Nonetheless, on your part, you still have to allow these changes to happen by taking the initiative to adopt new habits. Be more disciplined and punctual, for example, and your wealth will definitely increase.

 ## Relationships

For women who are single, you might be able to find someone new with the help of Peach Blossom Luck. For those already in a relationship, you might feel bored with your partner and this is a dangerous feeling to have. Try something new with your significant other. Do something that can bring excitement back to your love life.

Health

Migraines and headaches are something that you might have to deal with this year because of stress. Aside from that, you're also prone to injuries to your head so take precaution. Other parts of your body won't be causing you any issue this year.

Career

You'll be advancing in your career this year as fruitful developments are in store for you. Stay focused on your ambition so you would be able to complete your responsibilities easily. It's also favourable for you to be travelling so whenever you get the chance, go for it.

農曆正月

(February 4th - March 4th) 戊寅
This is a good month for you to be showcasing your talents and be recognized. Have confidence as you're more capable than you think.

農曆二月

(March 5th - April 3rd) 己卯
Your Wealth Luck is going strong this month. Men who are single are more likely to find love as there are plenty of opportunities for love.

農曆三月

(April 4th - May 4th) 庚辰
Even though there are positive developments in your career this month, the new responsibilities might give you additional stress. This may affect your relationship negatively.

農曆四月

(May 5th - June 4th) 辛巳
It's high time you go for a medical check-up. If you encountered any heart-related issues recently, it's more the reason to do so.

農曆五月

(June 5th - July 5th) 壬午
This month, you'll be blessed with a treasure trove of new ideas in the form of inspiration. Don't be afraid to share your ideas so that you can put them to good use.

農曆六月

(July 6th - August 6th) 癸未
Your relationship might be plagued by suspicion and insecurity this month. Put all your cards down on the table and come clean when you communicate with your partner to avoid unnecessary misunderstandings.

農曆七月

(August 7th - September 6th) 甲申
Try to stay calm this month as you are more temperamental than usual. Take some time off to travel, perhaps southwards, to clear your mind.

農曆八月

(September 7th - October 7th) 乙酉
Your wealth luck continues to go strong this month especially if you were born in summer or spring. For yourself, the best result would be from collaboration with others.

農曆九月

(October 8th - November 6th) 丙戌
It's possible that you feel unrecognized for your work and unappreciated. Having said that, don't let your emotions stop you from continuously performing your best.

農曆十月

(November 7th - December 6th) 丁亥
Again, it's another emotional month. As you have gone through this before sometime ago, you should be used to it by now so try to keep it in check.

農曆十一月

(December 7th 2020 - January 4th 2021) 戊子
Good Wealth Luck is yours to enjoy this month. Aside from that, the people at your workplace are also encouraging and supportive of you and your endeavours.

農曆十二月

(January 5th - February 2nd 2021) 己丑
If you're not careful with what you eat this month, you are likely to suffer from food poisoning.

乙卯 **Yi Mao Day**

Overview

For every opportunity that you find this year, there is an equal number of challenges that awaits. If you wish to achieve more, you have to do more. In your road to success, there will be those who wish to get in your way. You shouldn't be so forgiving, particularly to those who aren't appreciative of your kindness. This is a good year to see who your true friends are.

 ### Wealth

If you were born in winter, there's plenty of Wealth Luck that awaits you. This luck might manifest itself in the form of opportunities to be earning money from those who are appreciative of your talent. Of course, there will be competition. Even so, as long as you become the best, you'll be able to have the lion's share of the reward in the end.

 ### Relationships

There are plenty of issues related to insecurity and suspicion this year regardless of your relationship status. Try to take it seriously as your significant other might not be so patient with you. Examine the core of the problem and come up with a fix to it so that you can be happy with your romantic life.

 ### Health

If you were born in autumn, you might be affected by issues related to the stomach and digestive system. For everyone else, you might get headaches and migraines and the likeliest culprit behind it is probably stress. Physical well-being is also something you need to maintain as you're equally susceptible to physical problems than you are with mental ones.

 ### Career

If you wish to make a good impression to your boss this year, you have to rely on your creativity and innovate. However, in doing so, you might attract some unwanted attention in the process. Some of your peers who are jealous might try to remove you by any means necessary. Learn to safeguard your own position.

農曆正月
(February 4th - March 4th) 戊寅
You could find yourself a sizable boon this month through the help of your colleagues and social network.

農曆二月
(March 5th - April 3rd) 己卯
There might be some changes in the office, perhaps in the form of a new boss. This would be a good time for you to impress them so that you'll start your professional relationship on the right foot.

農曆三月
(April 4th - May 4th) 庚辰
You might be tempted this month to splurge on luxury materials that may seem like they're worth it but actually not in the long run. Before you spend your hard-earned money, think twice.

農曆四月
(May 5th - June 4th) 辛巳
At work, don't let your guard down as there are those who seek to bring you down. They may try to approach you on the pretence of being friendly so you have to be cautious of that. As long as you are able to avoid these people, this month would go on smoothly.

農曆五月
(June 5th - July 5th) 壬午
If you were born in spring, you would be able to find help from other people rather easily due to your luck. Make the best use of their assistance while you can.

農曆六月
(July 6th - August 6th) 癸未
In the office, it's getting more and more competitive. If you don't play the game, you might be pushed out of the way and all your efforts would be in vain. Be firm and don't let others step on you, though at the same time don't resort to their level.

農曆七月
(August 7th - September 6th) 甲申
Women would have problems in their relationship this month regardless whether they are married or not. The cause of it would probably be the feeling of underappreciation and lack of attention.

農曆八月
(September 7th - October 7th) 乙酉
Your finances might suffer this month because of some expensive. It might make you resort to alcohol but it doesn't really help with your stress. What does help however is for you to keep track of your money flow.

農曆九月
(October 8th - November 6th) 丙戌
This month, it's imperative for you to be making quick-decisions and not waste time with your hesitations. You'll be able to make the right decisions as long as you don't panic and remain calm.

農曆十月
(November 7th - December 6th) 丁亥
If you were born during winter or spring, be prepared to face some health issues this month. If this applies to you, be more aware of your health condition and perhaps go for a check-up just to be sure.

農曆十一月
(December 7th 2020 - January 4th 2021) 戊子
Wild mood swings can be expected for you this month. If you are aware of your feelings, you may be able to have some degree of control over it. If you are to travel this month, consider travelling south.

農曆十二月
(January 5th - February 2nd 2021) 己丑
For women, you might find your relationship troubled by a third party this month. Be prepared to handle these people and tread carefully.

丙辰 **Bing Chen Day**

Overview

If you wish to see success this year, focus on collaborating with your peers as the outcome would be highly favourable. Whatever you want, whatever your goals may be, the key to obtain it all is teamwork. Being independent is a positive trait, but there's nothing wrong with working with others either. Embrace their help and together you can achieve much more.

 ## Wealth

Your opportunities to increase your wealth this year can be found through your social circle. Therefore, look through your connections for them. The opportunity can come in many forms, including an advice, opinion or information that would prove to be beneficial for your wealth prospects.

 ## Relationships

If you're single and looking, it is likely you have your eyes on someone you may have got to know through your social circle. For those of you who are attached, expect some bumpy road along your relationship this year. As it's related to trust issues, being sincere is recommended.

 ## Health

You don't have to worry much about your health as the outlook is positive. However, if you are thirty years old or over, you might want to take note of your sugar intake as your cholesterol levels might rise. Take it easy with the sweets and go for medical check ups from time to time to maintain your health.

 ## Career

Your career can reach new heights if you are able to leverage off your social connections this year. If you're not the social type, it's still beneficial to rely on those you already know. While the outlook here is positive, it comes with a catch whereby you might be affected by rumours and gossip. Nonetheless, it's not too difficult to mitigate. Rely on your social connections still but simply watch what you say.

農曆正月

(February 4th - March 4th) 戊寅
Favouritism runs rampant in your workspace this month but don't let it get to you. Take the high road and focus on your job instead. If anyone asks for help, be helpful to them and be receptive for any opinion they might have. Sooner or later, people will see your value.

農曆二月

(March 5th - April 3rd) 己卯
This month would inspire you to have plenty of ideas and you should let your creativity flourish by finding an outlet. Discuss your ideas with anyone you can find to develop them further.

農曆三月

(April 4th - May 4th) 庚辰
In your office or workplace, you might be prone to be argumentative with your colleagues. Fortunately, it's nothing serious as long as you don't let your emotions take control.

農曆四月

(May 5th - June 4th) 辛巳
This is the month where all your prior effort will result in financial gain for you. Whatever you receive, manage it well. Try not to spend in things you don't really need.

農曆五月

(June 5th - July 5th) 壬午
It's looking to be a stressful month and as a result, your health might be negatively affected as well. From time to time, set aside some time for relaxation and opportunity to catch a break.

農曆六月

(July 6th - August 6th) 癸未
This month, you might unintentionally offend others with something you say. Watch what came out of your mouth; makes sure you communicate clearly to avoid misunderstandings.

農曆七月

(August 7th - September 6th) 甲申
For those born in the summer, you may find a boost in your Wealth Luck this month.

農曆八月

(September 7th - October 7th) 乙酉
This month, there's a chance for you to be travelling north. Whether or not it's something you want or would enjoy, keep an open mind. There's bound to be something you can gain from this.

農曆九月

(October 8th - November 6th) 丙戌
You may be unhappy with a certain person in your life at the moment. If you wish to have the tension between the two of you resolved, have an honest discussion with them.

農曆十月

(November 7th - December 6th) 丁亥
While you're trying to get your work done, your obligation to your friends and co-workers might get in the way. At the end of the day, try to remind yourself that your goals aren't going to be accomplished by themselves.

農曆十一月

(December 7th 2020 - January 4th 2021) 戊子
This month, there may be a promotion of some sort for you in your career if you were to travel southwards.

農曆十二月

(January 5th - February 2nd 2021) 己丑
Inspiration is all around you this month if you were to be receptive towards them. Accept the opinions and ideas of others with an open heart and if what they say is useful, don't forget to show gratitude towards them.

六十甲子 Forecast for 2020 based on Day of Birth

丁巳 Ding Si Day

Overview

Compared to yesteryears, your health outlook is improving. In your endeavours for this year, you will be able to find Noble People all around. Don't be afraid to rely on them especially on matters relating to your finances. Their opinion will lead you to make the right decisions. Whatever bad habits you might have, it's a good time for you to be discarding them and have new ones that are more positive and productive in their place.

Wealth

There are many roads to wealth if one possesses ingenuity and determination. As long as you're willing to innovate and seize the moment, you'll be able to benefit from the opportunities you are given. If you have a partner in your business, make sure you clarify everything as unclear communication might lead to misunderstandings. While opportunities are scarce, you would still be able to find success if you take full advantage of the ones you get.

Relationships

Single men will find favourable luck in love this year. As for women who are attached, frictions can be expected with their significant other this year. On top of that, they might be affected by troubles that involves an old friend and their partner. As there are multiple parties involved and emotions run high, it's easy to step on someone's toes. Tread carefully and try to practice empathy and compromise.

Health

For those of you born in springtime, this year you would be at the peak of your health. As for those who are born in other seasons, there might be some issues related to the stomach. This health concern may be recurring throughout the year.

Career

This year, it would be in your best interest to keep a low profile at your workplace and not get yourself involved in any office politics. There will come a time when you will have the chance to let your talents shine; but for the time being it's advisable to hold yourself back. If you've played your cards right, your efforts will come to fruition in June in the form of promotion or career advancement.

農曆正月

(February 4th - March 4th) 戊寅
This month, it's a good time to explore your options and seek new possibilities. Perhaps you can be on a look out for a new partner.

農曆二月

(March 5th - April 3rd) 己卯
Watch your words; you'll never know who you might offend unintentionally. Just as others might easily misunderstand you, it goes both ways. Give others the benefit of the doubt and don't be so quick to judge.

農曆三月

(April 4th - May 4th) 庚辰
It may get more competitive in the office this time of the year and this is likely to cause you stress. You can still resume your business as usual provided you keep your eyes on the prize.

農曆四月

(May 5th - June 4th) 辛巳
This month, if you have plans to travel, practice caution as there is an increased chance of getting yourself into an accident. As long as you remain vigilant, you should be able to make it through just fine.

農曆五月

(June 5th - July 5th) 壬午
If you have been working hard all this while, this month you may find a career advancement is in store for you. Know that all your effort hasn't been in vain.

農曆六月

(July 6th - August 6th) 癸未
If you mixed with the wrong crowd, you may find yourself entangled with litigation this month. Whatever problems others may have, let them solve it on their own if getting involved means putting your own self in hot water.

農曆七月

(August 7th - September 6th) 甲申
This isn't a good month for you to be putting your money into investment. At the moment, the market is not conducive for such endeavours and investments won't be profitable for you.

農曆八月

(September 7th - October 7th) 乙酉
Pregnant women may find their health at risk this month and as such should take better care of their health.

農曆九月

(October 8th - November 6th) 丙戌
You might be getting into a lot of arguments this month with your significant other over financial issues. These arguments may get out of control to the point that it may be the end of your relationship. Before it spirals out of control, keep your emotions in check.

農曆十月

(November 7th - December 6th) 丁亥
You might have petty people all around you this month and you'll hear all sort of baseless rumours and gossip. Subsequently, you might even get betrayed by the people you trust. In order to avoid this, choose your friends carefully.

農曆十一月

(December 7th 2020 - January 4th 2021) 戊子
It would serve you no benefit to appear callous and cold. It would be more favourable for you to be more warmth, empathic and approachable. Do that and let others rely on you.

農曆十二月

(January 5th - February 2nd 2021) 己丑
Don't procrastinate. Make sure you get your work done so that in the future, you don't have to deal with an avalanche of work all at once.

六十甲子 Forecast for 2020 based on Day of Birth

戊午 Wu Wu Day

Overview

It's going to be an excellent year for you as all the hard work you put in will come to fruition. For any opportunities that appear, make the best out of them as you'll have excellent Wealth Luck on your side. Be open-minded and say yes to positive changes and you'll be able to see considerable progress in your life.

 ## Wealth

If you see an opportunity to increase your financial standing, it would be wasted if you don't take it. Sometimes for opportunity to appear, you have to take the initiative yourself to make it happen. There's bound to be arguments over money matters if you have a partner, but it's nothing serious if you don't let it spiral out of control.

 ## Relationships

Married men are likely to be tempted by dalliances with a third party this year. Cherish the relationship you have and don't jeopardize it over short-term satisfactions. You have a responsibility to your significant other and as such have to put them first. If you are single, it's a good year for you to be getting married.

 ## Health

For those who are born in autumn or summer, your health outlook is more or less average for this year. Possible health issues that might affect you are just headaches and migraine so there's not much to worry about. Still, it wouldn't hurt to be careful with your health.

 ## Career

If you were born in spring, you might be able to see some form of advancement in your career be it a promotion or salary increment. This can only happen if you had put in effort to make it a reality. Keep up the good work and you will be rewarded eventually.

農曆正月

(February 4th - March 4th) 戊寅
Take good care of your head as your might suffer from head-related injuries. Additionally, it's a good month to end unproductive relationships. If you have anyone in your life that's not pulling their weight, go ahead and cut your ties with them.

農曆二月

(March 5th - April 3rd) 己卯
Your colleagues might coerce you into making difficult decisions. Don't submit to peer pressure. Instead, take your time when you're making your choices.

農曆三月

(April 4th - May 4th) 庚辰
It is likely you'll be pleasantly surprised this month due to unexpected monetary gains. This could be because of your recent contributions. As the reward is well-deserved, enjoy it.

農曆四月

(May 5th - June 4th) 辛巳
Whatever work you have to do, pay close attention to the details. Make sure that in the eyes of your boss, there is no wrongdoing. Cover all your bases so that nothing can be used against you.

農曆五月

(June 5th - July 5th) 壬午
If you have issues with the law in the past, it might resurface sometime this month. You have to put it to rest. It might be in the form of bills you have to settle. Before it gets worse, finish it once and for all.

農曆六月

(July 6th - August 6th) 癸未
Watch your diet this month as you might suffer from health issues related to the stomach. Always practice good hygiene.

農曆七月

(August 7th - September 6th) 甲申
There's an increased chance of head injuries this month, perhaps happening because you weren't cautious or focused. If you were born in summer, perhaps its your legs that gets injured.

農曆八月

(September 7th - October 7th) 乙酉
There might be new projects for you to work on this month. Perhaps you should pick up additional skills to better handle your new responsibility.

農曆九月

(October 8th - November 6th) 丙戌
It won't be a pleasant month for you in regards to your career. It could be that you'll have disagreements with certain colleagues. Don't let them get the upper hand and choose your allies carefully.

農曆十月

(November 7th - December 6th) 丁亥
It's possible that your eyes might be causing you problems this month. As soon as you notice any symptoms, go for a check up just to be on the safe side.

農曆十一月

(December 7th 2020 - January 4th 2021) 戊子
It might be possible for you to be travelling sometime this month. It would be advisable for you to come up with a budget on your expenditure then stick to that budget to prevent overspending. Additionally, keep your personal belongings safe.

農曆十二月

(January 5th - February 2nd 2021) 己丑
This month might give you a spell of lethargy that makes you feel like procrastinating. If you continue procrastinating, you'll only be troubling your own self later on. This can be avoided by having good discipline.

己未 Ji Wei Day

Overview

This year might see a lot of ups and down especially in terms of your career. There will be those who seek your downfall by spoiling your reputation because they are not as capable as you are. To best handle them, don't attract unnecessary attention and continue with your responsibilities. It's crucial for you to remain calm as the drama at work might put you in the spotlight.

 ## Wealth

Your Wealth Luck is looking good this year and as a result people might approach you to strengthen your ties with them. Look out for yourself first and foremost and pay less attention to them. As you progress through the year, sometime during the second half of the year, your luck would continue to improve particularly if you were born in summer or spring.

 ## Relationships

Relationships require effort to work. If you didn't work on it, you won't be able to enjoy it. For men, try to pay more attention to your partner even if you have other responsibilities to look after. Women on the other hand have to be more patient this year to maintain their relationship. Overall for both genders, the second half of the year is more favourable in terms of love.

 ## Health

Your number one focus this year ought to be your health. Key areas you need to monitor would be your eyes, heart and blood pressure. If you are a woman, watch out for gynaecological issues as well. Schedule a health check-up often and you should be fine.

 ## Career

Keep a low profile at the office and put 100% of your focus into your work. Petty people are around and they might just pick on you for seemingly no reason. It may be in the form of stealing credit for your hard work or pilfering your ideas. As such, choose who you trust carefully. Make sure you communicate everything clearly to avoid misunderstandings.

農曆正月

(February 4th - March 4th) 戊寅

Some people around you are looking to steal your ideas and pass it off as their own this month. Keep an eye out for such people to ensure your plans are not disrupted.

農曆二月

(March 5th - April 3rd) 己卯

This month, mothers-to-be might suffer from health issues. Don't take actions that might put your health in jeopardy. When you encounter the first sign of trouble, go for a medical check-up.

農曆三月

(April 4th - May 4th) 庚辰

You might feel inspired this month and instilled with the motivation to turn your plans into reality. Excellent results can be expected and you'll gain valuable experience through formulating new ideas.

農曆四月

(May 5th - June 4th) 辛巳

Overall, your luck is looking good at the moment. Despite of that, don't be complacent or take it for granted especially if you were to travel this month.

農曆五月

(June 5th - July 5th) 壬午

Your Wealth Luck takes a turn for the better this time around. While having this blessing, there's a price to be paid in the form of jealous eyes. Others might look at your well-earned success with envy. Don't let them get to you and focus on yourself instead.

農曆六月

(July 6th - August 6th) 癸未

If you are a a man who is in a committed relationship, expect verbal arguments with your partner this month. No matter how much you wish to win or have the final say, don't let it get personal as your relationship might deteriorate as a result.

農曆七月

(August 7th - September 6th) 甲申

If you have been putting in the effort and hard work, you career should be smooth-sailing at the moment. The reward that you get might be a salary increment or promotion.

農曆八月

(September 7th - October 7th) 乙酉

If you have to make any major decisions this month, try to delay your choice to another time. This is especially so if it concerns legal issues.

農曆九月

(October 8th - November 6th) 丙戌

If you wish to get ahead in life, you have to have the right skills. These skills can be acquired and trained with the right education. So, go for courses or programmes to enhance your overall capability.

農曆十月

(November 7th - December 6th) 丁亥

You might find yourself attending many social events this month. It might seem fun to meet new people, but remember that too much of a good thing can be bad. Practice moderation.

農曆十一月

(December 7th 2020 - January 4th 2021) 戊子

Whatever you have in mind might be conflicted to your boss' opinion and these differences may lead to conflict. Whatever it may be, these arguments should remain professional. Don't bring personal emotions to the table or even talk negatively of them behind their back.

農曆十二月

(January 5th - February 2nd 2021) 己丑

Your primary concern this month should be your health, especially if it's related to heart problems. If you are forty and above, you can mitigate this problem through regular check-ups.

庚申 Geng Shen Day

Overview

Overall, it would be a relatively stable year without major changes in your life or anything that would put you into jeopardy. While this means unpleasant surprises are less likely to happen, positive opportunities may also be hard to find. Nonetheless, it is good practice if you can make the most out of what you have. While you are having this period of stability, it would be a good time to be making plans.

 ## Wealth

Your wealth would see some form of stagnation this year. For what it's worth, your financial situation won't worsen. Just keep up your pace and do your best. Eventually, when an opportunity to improve your wealth does appear, at least you'd be well-prepared.

 ## Relationships

In terms of love and relationship, this aspect of your life would not undergo much changes as well. Perhaps it would be wise to focus on other pursuits. For those who are attached, this doesn't mean you won't be happy. As long as you are able to appreciate the small things, you can keep your relationship strong and going.

 ## Health

Overall, your outlook for health this year is positive aside from a slight risk of eye-related issues that are not very significant. Even so, if any symptoms were to appear, have it checked. If you're not too careful, you might also be susceptible to limb-related injuries.

 ## Career

If you're hoping for a career change this year, it's best not to go ahead with that plan just yet. As of current, it is unfavourable for you to be changing jobs. If you want to find more fulfilment in your current one, simply put more effort in it. You'll get your reward sooner or later if you were to do so.

農曆正月

(February 4th - March 4th) 戊寅
For those born in winter, you'll have excellent Financial Luck this month. If you were to travel, keep your expenditure in check so that you won't overspend regardless of the positive wealth outlook.

農曆二月

(March 5th - April 3rd) 己卯
Your Wealth Luck from the previous month continues. Having said that, it would mean nothing if you don't take the initiative. Make the best out of this opportunity and seek to improve your finances.

農曆三月

(April 4th - May 4th) 庚辰
Even after you achieved your goals, you should be maintaining your momentum. After you get what you want, you may feel like you should take it easy but being complacent won't do you any good. If you want to achieve more goals in the future, you should simply continue your efforts.

農曆四月

(May 5th - June 4th) 辛巳
Whatever success you achieve this month may earn the attention of jealous eyes. As long as what you achieved is well-deserved, don't even bother with the petty people and stay focused on your own ambition.

農曆五月

(June 5th - July 5th) 壬午
This month you will see competition escalating in the office and might get in the way of your work. With determination and grit, you'll be able to overcome this in one piece.

農曆六月

(July 6th - August 6th) 癸未
This month, you may find yourself to be your worst enemy. Instead of being self-critical, examine your own talents and what you have achieved with them thus far. Be confident and decisive.

農曆七月

(August 7th - September 6th) 甲申
With everything that is happening around you, it may seem unclear and confusing at the moment. Don't get distracted as making the wrong decision might worsen your problems.

農曆八月

(September 7th - October 7th) 乙酉
It will be an emotional month for you with wild mood swings and temperament. As long as you can keep these emotional issues to yourself and not act on them, it will simply pass over in due time.

農曆九月

(October 8th - November 6th) 丙戌
This month, men who are in relationships may be tempted to cheat on their partner. If you caught yourself in this situation, think it through and make the right choice. Think of the partner who have been with through thick and thin.

農曆十月

(November 7th - December 6th) 丁亥
You'll be able to enjoy good travelling luck this month and it may be related to your work. A breath of fresh air from the usual environment is nice and it may even be a financially rewarding endeavour.

農曆十一月

(December 7th 2020 - January 4th 2021) 戊子
If you encounter any legal or official paperwork, pay attention to the details. You might get yourself in trouble if you were to ignore the fine print. At the same time, you may have some toxic people in your vicinity that gives negative influence. Learn to tune them out.

農曆十二月

(January 5th - February 2nd 2021) 己丑
You might find some obstruction in getting your work completed and the culprit could be your superior. This is likely to be an uncomfortable scenario. Try to go for a mutual understanding by having clear communication with your boss in order to solve this dilemma.

六十甲子 Forecast for 2020 based on Day of Birth

辛酉 Xin You Day

Overview

You might feel like there's a lot of stagnation this year, but in actuality you just have to examine the bigger picture. There is some progress, though it's slow. It's a matter of perspective. If you feel like what you're doing is pointless, then it's hard to be productive. If you are able to shift your view, you would be able to persevere and maintain your determination. Focus on your goals and remain true to your vision.

 ## Wealth

In terms of finances, it's not a good year for you overall. It's more likely for you to lose money than the opposite especially if you are not cautious. At best, your luck in endeavours related to your finances are only mediocre. Despite of the conditions you are given, it shouldn't stop you from doing your best. Invest in education to acquire useful skills for the future. As long as you are able to persevere, your wealth luck would recover eventually.

 ## Relationships

For those of you who are married, try to find away to make your marriage exciting again. Remember what brought you two together and find the common ground. Show your appreciation towards one another and focus on the positive. If you are single, try to be happy with yourself first. It's advisable to look after your own self this year.

 ## Health

Throughout the year, your health is relatively stable. Having said that, it shouldn't be an excuse to skip medical check-ups or not taking up healthy habits. If you are thirty and above, you might be susceptible to heart-related issues.

 ## Career

If you wish you to advance in your career, you must take on new responsibilities. To do so, your capabilities must match the role you're looking for. Perhaps you should consider going for courses or classes that could train your current skillset or add to it to make you more competitive. No matter how old you are, always remember that education is a lifelong endeavour.

農曆正月

(February 4th - March 4th) 戊寅
This month, your Financial outlook is looking good. It's a good time to be making profits and exploring opportunities to increase your wealth.

農曆二月

(March 5th - April 3rd) 己卯
Success could be yours this month with the help with a couple of people. This is achievable through networking. They will be able to give you actionable advices that could lead you to where you want to be.

農曆三月

(April 4th - May 4th) 庚辰
Good news as you might be able to advance your career this month, especially if you were born in winter or autumn. When the opportunity appears, just take it first and think about it later. Otherwise, you might just miss out.

農曆四月

(May 5th - June 4th) 辛巳
Your emotions are volatile this month. As such, it would be wise to distant yourself from other people. It's easy for you to lose your patience so be mindful of your surroundings.

農曆五月

(June 5th - July 5th) 壬午
Whatever you learned will finally be of use this month as there are people who are willing to spend money for your expertise.

農曆六月

(July 6th - August 6th) 癸未
You might feel lazier than usual this month and your energy level is at an all-time low. Your health might also be at risk as your immune system is weakened.

農曆七月

(August 7th - September 6th) 甲申
You might receive help from others in terms of work, but only you can finish it. Focus your energy on getting things done.

農曆八月

(September 7th - October 7th) 乙酉
It's a good time for romance this month as your Peach Blossom Luck is blooming. You'll be able to find favourable outcomes if you were to go out and meet new people.

農曆九月

(October 8th - November 6th) 丙戌
There might be some changes at your workplace that is not in your favour. Regardless, take it with stride and learn from the experience. Don't let it distract you from your responsibilities.

農曆十月

(November 7th - December 6th) 丁亥
If you are planning to travel this month, it is advisable for you to travel south. It's also a good month for you to be collaborating with others.

農曆十一月

(December 7th 2020 - January 4th 2021) 戊子
This month, you can expect to face some issues regarding your health because of food allergies. You are also likely to be more irritable and temperamental. Be mindful of your physical and mental health.

農曆十二月

(January 5th - February 2nd 2021) 己丑
Individuals who are married will have to deal with some challenges in this month in the form of arguments. Have patience with your partner and try to compromise so it won't make the issue any worse.

六十甲子 Forecast for 2020 based on Day of Birth

壬戌 Ren Xu Day

Overview

All the hard work and effort you have accumulated in the past will now begin to pay off, especially if you're already in a stable job. Keep up the pace and your future is set. As long as you're keeping to your course, you'll be able to find success and respect.

Wealth

Where money is concerned, you have to take the initiative to see some financial improvements. You might want to consider options you've yet to try before. There's no harm in taking calculating risks by trying out new things. You can't get a different result if you keep doing the same thing, after all.

Relationships

If you're in a relationship and you've been with your partner for some time now, you can expect some emotional ups and down this year. Have patience and try to control your temper. There's no point in making things worse. Be diplomatic and try not to argue over trivial matters.

Health

There's a chance that you might suffer from blood-related illness and skin allergies this year provided that you don't pay much attention to your health. At the first sign of trouble, you should go for a medical check-up. You may also have to watch what you eat as well; there's a chance for you to get food poisoning. Don't take your health for granted.

Career

This is a good year for you to make a change in your career. You might even be able to travel more as a result. Whatever you choose to do, remember that opportunities appear if you are receptive to change. Business owners on the other hand need to focus their attention to their staff. Some of your employees might cause problems for you and your company and you need to handle it before it's too late.

農曆正月

(February 4th - March 4th) 戊寅
If you own a business, expect a competitive month ahead. Make the necessary preparations. Bare in mind that some of your employees might be leaving so you have to take this into account.

農曆二月

(March 5th - April 3rd) 己卯
Last month's competitive condition still hasn't died down. This is particularly true for those Summer babies. Reconsider your tactics and think of a different approach to gain the upper hand.

農曆三月

(April 4th - May 4th) 庚辰
If you make decisions on the spot, it might lead to unfavourable outcomes. Think it through before you make any choice whatsoever.

農曆四月

(May 5th - June 4th) 辛巳
Your health might suffer if you bite more than you can chew. Having too much stress might lead you to develop skin problems such as rashes and allergies. Give yourself a break once in a while.

農曆五月

(June 5th - July 5th) 壬午
You should be able to enjoy good Wealth Luck this month. This is particularly true if you were born in winter. One way to capitalize on this luck is to take the opportunity to ask for a raise or career advancement if it's well-deserved.

農曆六月

(July 6th - August 6th) 癸未
Your Wealth Luck continues well into this month. If you're itching to try out a new idea, it's an auspicious time to do so as the results are in your favour.

農曆七月

(August 7th - September 6th) 甲申
When things get difficult, you may be tempted to cut the corners and interpret the rules creatively. Doing so will only invite trouble. Stay true to the law.

農曆八月

(September 7th - October 7th) 乙酉
If you were born in winter or autumn, you would be able to gain favourable results from working closely with others.

農曆九月

(October 8th - November 6th) 丙戌
If you are in a relationship, you can expect a month full of arguments. The core of the problem could be trust issues that may come in the form of insecurity and envy.

農曆十月

(November 7th - December 6th) 丁亥
Your emotions are all over the place this month. As you can't tell heads from tails based on how you're feeling, try to get a second opinion on your decisions so that you would make informed choices.

農曆十一月

(December 7th 2020 - January 4th 2021) 戊子
Those looking to form partnerships and collaborate with others would benefit from this month's energy as they might be able to find the right person to do it with.

農曆十二月

(January 5th - February 2nd 2021) 己丑
A stressful month can be expected ahead and ample preparation are needed. Besides anticipating your obstacles, remember that it's okay to give yourself a break from time to time.

六十甲子

Forecast for 2020 based on Day of Birth

癸亥 Gui Hai Day

Overview
The effort you have been putting in your work is finally showing results. This should motivate you further to maintain your momentum and achieve much more than your initial goal. Keep up your pace and you'll eventually achieve unprecedented success. Collaborating with others is imperative for you this year as it will allow your endeavours to be smooth sailing.

 ## Wealth
Prioritize opportunities that allow you to collaborate with others as it would be the best way to utilize your Wealth Luck this year. In the process of obtaining your wealth, always remember that you're doing it out of passion. Being greedy will only make you lose sight of the bigger picture.

 ## Relationships
For those who are single, this year provides a good opportunity to find the right partner. Pay attention to the people you meet at your office or career-related endeavours. It's also possible that the people you meet might not live up to your expectation. But, if you persevere, you'll end up making the right connections.

 ## Health
Your health outlook doesn't look good and it might be declining due to work-related stress. As much as you'd like to prioritize your health, at the end of the day you need a healthy body to be efficient at your work. From time to time, give yourself a break and time to recuperate. When you're back on your feet, then you can resume work as per normal.

Career
No matter how capable you are, it's more rewarding to succeed together with others than to do it alone. Expand your social network, be open to working with others and you'll achieve much more. Besides that, remember that whatever resources you have at your disposal is limited. Be wise in handling them so that you're not using too much or too little.

農曆正月

(February 4th - March 4th) 戊寅
While there are many options to explore this month, be mindful of your limitations. It's not really necessary for you to suffer from exhaustion due to overworking just to get things done. Things can wait, your health comes first.

農曆二月

(March 5th - April 3rd) 己卯
It's an ideal month for you to show off your ideas to your peers and seek their advice on improvements. This may lead to future collaborations.

農曆三月

(April 4th - May 4th) 庚辰
This month, you might be feeling lethargic and lazy. Despite of this feeling, you shouldn't let it override your decisions. Don't settle for what you get when you don't do anything.

農曆四月

(May 5th - June 4th) 辛巳
There's a chance this month that you might hurt your legs. If you're thinking of doing any sports activity such as skiing or running, take due precaution. Additionally, pregnant women are more likely to find themselves in accidents.

農曆五月

(June 5th - July 5th) 壬午
If you're looking to start something new, now would be a good time. Maybe you could take some old ideas you had before and breathe new life into it. Once you get the ball rolling, you would able to overcome any hurdle that stand in your way.

農曆六月

(July 6th - August 6th) 癸未
It will be a stressful and tiring month for you. The quality of multiple aspects of your life would suffer as a result. Take the necessary steps to mitigate this condition.

農曆七月

(August 7th - September 6th) 甲申
After you're dealing with stress from the previous month, now you have to deal with financial issues. Get it done and over with before it spirals out of control.

農曆八月

(September 7th - October 7th) 乙酉
You might be met with a series of unfavourable incidents that might throw you off course and put unnecessary stress on your mind. The events that transpire would make less tolerable. As long as you practice self-awareness, you would be able to keep your emotions in check.

農曆九月

(October 8th - November 6th) 丙戌
At work, there might be a project that's been stalled for far too long. This month, with effort on your part, this project might finally see the light of day and be completed.

農曆十月

(November 7th - December 6th) 丁亥
As with the previous months, the workload increases further. Even if you're facing a mountain of work, keep calm. What you need to do is find balance; you need to get the job done but you have to do so without overworking yourself. You can't work when you're completely exhausted.

農曆十一月

(December 7th 2020 - January 4th 2021) 戊子
There's a chance that you might misunderstand something a friend says to you this month and subsequently be offended as a result. When such circumstance happens, keep an open mind. It's not worth it to burn bridges over something petty.

農曆十二月

(January 5th - February 2nd 2021) 己丑
Be on the lookout for certain people who are looking to spoil your reputation by spreading false rumours about you. Don't give them any attention whatsoever and pretend they don't exist.

JOEY YAP's
QI MEN DUN JIA MASTERY PROGRAM

This is the world's most comprehensive training program on the subject of Qi Men Dun Jia. Joey Yap is the Qi Men Strategist for some of Asia's wealthiest tycoons. This program is modelled after Joey Yap's personal application methods, covering techniques and strategies he applies for his high net worth clients. There is a huge difference between studying the subject as a scholar and learning how to use it successfully as a Qi Men strategist. In this program, Joey Yap shares with you what he personally uses to transform his own life and the lives of million others. In other words, he shares with his students what actually works and not just what looks good in theory with no real practical value. This means that the program covers his personal trade secrets in using the art of Qi Men Dun Jia.

There are five unique programs, with each of them covering one specific application aspect of the Joey Yap's Qi Men Dun Jia system.

Joey Yap's training program focuses on getting results. Theories and formulas are provided in the course workbook so that valuable class time are not wasted dwelling on formulas. Each course comes with its own comprehensive 400-plus pages workbook. Taught once a year exclusively by Joey Yap, seats to these programs are extremely limited.

Getting Whatever You Want from Whatever You've Got™ Spiritual Qi Men™

Qi Men Forecasting Methods™

Qi Men Destiny & Life Transformation™

Qi Men Feng Shui™

Qi Men Strategic Execution™

Qi Men Warcraft™

JOEY YAP CONSULTING GROUP

Pioneering Metaphysics-Centric Personal and Corporate Consultations

Founded in 2002, the Joey Yap Consulting Group is the pioneer in the provision of metaphysics-driven coaching and consultation services for professionals and individuals alike. Under the leadership of the renowned international Chinese Metaphysics consultant, author and trainer, Dato' Joey Yap, it has become a world-class specialised metaphysics consulting firm with a strong presence in four continents, meeting the metaphysics-centric needs of its A-list clientele, ranging from celebrities to multinational corporations.

The Group's core consultation practice areas include Feng Shui, BaZi and Qi Men Dun Jia, which are complemented by ancillary services such as Date Selection, Face Reading and Yi Jing. Its team of highly trained professional consultants, led by its Chief Consultant, Dato' Joey Yap, is well-equipped with unparalleled knowledge and experience to help clients achieve their ultimate potentials in various fields and specialisations. Given its credentials, the Group is certainly the firm of choice across the globe for metaphysics-related consultations.

The Peerless Industry Expert

Benchmarked against the standards of top international consulting firms, our consultants work closely with our clients to achieve the best possible outcomes. The possibilities are infinite as our expertise extends from consultations related to the forces of nature under the subject of Feng Shui, to those related to Destiny Analysis and effective strategising under BaZi and Qi Men Dun Jia respectively.

To date, we have consulted a great diversity of clients, ranging from corporate clients – from various industries such as real estate, finance and telecommunication, amongst others – to the hundreds of thousands of individuals in their key life aspects. Adopting up-to-date and pragmatic approaches, we provide comprehensive services while upholding the importance of clients' priorities and effective outcomes. Recognised as the epitome of Chinese Metaphysics, we possess significant testimonies from worldwide clients as a trusted Brand.

Feng Shui Consultation

Residential Properties
- Initial Land/Property Assessment
- Residential Feng Shui Consultation
- Residential Land Selection
- End-to-End Residential Consultation

Commercial Properties
- Initial Land/Property Assessment
- Commercial Feng Shui Consultation
- Commercial Land Selection
- End-to-End Commercial Consultation

Property Developers
- End-to-End Consultation
- Post-Consultation Advisory Services
- Panel Feng Shui Consultant

Property Investors
- Your Personal Feng Shui Consultant
- Tailor-Made Packages

Memorial Parks & Burial Sites
- Yin House Feng Shui

BaZi Consultation

Personal Destiny Analysis
- Individual BaZi Analysis
- BaZi Analysis for Families

Strategic Analysis for Corporate Organizations
- BaZi Consultations for Corporations
- BaZi Analysis for Human Resource Management

Entrepreneurs and Business Owners
- BaZi Analysis for Entrepreneurs

Career Pursuits
- BaZi Career Analysis

Relationships
- Marriage and Compatibility Analysis
- Partnership Analysis

General Public
- Annual BaZi Forecast
- Your Personal BaZi Coach

Date Selection Consultation

- **Marriage Date Selection**
- **Caesarean Birth Date Selection**
- **House-Moving Date Selection**
- **Renovation and Groundbreaking Dates**
- **Signing of Contracts**
- **O icial Openings**
- **Product Launches**

Qi Men Dun Jia Consultation

Strategic Execution
- Business and Investment Prospects

Forecasting
- Wealth and Life Pursuits
- People and Environmental Matters

Feng Shui
- Residential Properties
- Commercial Properties

Speaking Engagement

Many reputable organisations and institutions have worked closely with Joey Yap Consulting Group to build a synergistic business relationship by engaging our team of consultants, which are led by Joey Yap, as speakers at their corporate events.

We tailor our seminars and talks to suit the anticipated or pertinent group of audience. Be it department subsidiary, your clients or even the entire corporation, we aim to fit your requirements in delivering the intended message(s) across.

CHINESE METAPHYSICS REFERENCE SERIES

The Chinese Metaphysics Reference Series is a collection of reference texts, source material, and educational textbooks to be used as supplementary guides by scholars, students, researchers, teachers and practitioners of Chinese Metaphysics.

These comprehensive and structured books provide fast, easy reference to aid in the study and practice of various Chinese Metaphysics subjects including Feng Shui, BaZi, Yi Jing, Zi Wei, Liu Ren, Ze Ri, Ta Yi, Qi Men Dun Jia and Mian Xiang.

The Chinese Metaphysics Compendium

At over 1,000 pages, the Chinese Metaphysics Compendium is a unique one-volume reference book that compiles ALL the formulas relating to Feng Shui, BaZi (Four Pillars of Destiny), Zi Wei (Purple Star Astrology), Yi Jing (I-Ching), Qi Men (Mystical Doorways), Ze Ri (Date Selection), Mian Xiang (Face Reading) and other sources of Chinese Metaphysics.

It is presented in the form of easy-to-read tables, diagrams and reference charts, all of which are compiled into one handy book. This first-of-its-kind compendium is presented in both English and its original Chinese language, so that none of the meanings and contexts of the technical terminologies are lost.

The only essential and comprehensive reference on Chinese Metaphysics, and an absolute must-have for all students, scholars, and practitioners of Chinese Metaphysics.

The Ten Thousand Year Calendar (Pocket Edition)

The Ten Thousand Year Calendar

Dong Gong Date Selection

The Date Selection Compendium

Plum Blossoms Divination Reference Book

Xuan Kong Da Gua Ten Thousand Year Calendar

San Yuan Dragon Gate Eight Formations Water Method

BaZi Hour Pillar Useful Gods - Wood

BaZi Hour Pillar Useful Gods - Fire

BaZi Hour Pillar Useful Gods - Earth

BaZi Hour Pillar Useful Gods - Metal

BaZi Hour Pillar Useful Gods - Water

Xuan Kong Da Gua Structures Reference Book

Xuan Kong Da Gua 64 Gua Transformation Analysis

BaZi Structures and Structural Useful Gods - Wood

BaZi Structures and Structural Useful Gods - Fire

BaZi Structures and Structural Useful Gods - Earth

BaZi Structures and Structural Useful Gods - Metal

BaZi Structures and Structural Useful Gods - Water

Earth Study Discern Truth Second Edition

Eight Mansions Bright Mirror

Secret of Xuan Kong

Ode to Flying Stars

Xuan Kong Purple White Script

Ode to Mysticism

The Yin House Handbook

Water Water Everywhere

Xuan Kong Da Gua Not Exactly For Dummies

Joey Yap's BaZi Profiling System

Three Levels of BaZi Profiling (English & Chinese versions)

In BaZi Profiling, there are three levels that reflect three different stages of a person's personal nature and character structure.

Level 1 – The Day Master

The Day Master in a nutshell is the basic you. The inborn personality. It is your essential character. It answers the basic question "who am I". There are ten basic personality profiles – the ten Day Masters – each with its unique set of personality traits, likes and dislikes.

Level 2 – The Structure

The Structure is your behavior and attitude – in other words, it is about how you use your personality. It expands on the Day Master (Level 1). The structure reveals your natural tendencies in life – are you a controller, creator, supporter, thinker or connector? Each of the Ten Day Masters express themselves differently through the five Structures. Why do we do the things we do? Why do we like the things we like? The answers are in our BaZi Structure.

Level 3 – The Profile

The Profile depicts your role in your life. There are ten roles (Ten BaZi Profiles) related to us. As to each to his or her own - the roles we play are different from one another and it is unique to each Profile.

What success means to you, for instance, differs from your friends – this is similar to your sense of achievement or whatever you think of your purpose in life is.

Through the BaZi Profile, you will learn the deeper level of your personality. It helps you become aware of your personal strengths and works as a trigger for you to make all the positive changes to be a better version of you.

Keep in mind, only through awareness that you will be able to maximise your natural talents, abilities and skills. Only then, ultimately, you will get to enter into what we refer as 'flow' of life – a state where you have the powerful force to naturally succeed in life.

www.BaZiprofiling.com

THE BaZi
60 PILLARS SERIES

The BaZi 60 Pillars Series is a collection of ten volumes focusing on each of the Pillars or Jia Zi in BaZi Astrology. Learn how to see BaZi Chart in a new light through the Pictorial Method of BaZi analysis and elevate your proficiency in BaZi studies through this new understanding. Joey Yap's 60 Pillars Life Analysis Method is a refined and enhanced technique that is based on the fundamentals set by the true masters of olden times, and modified to fit to the sophistication of current times.

BaZi Collection

With these books, leading Chinese Astrology Master Trainer Joey Yap makes it easy to learn how to unlock your Destiny through your BaZi. BaZi or Four Pillars of Destiny is an ancient Chinese science which enables individuals to understand their personality, hidden talents and abilities, as well as their luck cycle - by examining the information contained within their birth data.

Understand and learn more about this accurate ancient science with this BaZi Collection.

| BOOK 1 | BOOK 2 | BOOK 3 | BOOK 4 | BOOK 5 | The 10 Gods |

(Available in English & Chinese)

Design Your Legacy

Design Your Legacy is Joey Yap's first book on the profound subject of Yin House Feng Shui, which is the study Feng Shui for burials and tombs. Although it is still pretty much a hidden practice that is largely unexplored by modern literature, the significance of Yin House Feng Shui has permeated through the centuries – from the creation of the imperial lineage of emperors in ancient times to the iconic leaders who founded modern China.

This book unveils the true essence of Yin House Feng Shui with its significant applications that are unlike the myths and superstition which have for years, overshadowed the genuine practice itself. Discover how Yin House Feng Shui – the true precursor to all modern Feng Shui practice, can be used to safeguard the future of your descendants and create a lasting legacy.

Must-Haves for Property Analysis!

For homeowners, those looking to build their own home or even investors who are looking to apply Feng Shui to their homes, these series of books provides valuable information from the classical Feng Shui therioes and applications.

In his trademark straight-to-the-point manner, Joey shares with you the Feng Shui do's and dont's when it comes to finding a property with favorable Feng Shui, which is condusive for home living.

Stories and Lessons on Feng Shui Series

All in all, this series is a delightful chronicle of Joey's articles, thoughts and vast experience - as a professional Feng Shui consultant and instructor - that have been purposely refined, edited and expanded upon to make for a light-hearted, interesting yet educational read. And with Feng Shui, BaZi, Mian Xiang and Yi Jing all thrown into this one dish, there's something for everyone.

(Available in English & Chinese)

More Titles under Joey Yap Books

Pure Feng Shui

Pure Feng Shui is Joey Yap's debut with an international publisher, CICO Books. It is a refreshing and elegant look at the intricacies of Classical Feng Shui - now compiled in a useful manner for modern day readers. This book is a comprehensive introduction to all the important precepts and techniques of Feng Shui practices.

Your Aquarium Here

This book is the first in Fengshuilogy Series, which is a series of matter-of-fact and useful Feng Shui books designed for the person who wants to do a fuss-free Feng Shui.

Walking the Dragons

Compiled in one book for the first time from Joey Yap's Feng Shui Mastery Excursion Series, the book highlights China's extensive, vibrant history with astute observations on the Feng Shui of important sites and places. Learn the landform formations of Yin Houses (tombs and burial places), as well as mountains, temples, castles and villages.

Walking the Dragons : Taiwan Excursion

A Guide to Classical Landform Feng Shui of Taiwan

From China to Tibet, Joey Yap turns his analytical eye towards Taiwan in this extensive Walking the Dragons series. Combined with beautiful images and detailed information about an island once known as Formosa, or "Beautiful Island" in Portuguese, this compelling series of essays highlights the colourful history and wonders of Taiwan. It also provides readers with fascinating insights into the living science of Feng Shui.

The Art of Date Selection: Personal Date Selection (Available in English & Chinese)

With the Art of Date Selection: Personal Date Selection, you can learn simple, practical methods to select not just good dates, but personalised good dates as well. Whether it is a personal activity such as a marriage or professional endeavour, such as launching a business - signing a contract or even acquiring assets, this book will show you how to pick the good dates and tailor them to suit the activity in question, and to avoid the negative ones too!

Your Head Here

Your Head Here is the first book by Sherwin Ng. She is an accomplished student of Joey Yap, and an experienced Feng Shui consultant and instructor with Joey Yap Consulting Group and Mastery Academy respectively. It is the second book under the Fengshuilogy series, which focuses on Bedroom Feng Shui, a specific topic dedicated to optimum bed location and placement.

If the Shoe Fits

This book is for those who want to make the effort to enhance their relationship.

In her debut release, Jessie Lee humbly shares with you the classical BaZi method of the Ten Day Masters and the combination of a new profiling system developed by Joey Yap, to understand and deal with the people around you.

Being Happy and Successful at Work and in your Career

Have you ever wondered why some of us are so successful in our careers while others are dragging their feet to work or switching from one job to another? Janet Yung hopes to answer this question by helping others through the knowledge and application of BaZi and Chinese Astrology. In her debut release, she shares with the readers the right way of using BaZi to understand themselves: their inborn talents, motivations, skills, and passions, to find their own place in the path of professional development.

Being Happy & Successful - Managing Yourself & Others

Manage Your Talent & Have Effective Relationships at the Workplace

While many strive for efficiency in the workplace, it is vital to know how to utilize your talents. In this book, Janet Yung will take you further on how to use the BaZi profiling system as a tool to assess your personality and understanding your approach to the job. From ways in communicating with your colleagues to understanding your boss, you will be astounded by what this ancient system can reveal about you and the people in your life. Tips and guidance will also be given in this book so that you will make better decisions for your next step in advancing in your career.

The BaZi Road to Success

The BaZi Road to Success explains your journey in life through a chart that is obtained just from looking at the date you were born and its connection with key BaZi elements.

Your Day Pillar, Hour Pillar, Luck Pillar and Annual Pillar all come together to paint a BaZi chart that churns out a combination of different elements, which the book helps interpret. From relationships, career advice, future plans and possibility of wealth accumulation - this book covers it all!

Face Reading Collection

The Chinese Art of Face Reading: The Book of Moles

The Book of Moles by Joey Yap delves into the inner meanings of moles and what they reveal about the personality and destiny of an individual. Complemented by fascinating illustrations and Joey Yap's easy-to-understand commentaries and guides, this book takes a deeper focus into a Face Reading subject, which can be used for everyday decisions – from personal relationships to professional dealings and many others.

Discover Face Reading (Available in English & Chinese)

This is a comprehensive book on all areas of Face Reading, covering some of the most important facial features, including the forehead, mouth, ears and even philtrum above your lips. This book will help you analyse not just your Destiny but also help you achieve your full potential and achieve life fulfillment.

Joey Yap's Art of Face Reading

The Art of Face Reading is Joey Yap's second effort with CICO Books, and it takes a lighter, more practical approach to Face Reading. This book does not focus on the individual features as it does on reading the entire face. It is about identifying common personality types and characters.

Faces of Fortune 2

We don't need to go far to look for entrepreneurs with the X-Factor. Malaysia produces some of the best entrepreneurs in the world. In this book, we will tell you the rags -to- riches stories of 9 ordinary people who has no special privileges, and how they made it on their own.

Easy Guide on Face Reading (Available in English & Chinese)

The Face Reading Essentials series of books comprises of five individual books on the key features of the face – the Eyes, the Eyebrows, the Ears, the Nose, and the Mouth. Each book provides a detailed illustration and a simple yet descriptive explanation on the individual types of the features.

The books are equally useful and effective for beginners, enthusiasts and those who are curious. The series is designed to enable people who are new to Face Reading to make the most out of first impressions and learn to apply Face Reading skills to understand the personality and character of their friends, family, co-workers and business associates.

2020 Annual Releases

| Chinese Astrology for 2020 | Feng Shui for 2020 | Tong Shu Desktop Calendar 2020 | Daily Wall Calendar 2020 | Professional Tong Shu Diary 2020 | Tong Shu Monthly Planner 2020 | Weekly Tong Shu Diary 2020 |

Cultural Series

Discover the True Significance of the Ancient Art of Lion Dance

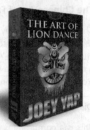

The Lion has long been a symbol of power and strength. That powerful symbol has evolved into an incredible display of a mixture of martial arts and ritualism that is the Lion Dance. Throughout ancient and modern times, the Lion Dance has stamped itself as a popular part of culture, but is there a meaning lost behind this magnificent spectacle?

The Art of Lion Dance written by the world's number one man in Chinese Metaphysics, Dato' Joey Yap, explains the history and origins of the art and its connection to Qi Men Dun Jia. By creating that bridge with Qi Men, the Lion Dance is able to ritualise any type of ceremony, celebrations and mourning alike.

The book is the perfect companion to the modern interpretation of the art as it reveals the significance behind each part of the Lion costume, as well as rituals that are put in place to bring the costume and its spectacle to life.

Chinese Traditions & Practices

China has a long, rich history spanning centuries. As Chinese culture has evolved over the centuries, so have the country's many customs and traditions. Today, there's a Chinese custom for just about every important event in a person's life – from cradle to the grave.

Although many China's customs have survived to the present day, some have been all but forgotten: rendered obsolete by modern day technology. This book explores the history of Chinese traditions and cultural practices, their purpose, and the differences between the traditions of the past and their modern incarnations.

If you are a westerner or less informed about Chinese culture, you may find this book particularly useful, especially when it comes to doing business with the Chinese – whether it be in China itself or some other country with a considerable Chinese population. If anything, it will allow you to have a better casual understanding of the culture and traditions of your Chinese friends or acquaintances. An understanding of Chinese traditions leads to a more informed, richer appreciation of Chinese culture and China itself.

Educational Tools and Software

Joey Yap's Feng Shui Template Set

Directions are the cornerstone of any successful Feng Shui audit or application. The Joey Yap Feng Shui Template Set is a set of three templates to simplify the process of taking directions and determining locations and positions, whether it is for a building, a house, or an open area such as a plot of land - all of it done with just a floor plan or area map.

The Set comprises three basic templates: The Basic Feng Shui Template, Eight Mansions Feng Shui Template, and the Flying Stars Feng Shui Template.

Mini Feng Shui Compass

The Mini Feng Shui Compass is a self-aligning compass that is not only light at 100gms but also built sturdily to ensure it will be convenient to use anywhere. The rings on the Mini Feng Shui Compass are bilingual and incorporate the 24 Mountain Rings that is used in your traditional Luo Pan.

The comprehensive booklet included with this, will guide you in applying the 24 Mountain Directions on your Mini Feng Shui Compass effectively and the Eight Mansions Feng Shui to locate the most auspicious locations within your home, office and surroundings. You can also use the Mini Feng Shui Compass when measuring the direction of your property for the purpose of applying Flying Stars Feng Shui.

MASTERY ACADEMY
OF CHINESE METAPHYSICS
Your **Preferred** Choice to the Art & Science of
Classical Chinese Metaphysics Studies

Bringing **innovative** techniques and **creative** teaching methods to an ancient study.

Mastery Academy of Chinese Metaphysics was established by Joey Yap to play the role of disseminating this Eastern knowledge to the modern world with the belief that this valuable knowledge should be accessible to everyone and everywhere.

Its goal is to enrich people's lives through accurate, professional teaching and practice of Chinese Metaphysics knowledge globally. It is the first academic institution of its kind in the world to adopt the tradition of Western institutions of higher learning - where students are encouraged to explore, question and challenge themselves, as well as to respect different fields and branches of studies. This is done together with the appreciation and respect of classical ideas and applications that have stood the test of time.

The Art and Science of Chinese Metaphysics – be it Feng Shui, BaZi (Astrology), Qi Men Dun Jia, Mian Xiang (Face Reading), ZeRi (Date Selection) or Yi Jing – is no longer a field shrouded with mystery and superstition. In light of new technology, fresher interpretations and innovative methods, as well as modern teaching tools like the Internet, interactive learning, e-learning and distance learning, anyone from virtually any corner of the globe, who is keen to master these disciplines can do so with ease and confidence under the guidance and support of the Academy.

It has indeed proven to be a centre of educational excellence for thousands of students from over thirty countries across the world; many of whom have moved on to practice classical Chinese Metaphysics professionally in their home countries.

At the Academy, we believe in enriching people's lives by empowering their destinies through the disciplines of Chinese Metaphysics. Learning is not an option - it is a way of life!

MASTERY ACADEMY
OF CHINESE METAPHYSICS™

MALAYSIA
19-3, The Boulevard, Mid Valley City, 59200 Kuala Lumpur, Malaysia
Tel : +6(03)-2284 8080 | Fax : +6(03)-2284 1218
Email   : info@masteryacademy.com
Website : www.masteryacademy.com

Australia, Austria, Canada, China, Croatia, Cyprus, Czech Republic, Denmark, France, Germany, Greece, Hungary, India, Italy, Kazakhstan, Malaysia, Netherlands (Holland), New Zealand, Philippines, Poland, Russian Federation, Singapore, Slovenia, South Africa, Switzerland, Turkey, United States of America, Ukraine, United Kingdom

www.masteryacademy.com | +6(03) - 2284 8080

The Mastery Academy around the world!

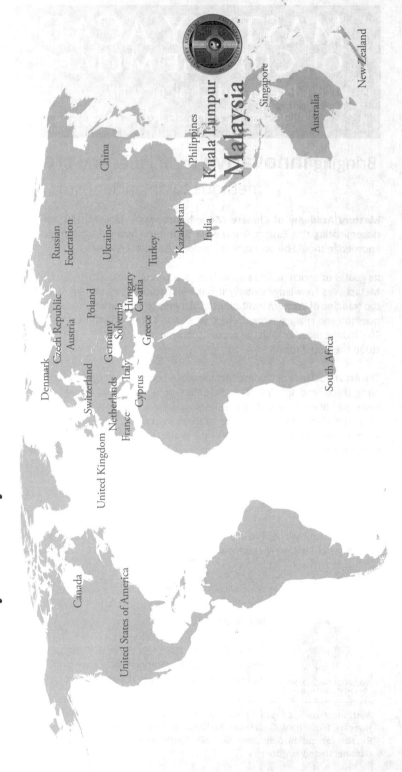

Canada

United States of America

Denmark
Czech Republic
Austria
Poland
Switzerland
Germany
Netherlands
Solvenia
France
Italy
Cyprus
Hungary
Croatia
Greece

United Kingdom

Russian Federation

Ukraine

Turkey

Kazakhstan

India

China

Philippines
Kuala Lumpur
Malaysia

Singapore

Australia

New Zealand

South Africa

Feng Shui Mastery™
LIVE COURSES (MODULES ONE TO FOUR)

This an ideal program for those who wants to achieve mastery in Feng Shui from the comfort of their homes. This comprehensive program covers the foundation up to the advanced practitioner levels, touching upon the important theories from various classical Feng Shui systems including Ba Zhai, San Yuan, San He and Xuan Kong.

Module One:
Beginners
Course

Module Two:
Practitioners
Course

Module Three:
Advanced
Practitioners Course

Module Four:
Master Course

BaZi Mastery™
LIVE COURSES (MODULES ONE TO FOUR)

This lesson-based program brings a thorough introduction to BaZi and guides the student step-by-step, all the way to the professional practitioner level. From the theories to the practical, BaZi students along with serious Feng Shui practitioners, can master its application with accuracy and confidence.

Module One:
Intensive
Foundation Course

Module Two:
Practitioners
Course

Module Three:
Advanced
Practitioners Course

Module Four:
Master Course in BaZi

Xuan Kong Mastery™
LIVE COURSES (MODULES ONE TO THREE)
* Advanced Courses For Master Practitioners

Xuan Kong is a sophisticated branch of Feng Shui, replete with many techniques and formulae, which encompass numerology, symbology and the science of the Ba Gua, along with the mathematics of time. This program is ideal for practitioners looking to bring their practice to a more in-depth level.

Module One:
Advanced
Foundation Course

Module Two A:
Advanced Xuan
Kong Methodologies

Module Two B:
Purple White

Module Three:
Advanced Xuan Kong
Da Gua

Mian Xiang Mastery™
LIVE COURSES (MODULES ONE AND TWO)

This program comprises of two modules, each carefully developed to allow students to familiarise with the fundamentals of Mian Xiang or Face Reading and the intricacies of its theories and principles. With lessons guided by video lectures, presentations and notes, students are able to understand and practice Mian Xiang with greater depth.

Module One:
Basic Face
Reading

Module Two:
Practical Face
Reading

Yi Jing Mastery™
LIVE COURSES (MODULES ONE AND TWO)

Whether you are a casual or serious Yi Jing enthusiast, this lesson-based program contains two modules that brings students deeper into the Chinese science of divination. The lessons will guide students on the mastery of its sophisticated formulas and calculations to derive answers to questions we pose.

Module One:
Traditional Yi Jing

Module Two:
Plum Blossom
Numerology

Ze Ri Mastery™
LIVE COURSES (MODULES ONE AND TWO)

In two modules, students will undergo a thorough instruction on the fundamentals of ZeRi or Date Selection. The comprehensive program covers Date Selection for both Personal and Feng Shui purposes to Xuan Kong Da Gua Date Selection.

Module One:
Personal and
Feng Shui Date
Selection

Module Two:
Xuan Kong
Da Gua Date
Selection

Joey Yap's
SAN YUAN QI MEN XUAN KONG DA GUA™

This is an advanced level program which can be summed up as the Integral Vision of San Yuan studies – an integration of the ancient potent discipline of Qi Men Dun Jia and the highly popular Xuan Kong 64 Hexagrams. Often regarded as two independent systems, San Yuan Qi Men and San Yuan Xuan Kong Da Gua can trace their origins to the same source and were actually used together in ancient times by great Chinese sages.

This method enables practitioners to harness the Qi of time and space, and predict the outcomes through a highly-detailed analysis of landforms, places and sites.

BaZi 10X

Emphasising on the practical aspects of BaZi, this programme is rich with numerous applications and techniques pertaining to the pursuit of wealth, health, relationship and career, all of which constitute the formula of success. This programme is designed for all levels of practitioners and is supplemented with innovative learning materials to enable easy learning. Discover the different layers of BaZi from a brand new perspective with BaZi 10X.

Feng Shui for Life

This is an entry-level five-day course designed for the Feng Shui beginner to learn the application of practical Feng Shui in day-to-day living. Lessons include quick tips on analysing the BaZi chart, simple Feng Shui solutions for the home, basic Date Selection, useful Face Reading techniques and practical Water formulas. A great introduction course on Chinese Metaphysics studies for beginners.

Joey Yap's
Design Your Destiny

This is a three-day life transformation program designed to inspire awareness and action for you to create a better quality of life. It introduces the DRT™ (Decision Referential Technology) method, which utilises the BaZi Personality Profiling system to determine the right version of you, and serves as a tool to help you make better decisions and achieve a better life in the least resistant way possible, based on your Personality Profile Type.

Millionaire Feng Shui Secrets Programme

This program is geared towards maximising your financial goals and dreams through the use of Feng Shui. Focusing mainly on the execution of Wealth Feng Shui techniques such as Luo Shu sectors and more, it is perfect for boosting careers, businesses and investment opportunities.

Grow Rich With BaZi Programme

This comprehensive programme covers the foundation of BaZi studies and presents information from the career, wealth and business standpoint. This course is ideal for those who want to maximise their wealth potential and live the life they deserve. Knowledge gained in this course will be used as driving factors to encourage personal development towards a better future.

Walk the Mountains!
Learn Feng Shui in a Practical and Hands-on Program

 Feng Shui Mastery Excursion™

Learn landform (Luan Tou) Feng Shui by walking the mountains and chasing the Dragon's vein in China. This program takes the students in a study tour to examine notable Feng Shui landmarks, mountains, hills, valleys, ancient palaces, famous mansions, houses and tombs in China. The excursion is a practical hands-on course where students are shown to perform readings using the formulas they have learnt and to recognise and read Feng Shui Landform (Luan Tou) formations.

Read about the China Excursion here:
http://www.fengshuiexcursion.com

Mastery Academy courses are conducted around the world. Find out when will Joey Yap be in your area by visiting
www.masteryacademy.com
or call our offices at **+6(03)-2284 8080**.